Foodplant List

for the Caterpillars of Britain's Butterflies and Larger Moths

Compiled by
Tim Crafer

Published by Atropos Publishing

Published by Atropos Publishing,
36 Tinker Lane, Meltham, Holmfirth, HD9 4EX.
www.atropos.info
Email atropos@atroposed.freeserve.co.uk
Tel. 01326 290287

Copyright © Tim Crafer

First published 2005

ISBN 0-9551086-0-8

Front cover illustration: Caterpillar of Black Hairstreak *Satyrium pruni*
Front cover design and photography by Cell Creative.

Printed in England.

All rights reserved. No part of this publication may be reproduced, stored in a retrieval system or transmitted in any form or by any means, electronic, mechanical, photocopying, recording or otherwise, without the prior written permission of the publisher or copyright holder.

CONTENTS

Foreword 4
About the Publisher 5
Introduction 6
Key 9
Plant List 11
Index 116

FOREWORD

Butterfly Conservation is delighted to be associated with this book and its comprehensive list of moth and butterfly foodplants. We appreciate the efforts of the author, Tim Crafer, who has so painstakingly brought together such a wealth of information. The list is invaluable to anyone who wants to help conserve these fascinating and often endangered insects, or simply to study and enjoy them. As Tim says in his introduction, there is ample scope for amateur as well as professional Lepidopterists to make new discoveries and add to this list in the future. We also greatly welcome the association with *Atropos* and will put the funds raised from the book towards practical projects to conserve moths and butterflies for future generations to enjoy.

Martin Warren
Chief Executive,
Butterfly Conservation

About the Publisher

Atropos is the only British periodical devoted to butterflies, moths and dragonflies. It appears three times a year, publishing news and feature articles of interest to both amateur and professional naturalists. For further details visit the website or write to 36 Tinker Lane, Meltham, Holmfirth, HD9 4EX for a sample copy (please enclose an A5 SAE with 2 x 1st class stamps).

Atropos also runs a mail-order book service specialising in key titles for butterfly, moth and dragonfly enthusiasts. A catalogue is available on request from: 1 Myrtle Villas, Sussex Road, New Romney, Kent, TN28 8DY.

www.atropos.info

£1 from the purchase of this book will be donated to the charity Butterfly Conservation

About Butterfly Conservation

Founded in 1968, Butterfly Conservation is the UK charity taking action to save butterflies, moths and their habitats. The Society runs a wide variety of conservation projects and is taking the lead in conserving the UK's butterfly and moth populations, particularly through the UK Biodiversity Action Plan and the Society's own Regional Action Plans.

Butterfly Conservation has developed a strategy to protect important butterfly and moth populations through the establishment of nature reserves. Our staff and local Branches also advise on habitat management on many hundreds of other key sites owned by private individuals.

The Society runs several high profile recording and monitoring programmes and collaborates with Rothamsted Research on the analysis of trends in common moths obtained from their long-running light trap network.

A strong membership makes up 31 branches throughout the UK. Every year these branches organise hundreds of field trips, talks and educational courses across the country. Volunteers are also involved in monitoring hundreds of important localities, and give practical help by attending work-parties to manage habitats.

Join Butterfly Conservation and save butterflies, moths and their habitats

By becoming a member of Butterfly Conservation you will receive:

- *Butterfly* magazine three times a year
- Membership of your local Branch, including regular newsletters
- Details of guided walks, talks and other social events in your area
- Advice and information about identifying butterflies and moths and attracting them to your garden

Further information on Butterfly Conservation's work and becoming a member can be found at:

www.butterfly-conservation.org

or contact:

Butterfly Conservation,
Manor Yard, East Lulworth,
Wareham, Dorset, BH20 5QP
Tel: 0870 7744309
Fax: 0870 7706150
Email: info@butterfly-conservation.org

INTRODUCTION

The concept of this project was born in 2002 when I realised that whilst there were some excellent works available that illustrated the caterpillars (larvae) of the British macrolepidoptera (butterflies and larger moths) there was no comprehensive foodplant list available as an aid to identification. Here was something that might be useful, as whilst the caterpillars of some species are very general in the range of plants upon which they will feed (so called polyphagous species), others are specific to a very narrow range of plants. The plant that a caterpillar consumes can therefore be an important part of the identification process. I decided to look into the practicality of producing a foodplant-caterpillar index and it quickly became apparent why nobody else had comprehensively tackled the problem before. There are a considerable number of foodplants listed in the literature, some with more than 100 different macrolepidoptera species consuming them. However, with modern technology it seemed feasible to produce a reasonably complete list.

It is hoped that this book will aid the identification of caterpillars by listing them under their respective foodplants and the periods when they are active. However, it is only a guide and can never be complete as observers will always be finding caterpillars feeding on new hostplants. It covers the macrolepidoptera only, and there are approximately 500 plants and 4,800 caterpillar listings contained within these pages. The list should be used purely as a starting point for those wishing to identify a caterpillar. **It is likely that some of the plants listed will not be eaten by caterpillars in the wild (see later) so the information contained in this book should not be cited as comprehensive foodplant listings for wild larvae.**

How to Use this Book

The reader is referred to the key that follows this introductory section for details of the symbols and abbreviations used. Almost all of the information provided has been taken from the key publications listed in the Bibliography. No attempt has been made to comprehensively search the various entomological journals for additional foodplant pairings, though some additional references that were casually encountered in such literature have been added. No information is given regarding recognition of the various caterpillars, for which the reader is referred to the Bibliography.

J.D. Bradley's *Checklist of Lepidoptera Recorded from the British Isles* (revised edition, 2000) formed the basis of nomenclature for the Lepidoptera and Clive Stace's *New Flora of the British Isles* (1997) for plants. Extinct Lepidoptera species have been excluded, as have non-breeding immigrants.

The primary order of the plant list is alphabetical by English name with members of some of the larger families being grouped together. Thus the various bedstraws are listed under bedstraw. Usually the first part of a vernacular name has been used to allocate alphabetical order, except for some species that are more widely recognised by the second part of the vernacular name. Thus Common Juniper is listed under Juniper.

Macrolepidoptera species appear within the list under the various known foodplants with which they are associated, thus species that feed on a wide variety of plants will appear many times throughout the list. Where more than five macrolepidoptera species are listed under a given plant, every fifth line has been highlighted to assist the eye as it looks across the various columns.

At the beginning of the list there is a special category for polyphagous caterpillars. While these macrolepidoptera are also listed under specific plant species it is impossible to cover every foodplant that they consume. The polyphagous section should thus always be checked when difficulty is experienced in identification.

The published works used in constructing this list often differ in the foodplants listed for a particular species, but all are listed here. This is because one cannot prove a negative and if the caterpillar of a certain species of moth was reported consuming a particular plant in the nineteenth century, how does one disprove it? It should also be considered that caterpillars move, especially if they denude their foodplant, and they may be reported on another plant when on passage, while not actually consuming it. Foodplants used in captivity have been disregarded where this was stated in the source, but this is not always clear from the sources used so it has to be accepted that some of the named foodplants may be based on captive feeding and possibly even continental literature in some cases.

Careful consideration was given to using information contained within Allan (1979), as some of this relates to plants eaten in captivity that may not be used in the wild. However, under the remit of providing a starting point for caterpillar identification I felt it was better to provide the reader with longer lists (perhaps containing Lepidoptera species that do not actually feed upon that particular plant in the wild); after all, if a caterpillar eats a particular plant species in captivity then there must be the potential for it to be used in the wild, even if only under rare circumstances. Thus the reader may find reference to foodplants for species whose feeding habits are not known in the wild, e.g. Pale Shining Brown.

Some plants are host to enormous numbers of macrolepidoptera species, which makes the task more difficult for those wanting to identify a caterpillar found on one of these plants. For example, willows/sallows (>180 species listed), birches (152), oaks (125), hawthorn (116), blackthorn (96), heathers (82), brambles (63), docks (96), grasses (>80), dandelions and plantains (66 each). The periods of caterpillar activity shown in the list may help identification in these cases. It is interesting to speculate what makes some plants more palatable than others. A comparatively recently imported garden shrub like Buddleia, which was collected in the Victorian era, is now a common garden and feral plant. It is very attractive as a nectar source for adult Lepidoptera, but amazingly only three macrolepidoptera species are listed as feeding upon it. On the other hand, older established plants, often the first to arrive after the ice age, seem to be eaten by a wider variety of caterpillars (see above).

In many cases plants are listed by genera rather than species, e.g. heathers. The separation of the species within certain genera can be very difficult. It is common for the sources used in compiling this list to only mention the plant genera, so often I have included an 'unspecified' section under the genus before the specific foodplant species are listed. Even if the observer is confident of plant identity the 'unspecified' section should still be consulted as the caterpillar could be listed there. Similarly, if the plant species has not been identified to species level the whole genus should be checked.

Willows are a special case and have been treated differently in the list. Many authorities use the word 'sallow' as a foodplant without specifying a species. The term 'sallow' is not listed in most floras, including Stace (1997). Lepidopterists generally use it to indicate an unspecified broad-leafed shrub willow *Salix* spp. In order to break down the genus *Salix* it has been divided into three sections: Trees >10m High, Shrubs and Small Trees <10m High, and Dwarf Shrubs <1.5m High. The heights used are taken from Stace (1997) but are only indications as exceptional specimens can be taller and young plants may be shorter. The 'Unspecified Willows' section that precedes these categories refers to all species of willow. At the start of the 'Shrub and Small Tree' section is an 'Unspecified' list of caterpillars that various authors have listed under 'sallow'; these should be checked with all the shrub willows.

The period of caterpillar activity is given by month for each entry, but this should be used only as a guide, as periods will vary considerably with latitude, unseasonal weather, etc. Some species are double-brooded, particularly in the south of England, whilst others have a second brood only if the season is favourable. The list presents such information where it is known. Some caterpillars are active in favourable conditions throughout the winter, whilst others hibernate; this is indicated in the lists.

The geographical ranges given should also only be used as guides. Global warming and other climatic and vegetative changes mean that species are often on the move, either advancing or retreating geographically. Also there may well be local populations existing outside the indicated areas.

Errors, Corrections and Additions

Although every care has been taken with the preparation of this extensive list, it is inevitable that there will be omissions, particularly as there is likely to be much unpublished information in the records of naturalists. There is considerable scope for both amateur and professional to contribute to knowledge in this area. We hope to publish a revised second edition in the near future, containing refinements and the additional information that will inevitably follow.

I would be most grateful if any reader who spots either mistakes or omissions, or could suggest amendments for future reprints, would communicate with the assembler (details below), preferably by Email. If providing information about additional larval foodplants please state where and when your observations were made, and whether the observations relate to field observations or were made in captivity.

Tim Crafer
Tel & Fax: 01328 830242
E–mail: tcrafer@msn.com
Address: Lodge Barn, Stiffkey,
Wells–next–the–Sea,
Norfolk, NR23 1QP
England

Bibliography

Allan, P.B.M., 1979. *Larval Foodplants*. Watkins & Doncaster, Hawkhurst.

Asher, J., Warren, M., Fox, R., Harding, P. & Jeffcoate, G. & S., 2001. *The Millennium Atlas of Butterflies in Britain and Ireland*. Oxford University Press. Oxford.

Bradley, J.D., 2000. *Checklist of Lepidoptera Recorded from the British Isles*. Second edition (revised). D. Bradley, Fordingbridge.

Heath. J. & Emmet, A.M., 1983. *The Moths and Butterflies of Great Britain and Ireland*. Vol. 7 (2). Harley Books, Colchester.

Porter, J., 1997. *The Colour Identification Guide to Caterpillars of the British Isles*. Viking, London.

Riley, A.M. & Prior, G., 2003. *British and Irish Pug Moths*. Harley Books, Colchester.

Skinner, B., 1998. *The Colour Identification Guide to Moths of the British Isles*. Viking, London.

South, R., 1939. *The Moths of the British Isles*. Frederick Warne, London.

Stace, C., 1997. *New Flora of the British Isles*. Cambridge University Press, Cambridge.

Thomas, J. & Lewington, R., 1991. *The Butterflies of Britain and Ireland*. Dorling Kindersley, London.

Waring, P., Townsend, M. & Lewington, R., 2003. *Field Guide to the Moths of Great Britain and Ireland*. British Wildlife Publishing, Hook.

Young, M., 1997. *The Natural History of Moths*. T & A.D. Poyser, London.

Many of the above titles may be purchased from book suppliers, though some are now out of print and may have to be sought second-hand.

Acknowledgements

My thanks go to all those who have helped generate this book. Many assisted without realising that they had done so, like Ivan and Janet West who pointed out a Vapourer *Orgyia antiqua* caterpillar feeding on their Pyracantha one morning (new to the list).

Jim Porter, whose *Colour Identification Guide to Caterpillars of the British Isles* (1997) is the standard work on the subject, bore the brunt of inspecting the early drafts and made some most useful suggestions. Sean Clancy, Peter Davey, Mark Parsons, Martin Townsend and Mark Tunmore also provided valuable assistance with aspects of proof-reading and list construction. I am also grateful to Jill Marsden and Gillian Beckett for assisting with the botanical aspects of proof-reading.

Finally, I must thank my very patient wife who not only encouraged in the dark days but made many most useful suggestions.

KEY

Including symbols & abbreviations

The key to this list is necessarily complicated as a lot of information is squeezed into each line by the use of codes. While this may cause some difficulty initially, the reader will soon get used to both the system and the codes.

Plant names: These are in alphabetical order of their vernacular names, followed by the scientific name in italics. At the end of the list there is an index of scientific names for the plants with their vernacular equivalent to assist those used to working with scientific names.

Caterpillars: There are six columns for each caterpillar entry: species name, main activity period(s), secondary activity period, plant parts, distribution, and rarity status.

Column 1: Caterpillar names. Both the vernacular and the scientific names are given. Species are primarily sorted by the commencement of their main caterpillar activity period, thus those that first emerge from the egg in March are grouped together. Species are secondarily sorted by the time of their pupation, e.g. March–May is grouped before March–June. Thus species with identical main caterpillar activity periods are grouped together, within which groupings they are ordered alphabetically by English name. Second brood periods are ignored for the list order.

Column 2: Main activity period(s). This column shows the approximate months when caterpillars are active, the beginning and end periods being separated by a hyphen. If the species is double-brooded, there is an ampersand (&) between the two brood periods. In both this and the next column it should be noted that where the time period stretches through the winter the species may hibernate as a caterpillar, and this is indicated by a wavy dash (~) in place of a hyphen. Some caterpillars remain active in favourable weather conditions throughout the winter and these have the normal hyphen.

Column 3: Secondary activity period. If a period is shown it indicates that the species is double-brooded in the south but single-brooded in the north, the period of the northern single brood activity being included in this column (hibernators are treated as described in column 2 above).

For example:

1	2	3
Purple Thorn *Selenia tetralunaria*	5–7 & 8–9	6–7

This indicates that the Purple Thorn is double-brooded in the south during the periods shown in column 2, and single brooded in the north with that period included in column 3.

If a plus sign (+) is shown in this third column, there may be a second brood of caterpillars in favourable seasons, usually in the south.

If a star (∗) is shown, the species may have a lifecycle (egg to adult) of more than 12 months and can spend a considerable time as a caterpillar and/or a pupa (as much as four years).

If there is no entry in this column none of the above attributes apply.

Column 4: Parts of the plant that the caterpillar may eat. These are indicated as follows: B = buds, F = flowers, S = seeds, fruit, etc., St = stem, R = roots, L = leaves, I = inside (e.g. ISt = inside the stem), D = dead (e.g. DL = dead leaves). If there is no entry in this column it indicates that normally the caterpillar eats the leaves. The information in this column should be treated with caution and not used as the primary means of identification.

Column 5: Geographical range. The system used is based mainly on that used in Waring, Townsend & Lewington (2003) with some additional refinements.

The codes used are as follows:

S	= Southern Britain. England south of a line from the Wash to the Severn estuary, and southern counties of Wales.
C	= Central Britain. From Yorkshire south to the Wash, the midland counties and most of Wales.
N	= Northern Britain. The northern third of the land area, including Scotland, associated islands and northernmost counties of England.
E	= Eastern Britain. The east coast and land east of a line bisecting the Isle of Wight.
W	= Western Britain. The west coast and land west of a line bisecting the Isle of Wight.

If not separated by commas, i.e. NW (not N, W which signifies North **and** West) the codes are as follows:

SE	= South-eastern Britain. England east of a line approximately from The Wash to the Isle of Wight.
SW	= South-western Britain. England west of a line approximately from the River Severn to the Isle of Wight, and the seaboard counties of south Wales.
NE	= North-eastern Britain. Eastern Scotland and the eastern coastal counties as far south as the Humber.
NW	= North-western Britain. Western Scotland, much of Wales and the western counties of England in between.
EC	= East-central. The eastern half of Central Britain.
WC	= West-central. The western half of Central Britain.
SN	= Southern-north. Northern England but not Scotland.
Brackets ( )	= present, but more sparsely distributed.

If no area is indicated the species occurs widely throughout Britain, but may be local in certain areas.

Column 6: Rarity status.

Moth species have been allotted a category based on the number of 10km squares within Britain from which they have been reported since 1980. This follows the system used in Waring, Townsend & Lewington (2003).

RDB	= Red Data Book species. Recorded from less than 15 x 10 km squares.
Na	= Nationally Scarce A. Very restricted; only recorded from 16–30 x 10km squares.
Nb	= Nationally Scarce B. Restricted national distribution; recorded from 31–100 x 10km squares.
UC	= Uncommon on introduced foodplant. Recorded from less than 100 x 10km squares.
L	= Localised in Britain, known from 100–300 x 10km squares.
Bm	= Breeding immigrants which breed, but normally do not survive the winter, in Britain.

If this column is blank the species is considered to be common throughout.

Butterflies have been allotted a category based mainly on information from *The Millennium Atlas of Butterflies in Britain and Ireland* (Asher *et al.* 2001).

R	= Rare, reported from <100 x 10km squares.
S	= Scarce, reported from 100–400 x 10km squares.
L	= Local, reported from 400–999 x 10km squares.
Bm	= Breeding immigrants which normally do not survive the winter in Britain.

If this column is blank the species is considered to be widespread.

Note that species can be abundant where they occur and yet have a very restricted national distribution.

PLANT LIST

Columns	1	2	3	4	5	6
Polyphagous Caterpillars						
Angle Shades	*Phlogophora meticulosa*	All				
Brimstone Moth	*Opisthograptis luteolata*	All	7–9			
Oak Eggar	*Lasiocampa quercus*	All	*			
Garden Dart	*Euxoa nigricans*	2–6				
Beaded Chestnut	*Agrochola lychnidis*	3–6			S, C, (N)	
Dotted Chestnut	*Conistra rubiginea*	3–6			S, (C)	Nb
Grass Eggar	*Lasiocampa trifolii*	3–7			S, WC	Na
Scalloped Oak	*Crocallis elinguaria*	3–7				
White-line Dart	*Euxoa tritici*	3–7				
Brown-spot Pinion	*Agrochola litura*	4–6				
Clouded Drab	*Orthosia incerta*	4–6				
Common Quaker	*Orthosia cerasi*	4–6				
Copper Underwing	*Amphipyra pyramidea*	4–6			S, C, (N)	
Chestnut	*Conistra vaccinii*	5–6				
Dark Chestnut	*Conistra ligula*	4–6			S, C, (N)	
December Moth	*Poecilocampa populi*	4–6				
Dotted Border	*Agriopis marginaria*	4–6				
Dun-bar	*Cosmia trapezina*	4–6				
Engrailed	*Ectropis bistortata*	4–6 & 7–9	5–7			
Feathered Thorn	*Colotois pennaria*	4–6				
Flounced Chestnut	*Agrochola helvola*	4–6				
Grey Chi	*Antitype chi*	4–6			C, N, (S)	
Lackey	*Malacosoma neustria*	4–6			S, C, (N)	
Lunar-spotted Pinion	*Cosmia pyralina*	4–6			S, (C)	L
Mottled Umber	*Erannis defoliaria*	4–6				
Mouse	*Amphipyra tragopoginis*	4–6		L & F		
November Moth	*Epirrita dilutata*	4–6				
Pale Brindled Beauty	*Phigalia pilosaria*	4–6				
Pale Eggar	*Trichiura crataegi*	4–6				
Pale November Moth	*Epirrita christyi*	4–6			S, C, (N)	
Satellite	*Eupsilia transversa*	4–6				
Scarce Umber	*Agriopis aurantiaria*	4–6				
Small Quaker	*Orthosia cruda*	4–6				
Sprawler	*Asteroscopus sphinx*	4–6			S, C	
Twin-spot Carpet	*Perizoma didymata*	4–6				
Twin-spotted Quaker	*Orthosia munda*	4–6			S, C, (N)	
White-marked	*Cerastis leucographa*	4–6			S, C	L
Winter Moth	*Operophtera brumata*	4–6				
Yellow-line Quaker	*Agrochola macilenta*	4–6				
Ground Lackey	*Malacosoma castrensis*	4–7			SE, (SW)	Na
Hebrew Character	*Orthosia gothica*	4–7				
Large Ranunculus	*Polymixis flavicincta*	4–7			S, (C)	L
Blossom Underwing	*Orthosia miniosa*	5–6			S, C	L
Double-striped Pug	*Gymnoscelis rufifasciata*	5–6 & 9–10		F		
Early Thorn	*Selenia dentaria*	5–6 & 8–9	6–8			
March Moth	*Alsophila aescularia*	5–6				
Red Chestnut	*Cerastis rubricosa*	5–6				
August Thorn	*Ennomos quercinaria*	5–7			S, C, (N)	L
Belted Beauty	*Lycia zonaria*	5–7			NW	Na

Species	Months				
Brindled Beauty *Lycia hirtaria*	5–7			S, C, (N)	
Canary-shouldered Thorn *Ennomos alniaria*	5–7				
Northern Drab *Orthosia opima*	5–7				L
Nut-tree Tussock *Colocasia coryli*	5–7 & 9–10	7–9			
Oak Beauty *Biston strataria*	5–7			S, C, (N)	
Pale Pinion *Lithophane hepatica*	5–7			S, WC	L
Powdered Quaker *Orthosia gracilis*	5–7				
Purple Thorn *Selenia tetralunaria*	5–7 & 8–9	6–7		S, C, (N)	
Red Sword-grass *Xylena vetusta*	5–7				L
Ruby Tiger *Phragmatobia fuliginosa*	5–7 & 7~4	7–5			
Setaceous Hebrew Character *Xestia c-nigrum*	5–7 & 9~4	9–5			
Sword-grass *Xylena exsoleta*	5–7			C, N	Nb
V-Pug *Chloroclystis v-ata*	5–7 & 8–10	7–9	F	S, C, (N)	
Large Thorn *Ennomos autumnaria*	5–8			SE	Nb
Rosy Rustic *Hydraecia micacea*	5–8		lSt & R		
Vapourer *Orgyia antiqua*	5–8	+			
Cabbage Moth *Mamestra brassicae*	5–10	+			
Lime-speck Pug *Eupithecia centaureata*	5–10	+	F		
Silver Y *Autographa gamma*	5–10	+			Bm
Common Pug *Eupithecia vulgata*	6–7 & 8–10	7–8			
Coxcomb Prominent *Ptilodon capucina*	6–7 & 8–9	6–8			
Dark-barred Twin-spot Carpet *Xanthorhoe ferrugata*	6–7 & 9	6–8		S, C, (N)	
Dog's Tooth *Lacanobia suasa*	6–7 & 8–9	7–8		S, C, (N)	L
Flame Shoulder *Ochropleura plecta*	6–7 & 9–10	8–9			
Small Square-spot *Diarsia rubi*	6–7 & 9~4	8~5			
White Colon *Sideridis albicolon*	6–7 & 9		F		Nb
Autumn Green Carpet *Chloroclysta miata*	6–8				L
Lunar Thorn *Selenia lunularia*	6–8				L
Red-green Carpet *Chloroclysta siterata*	6–8				
Small Engrailed *Ectropis crepuscularia*	6–8			S, C, (N)	L
Square Spot *Paradarisa consonaria*	6–8			S, C, SN	L
Dark Brocade *Blepharita adusta*	6–9				
Satyr Pug *Eupithecia satyrata*	6–9		F		L
Scalloped Hazel *Odontopera bidentata*	6–9				
Common White Wave *Cabera pusaria*	6–10				
Grey Pug *Eupithecia subfuscata*	6–10		F & L		
Muslin Moth *Diaphora mendica*	6–10			S, C, (N)	
Pale Tussock *Calliteara pudibunda*	6–10			S, C	
Shuttle-shaped Dart *Agrotis puta*	6–4	+		S, C, (N)	
Treble Lines *Charanyca trigrammica*	6–4			S, C	
Mullein Wave *Scopula marginepunctata*	7 & 9–5	9–5		S, C, (N)	L
Red Twin-spot Carpet *Xanthorhoe spadicearia*	7 & 9	6–8			
Alder Moth *Acronicta alni*	7–8			S, C, (N)	L
Common Marbled Carpet *Chloroclysta truncata*	7–8 & 9~5	8~6			
Dark Sword-grass *Agrotis ipsilon*	7–8		L & R		Bm
Light Brocade *Lacanobia w-latinum*	7–8			S, C, (N)	L
Bordered Gothic *Heliophobus reticulata*	7–9		F	S, C	RDB
Bright-line Brown-eye *Lacanobia oleracea*	7–9	+			
Broken-barred Carpet *Electrophaes corylata*	7–9				
Broom Moth *Melanchra pisi*	7–9				
Green Silver-lines *Pseudoips prasinana*	7–9	+			
Grey Dagger *Acronicta psi*	7–9	+			
Knot Grass *Acronicta rumicis*	7–9	+			
Pale-shouldered Brocade *Lacanobia thalassina*	7–9	+			
Peppered Moth *Biston betularia*	7–9				

Species	Dates				
Shaded Pug *Eupithecia subumbrata*	7–9		F	S, (C)	L
White Ermine *Spilosoma lubricipeda*	7–9				
Buff Ermine *Spilosoma luteum*	7–10				
Buff-tip *Phalera bucephala*	7–10				
Flame *Axylia putris*	7–10			S, C, (N)	
Little Emerald *Jodis lactearia*	7–10			S, C, NW	
Heart and Dart *Agrotis exclamationis*	7~3	+			
Turnip Moth *Agrotis segetum*	7–4	+	St & R		
Clouded Buff *Diacrisia sannio*	7~5				L
Riband Wave *Idaea aversata*	7~5	+			
Yellow Shell *Camptogramma bilineata*	7~5				
Willow Beauty *Peribatodes rhomboidaria*	7~6	+			
Dot Moth *Melanchra persicariae*	8–10			S, C, (N)	
Wormwood Pug *Eupithecia absinthiata*	8–10		F		
Mottled Rustic *Caradrina morpheus*	8–11				
Crescent Dart *Agrotis trux*	8–3			SW, WC, NW	L
Gothic *Naenia typica*	8–3				L
Beautiful Golden Y *Autographa pulchrina*	8~5				
Bright Wave *Idaea ochrata*	8~5			SE	RDB
Brown Rustic *Rusina ferruginea*	8~5				
Common Emerald *Hemithea aestivaria*	8~5			S, C, (N)	
Cream-spot Tiger *Arctia villica*	8~5			S	L
Double Dart *Graphiphora augur*	8~5				
Double Square-spot *Xestia triangulum*	8~5				
Grey Arches *Polia nebulosa*	8~5				
Lappet *Gastropacha quercifolia*	8~5			S, EC	
Light Emerald *Campaea margaritata*	8~5	+			
Mottled Beauty *Alcis repandata*	8~5				
Orange Moth *Angerona prunaria*	8~5			S, (C)	L
Plain Golden Y *Autographa jota*	8~5				
Plain Wave *Idaea straminata*	8~5				L
Purple Clay *Diarsia brunnea*	8~5				
Scarlet Tiger *Callimorpha dominula*	8~5			S, (WC)	L
Treble Brown Spot *Idaea trigeminata*	8~5	+		S, (C)	L
Triple-spotted Clay *Xestia ditrapezium*	8~5		B		L
Wood Tiger *Parasemia plantaginis*	8~5				L
Ashworth's Rustic *Xestia ashworthii*	8~6			WC	Na
Garden Tiger *Arctia caja*	8~6				
Gold Spangle *Autographa bractea*	8~6			C, N	
Lesser Yellow Underwing *Noctua comes*	8–6				
Scarce Vapourer *Orgyia recens*	8–6			EC	RDB
Swallow-tailed Moth *Ourapteryx sambucaria*	8–6				
Yellow-tail *Euproctis similis*	8–6			S, C, (N)	
Beautiful Brocade *Lacanobia contigua*	8–9				L
Broad-bordered Yellow Underwing *Noctua fimbriata*	9~4				
Ingrailed Clay *Diarsia mendica*	9~4				
Lesser Broad-bordered Yellow Underwing *Noctua janthe*	9~4				
Six-striped Rustic *Xestia sexstrigata*	9~4				
Square-spot Rustic *Xestia xanthographa*	9~4				
Vine's Rustic *Hoplodrina ambigua*	9–4 & 7–8			S, (C)	L
Dotted Clay *Xestia baja*	9~5				
Gold Spot *Plusia festucae*	9~5 & 7–8	9~5			
Large Yellow Underwing *Noctua pronuba*	9–5				
Least Yellow Underwing *Noctua interjecta*	9–5			S, C, (SN)	
Lunar Yellow Underwing *Noctua orbona*	9–5				Nb

Plain Clay *Eugnorisma depuncta*	9–5		SW, WC, N	Nb
Brown-tail *Euproctis chrysorrhoea*	9–6		S, (EC)	L
Jersey Tiger *Euplagia quadripunctaria*	9–6		SW	Nb
Magpie *Abraxas grossulariata*	9–6			
Autumnal Rustic *Eugnorisma glareosa*	10–5			
Black Rustic *Aporophyla nigra*	10–5			
Feathered Ranunculus *Polymixis lichenea*	10–5		S, C, (N)	L

Agrimony *Agrimonia eupatoria*

Grizzled Skipper *Pyrgus malvae*	7–9	+	S, C	S

Alder *Alnus glutinosa*

Autumnal Moth *Epirrita autumnata*	4–6			
Blue-bordered Carpet *Plemyria rubiginata*	4–6			
Brown-spot Pinion *Agrochola litura*	4–6			
Common Quaker *Orthosia cerasi*	4–6			
December Moth *Poecilocampa populi*	4–6			
Dotted Border *Agriopis marginaria*	4–6			
Northern Winter Moth *Operophtera fagata*	4–6			
Pale Brindled Beauty *Phigalia pilosaria*	4–6			
Pale November Moth *Epirrita christyi*	4–6		S, C, (N)	
Hebrew Character *Orthosia gothica*	4–7			
Early Thorn *Selenia dentaria*	5–6 & 8–9	6–8		
Bordered Beauty *Epione repandaria*	5–7			
Brindled Beauty *Lycia hirtaria*	5–7		S, C, (N)	
Canary-shouldered Thorn *Ennomos alniaria*	5–7			
Early Tooth-striped *Trichopteryx carpinata*	5–7			
Nut-tree Tussock *Colocasia coryli*	5–7 & 9–10	7–9		
Oak Beauty *Biston strataria*	5–7		S, C, (N)	
Purple Thorn *Selenia tetralunaria*	5–7 & 8–9	6–7	S, C, (N)	
Emperor Moth *Saturnia pavonia*	5–8			
Grey Birch *Aethalura punctulata*	5–8			
Large Thorn *Ennomos autumnaria*	5–8		SE	Nb
Common Wave *Cabera exanthemata*	6–7 & 8–9	7–8		
Coxcomb Prominent *Ptilodon capucina*	6–7 & 8–9	6–8		
Dingy Mocha *Cyclophora pendularia*	6–7 & 8–9		S	RDB
Iron Prominent *Notodonta dromedarius*	6–7 & 9–10	8		
Pebble Hook-tip *Drepana falcataria*	6–7 & 9	7–8		
Autumn Green Carpet *Chloroclysta miata*	6–8			L
Kentish Glory *Endromis versicolora*	6–8		NE	Na
Alder Kitten *Furcula bicuspis*	6–9		S, C	L
Brindled White-spot *Parectropis similaria*	6–9		S, (C)	L
Common White Wave *Cabera pusaria*	6–10			
Dark Brocade *Blepharita adusta*	6–9			
Lime Hawk-moth *Mimas tiliae*	6–9		S, C	
Mottled Pug *Eupithecia exiguata*	6–10		S, C, (N)	
Sharp-angled Peacock *Macaria alternata*	7 & 9		S, (C)	L
Alder Moth *Acronicta alni*	7–8		S, C, (N)	L
Dingy Shell *Euchoeca nebulata*	7–9		S, C, (N)	L
Knot Grass *Acronicta rumicis*	7–9	+		
Lobster Moth *Stauropus fagi*	7–9		S, (WC)	
Small Yellow Wave *Hydrelia flammeolaria*	7–9		S, C, (N)	
Waved Carpet *Hydrelia sylvata*	7–9		S, W	Nb
Buff-tip *Phalera bucephala*	7–10			
Common Lutestring *Ochropacha duplaris*	7–10			

May Highflyer *Hydriomena impluviata*	7–10				
Miller *Acronicta leporina*	7–10				
Small Fan-foot *Herminia grisealis*	7–10		L & DL		
Common Fan-foot *Pechipogo strigilata*	7–4		DL	S, C	Na
Large Red-belted Clearwing *Synanthedon culiciformis*	7–5	*	ISt		Nb
Coronet *Craniophora ligustri*	8–9				L
Satin Lutestring *Tetheella fluctuosa*	8–9			SE, W	L
Goat Moth *Cossus cossus*	8–5	*	ISt		Nb
White-barred Clearwing *Synanthedon spheciformis*	8–5	*	ISt	S, C	Nb
Large Emerald *Geometra papilionaria*	9–5				

Alder Buckthorn *Frangula alnus* see Buckthorns

Algae see also Lichens

Orange Footman *Eilema sororcula*	6–9			S	L
Red-necked Footman *Atolmis rubricollis*	8–10			S, WC, (N)	L
Common Footman *Eilema lurideola*	8–5			S, C, (N)	
Four-dotted Footman *Cybosia mesomella*	8–5				L
Dingy Footman *Eilema griseola*	8–6			S, (C)	
Dotted Footman *Pelosia muscerda*	8–6			SE	RDB
Muslin Footman *Nudaria mundana*	8–6				L
Northern Footman *Eilema sericea*	8–6			WC	RDB
Pigmy Footman *Eilema pygmaeola*	8–6			SE	RDB
Scarce Footman *Eilema complana*	8–6			S, C	L
Small Dotted Footman *Pelosia obtusa*	8–6			SE	RDB
Rosy Footman *Miltochrista miniata*	9–5			S, (C)	L
Round-winged Muslin *Thumatha senex*	9–5			S, C, (N)	L
Buff Footman *Eilema depressa*	9–6			S, (C)	L
Four-spotted Footman *Lithosia quadra*	9–6			SW	Na
Hoary Footman *Eilema caniola*	9–6			SW, (WC)	Nb

Almond *Prunus dulcis*

Figure of Eight *Diloba caeruleocephala*	5–7			S, C, (N)	
Red-belted Clearwing *Synanthedon myopaeformis*	7–5	*	ISt	S, (C)	Nb

Alter Lilly *Zantedeschia aethiopica* see Arum Lily

Alyssum (Garden) *Alyssum* spp.

Garden Carpet *Xanthorhoe fluctuata*	6–10				
Least Carpet *Idaea rusticata*	8–5			SE	L

Angelica *Angelica sylvestris*

Brindled Ochre *Dasypolia templi*	4–8		ISt & R	SW, C, N	L
Lime-speck Pug *Eupithecia centaureata*	5–10	+	F		
V-Pug *Chloroclystis v-ata*	5–7 & 8–10	7–9	F	S, C, (N)	
White-spotted Pug *Eupithecia tripunctaria*	6–7 & 9–10		F & S	S, C, (N)	L
Swallowtail *Papilio machaon*	6–8	+		SE	R
Grey Pug *Eupithecia subfuscata*	6–10		F & L		
Triple-spotted Pug *Eupithecia trisignaria*	8–10		F & S	S, C, (N)	L
Mottled Beauty *Alcis repandata*	8–5				

Apples, Cultivated & Crab *Malus* spp.

Brimstone Moth *Opisthograptis luteolata*	All	7–9			
Dotted Chestnut *Conistra rubiginea*	3–6			S, (C)	Nb
Green Pug *Pasiphila rectangulata*	4–5		F		
Black Arches *Lymantria monacha*	4–6			S, C	L

Blue-bordered Carpet *Plemyria rubiginata*	4–6			S, C, (N)	
Copper Underwing *Amphipyra pyramidea*	4–6			S, C, (N)	
Dotted Border *Agriopis marginaria*	4–6				
Feathered Thorn *Colotois pennaria*	4–6				
Green-brindled Crescent *Allophyes oxyacanthae*	4–6				
Lackey *Malacosoma neustria*	4–6			S, C, (N)	
Lunar-spotted Pinion *Cosmia pyralina*	4–6			S, (C)	L
Mottled Umber *Erannis defoliaria*	4–6				
Northern Winter Moth *Operophtera fagata*	4–6				
November Moth *Epirrita dilutata*	4–6				
Pale Brindled Beauty *Phigalia pilosaria*	4–6				
Pale Eggar *Trichiura crataegi*	4–6				
Satellite *Eupsilia transversa*	4–6				
Spring Usher *Agriopis leucophaearia*	4–6			S, C, (N)	
Sprawler *Asteroscopus sphinx*	4–6			S, C	
Winter Moth *Operophtera brumata*	4–6				
Small Eggar *Eriogaster lanestris*	4–7	*		S, C	Nb
Clouded Drab *Orthosia incerta*	4–6				
March Moth *Alsophila aescularia*	5–6				
Figure of Eight *Diloba caeruleocephala*	5–7			S, C, (N)	
Pale Pinion *Lithophane hepatica*	5–7			S, WC	L
V-Pug *Chloroclystis v-ata*	5–7 & 8–10	7–9	F	S, C, (N)	
Chinese Character *Cilix glaucata*	6–7 & 8–9			S, C, (N)	
Least Black Arches *Nola confusalis*	6–8			S, C, (N)	L
Pinion-spotted Pug *Eupithecia insigniata*	6–8		F	S, C	Nb
Red-green Carpet *Chloroclysta siterata*	6–8				
Eyed Hawk-moth *Smerinthus ocellata*	6–9			S, C	
Pale Tussock *Calliteara pudibunda*	6–10			S, C	
Clouded Silver *Lomographa temerata*	7–8			S, C, (N)	
Pale Oak Beauty *Hypomecis punctinalis*	7–8			S, (C)	
Dark Dagger *Acronicta tridens*	7–9	+		S, C, (N)	
Grey Dagger *Acronicta psi*	7–9	+			
Lobster Moth *Stauropus fagi*	7–9			S, (WC)	
Pale-shouldered Brocade *Lacanobia thalassina*	7–9	+			
Red-belted Clearwing *Synanthedon myopaeformis*	7–5		ISt	S, (C)	Nb
Gothic *Naenia typica*	8–3				L
Goat Moth *Cossus cossus*	8–5	*	ISt		Nb
Lappet *Gastropacha quercifolia*	8–5			S, EC	
Leopard Moth *Zeuzera pyrina*	8–5	*	ISt	S, C	
Short-cloaked Moth *Nola cucullatella*	8–5			S, C	
Triple-spotted Clay *Xestia ditrapezium*	8–5		B		L
Yellow-tail *Euproctis similis*	8–6			S, C, (N)	
Brown-tail *Euproctis chrysorrhoea*	9–6			S, (EC)	L
Magpie *Abraxas grossulariata*	9–6				

Artichoke, Globe *Cynara cardunculus*

Painted Lady *Vanessa cardui*	5–10				Bm

Arum Lily *Zantedeschia aethiopica*

Lesser Broad-bordered Yellow Underwing *Noctua janthe*	9–4				

Ash *Fraxinus excelsior*

Barred Tooth-striped *Trichopteryx polycommata*	4–6			S, N, (C)	Na
Brown-spot Pinion *Agrochola litura*	4–6				
Brick *Agrochola circellaris*	4–6		F, S & L		

Centre-barred Sallow *Atethmia centrago*	4–6		B & F		
Copper Underwing *Amphipyra pyramidea*	4–6			S, C, (N)	
December Moth *Poecilocampa populi*	4–6				
November Moth *Epirrita dilutata*	4–6				
Pale Brindled Beauty *Phigalia pilosaria*	4–6				
Sprawler *Asteroscopus sphinx*	4–6			S, C	
Twin-spotted Quaker *Orthosia munda*	4–6			S, C, (N)	
Dusky Thorn *Ennomos fuscantaria*	5–7			S, C	
Purple Thorn *Selenia tetralunaria*	5–7 & 8–9	6–7		S, C, (N)	
Tawny Pinion *Lithophane semibrunnea*	5–7			S, C	L
Ash Pug *Eupithecia fraxinata*	6–7 & 8–9				
Barred Umber *Plagodis pulveraria*	6–8				L
Lunar Thorn *Selenia lunularia*	6–8				L
Red-green Carpet *Chloroclysta siterata*	6–8				
Mottled Pug *Eupithecia exiguata*	6–10			S, C, (N)	
Little Thorn *Cepphis advenaria*	7–8			S, (C)	Nb
Privet Hawk-moth *Sphinx ligustri*	7–9			S, (C)	
Coronet *Craniophora ligustri*	8–9				L
Goat Moth *Cossus cossus*	8–5	*	ISt		Nb
Leopard Moth *Zeuzera pyrina*	8–5	*	ISt	S, C	
Light Emerald *Campaea margaritata*	8–5	+			
Lilac Beauty *Apeira syringaria*	9–5			S, C, (N)	L

Aspen *Populus tremula* see under Poplars & Aspen

Azaleas *Rhododendron* spp. see Rhododendrons

Balsams *Impatiens* spp.

Balsam Carpet *Xanthorhoe biriviata*	6 & 8–9			S, SE, (EC)	UC
Small Phoenix *Ecliptopera silaceata*	6–7	+			
Elephant Hawk-moth *Deilephila elpenor*	7–9	+		S, C, (N)	
Netted Carpet *Eustroma reticulatum*	8–9		F, S & L	WC	RDB

Baneberry *Actaea spicata*

Fern *Horisme tersata*	7–9			S, (C)	

Barberry or Berberis *Berberis* spp.

Angle Shades *Phlogophora meticulosa*	All				
Barberry Carpet *Pareulype berberata*	6–7 & 8–9			S	RDB
Scarce Tissue *Rheumaptera cervinalis*	6–7			S, C	L
Scalloped Hazel *Odontopera bidentata*	6–9				
Grey Pug *Eupithecia subfuscata*	6–10		F & L		
Mottled Pug *Eupithecia exiguata*	6–10			S, C, (N)	
Pale Tussock *Calliteara pudibunda*	6–10			S, C	
Pale-shouldered Brocade *Lacanobia thalassina*	7–9	+			
Buff Ermine *Spilosoma luteum*	7–10				
Dot Moth *Melanchra persicariae*	8–10			S, C, (N)	
Common Emerald *Hemithea aestivaria*	8–5			S, C, (N)	
Mottled Beauty *Alcis repandata*	8–5				
Yellow-tail *Euproctis similis*	8–6			S, C, (N)	

Barley *Hordeum* spp. see under Cereals

Bearberry *Arctostaphylos uva-ursi*

Northern Dart *Xestia alpicola*	4–5	*		N	Na
Golden-rod Brindle *Lithomoia solidaginis*	4–7			WC, N	L

Netted Mountain Moth *Macaria carbonaria*	5–7			N	RDB
Green Hairstreak *Callophrys rubi*	5–8		F & L		L
Small Dark Yellow Underwing *Anarta cordigera*	6–7			N	Na
Satyr Pug *Eupithecia satyrata*	6–9		F		L
Broad-bordered White Underwing *Anarta melanopa*	7–8			N	RDB
Saxon *Hyppa rectilinea*	7–10			N	Nb

Bedstraws *Galium* spp.

Unspecified

Barred Straw *Eulithis pyraliata*	4–6				
Red Chestnut *Cerastis rubricosa*	5–6				
Silver Y *Autographa gamma*	5–10	+			Bm
White-banded Carpet *Spargania luctuata*	6–7 & 9			SE	Na
Satyr Pug *Eupithecia satyrata*	6–9		F		L
Bedstraw Hawk-moth *Hyles gallii*	7–9				Bm
Cream Wave *Scopula floslactata*	7–4				L
Yellow Shell *Camptogramma bilineata*	7–5				
Large Twin-spot Carpet *Xanthorhoe quadrifasiata*	8–5			S, C	L
Plain Wave *Idaea straminata*	8–5				L
Autumnal Rustic *Eugnorisma glareosa*	10–5				

Common Marsh-bedstraw *G. palustre*

Devon Carpet *Lampropteryx otregiata*	6–7 & 9–10			SW	Nb
Purple Bar *Cosmorhoe ocellata*	6–7 & 9–4	7–8			
Oblique Carpet *Orthonama vittata*	7 & 9–4	8–6			L
Elephant Hawk-moth *Dcilcphila elpenor*	7–9	+		S, C, (N)	
Small Elephant Hawk-moth *Deilephila porcellus*	7–9			S, C, (N)	L

Fen Bedstraw *G. uliginosum*

Devon Carpet *Lampropteryx otregiata*	6–7 & 9–10			S, SW	Nb
Elephant Hawk-moth *Deilephila elpenor*	7–9	+		S, C, (N)	
Small Elephant Hawk-moth *Deilephila porcellus*	7–9			S, C, (N)	L

Goosegrass (Cleavers) *G. aparine*

Barred Straw *Eulithis pyraliata*	4–6				
Mottled Grey *Colostygia multistrigaria*	5–6				
Water Carpet *Lampropteryx suffumata*	5–6				
Common Carpet *Epirrhoe alternata*	6–7 & 9–10	7–8			
Red Twin-spot Carpet *Xanthorhoe spadicearia*	7 & 9	6–8			
Small Elephant Hawk-moth *Deilephila porcellus*	7–9			S, C, (N)	L
Striped Twin-spot Carpet *Nebula salicata*	7–9	+		W, N, (SW)	
Silver-ground Carpet *Xanthorhoe montanata*	7–5				
Yellow Shell *Camptogramma bilineata*	7–5				
Gothic *Naenia typica*	8–3				L
Square-spot Rustic *Xestia xanthographa*	9–4				

Heath Bedstraw *G. saxatile*

Mottled Grey *Colostygia multistrigaria*	5–6				
Water Carpet *Lampropteryx suffumata*	5–6				
Galium Carpet *Epirrhoe galiata*	6–7 & 9	8		S, C, (N)	L
Green Carpet *Colostygia pectinataria*	6–7 & 9–5	8–5			
Purple Bar *Cosmorhoe ocellata*	6–7 & 9–4	7–8			
Small Argent & Sable *Epirrhoe tristata*	6–8	+	F	C, N, (SW)	
Oblique Carpet *Orthonama vittata*	7 & 9–4	8–6			L
Bedstraw Hawk-moth *Hyles gallii*	7–9				Bm

Elephant Hawk-moth *Deilephila elpenor*	7–9	+		S, C, (N)	
Small Elephant Hawk-moth *Deilephila porcellus*	7–9			S, C, (N)	L
Striped Twin-spot Carpet *Nebula salicata*	7–9	+		W, N, (SW)	
Silurian *Eriopygodes imbecilla*	8–5			WC	RDB
Beech-green Carpet *Colostygia olivata*	9–5			WC, N, (S)	L

Hedge Bedstraw *G. mollugo*

White-line Dart *Euxoa tritici*	3–7				
Barred Straw *Eulithis pyraliata*	4–6				
Water Carpet *Lampropteryx suffumata*	5–6				
Common Carpet *Epirrhoe alternata*	6–7 & 9–10	7–8			
Galium Carpet *Epirrhoe galiata*	6–7 & 9	8		S, C, (N)	L
Green Carpet *Colostygia pectinataria*	6–7 & 9–5	8–5			
Purple Bar *Cosmorhoe ocellata*	6–7 & 9–4	7–8			
Striped Hawk-moth *Hyles livornica*	6–7 & 9–10				Bm
Small Argent & Sable *Epirrhoe tristata*	6–8	+	F	C, N, (SW)	
Humming-bird Hawk-moth *Macroglossum stellatarum*	6–9				Bm
Oblique Carpet *Orthonama vittata*	7 & 9–4	8–6			L
Red Twin-spot Carpet *Xanthorhoe spadicearia*	7 & 9	6–8			
Ruddy Carpet *Catarhoe rubidata*	7–8			S,C	Nb
Bedstraw Hawk-moth *Hyles gallii*	7–9				Bm
Elephant Hawk-moth *Deilephila elpenor*	7–9	+		S, C, (N)	
Flame *Axylia putris*	7–9			S, C, (N)	
Royal Mantle *Catarhoe cuculata*	7–9		F	S, (N)	L
Small Elephant Hawk-moth *Deilephila porcellus*	7–9			S, C, (N)	L
Striped Twin-spot Carpet *Nebula salicata*	7–9	+		W, N, (SW)	
Silver-ground Carpet *Xanthorhoe montanata*	7–5				
Wood Carpet *Epirrhoe rivata*	8–9			S, C, (N)	L
Mottled Rustic *Caradrina morpheus*	8–11				
Single-dotted Wave *Idaea dimidiata*	8–5		F & L	S, C, NW	
Small Scallop *Idaea emarginata*	8–5			S, C	L
Six-striped Rustic *Xestia sexstrigata*	9–4				
Beech-green Carpet *Colostygia olivata*	9–5			WC, N, (S)	L
Archer's Dart *Agrotis vestigialis*	9–6				L
Black Rustic *Aporophyla nigra*	10–5				

Lady's Bedstraw *G. verum*

Square-spot Dart *Euxoa obelisca*	3–7				Nb
White-line Dart *Euxoa tritici*	3–7				
Barred Straw *Eulithis pyraliata*	4–6				
Mottled Grey *Colostygia multistrigaria*	5–6				
Oblique Striped *Phibalapteryx virgata*	5–6 & 8–9			S, WC, (SN)	Nb
Water Carpet *Lampropteryx suffumata*	5–6				
Common Carpet *Epirrhoe alternata*	6–7 & 9–10	7–8			
Dark-barred Twin-spot Carpet *Xanthorhoe ferrugata*	6–7 & 9	6–8		S, C, (N)	
Flame Shoulder *Ochropleura plecta*	6–7 & 9–10	8–9			
Galium Carpet *Epirrhoe galiata*	6–7 & 9	8		S, C, (N)	L
Green Carpet *Colostygia pectinataria*	6–7 & 9–5	8–5			
Humming-bird Hawk-moth *Macroglossum stellatarum*	6–9				Bm
Purple Bar *Cosmorhoe ocellata*	6–7 & 9–4	7–8			
Striped Hawk-moth *Hyles livornica*	6–7 & 9–10				Bm
Oblique Carpet *Orthonama vittata*	7 & 9–4	8–6			L
Red Twin-spot Carpet *Xanthorhoe spadicearia*	7 & 9	6–8			
Ruddy Carpet *Catarhoe rubidata*	7–8			S,C	Nb
Bedstraw Hawk-moth *Hyles gallii*	7–9				Bm

Elephant Hawk-moth *Deilephila elpenor*	7–9	+		S, C, (N)	
Flame *Axylia putris*	7–9			S, C, (N)	
Royal Mantle *Catarhoe cuculata*	7–9		F	S, (N)	L
Small Elephant Hawk-moth *Deilephila porcellus*	7–9			S, C, (N)	L
Striped Twin-spot Carpet *Nebula salicata*	7–9	+		W, N, (SW)	
Riband Wave *Idaea aversata*	7–5	+			
Wood Carpet *Epirrhoe rivata*	8–9			S, C, (N)	L
Small Scallop *Idaea emarginata*	8–5			S, C	L
Ashworth's Rustic *Xestia ashworthii*	8–6			WC	Na
Beech-green Carpet *Colostygia olivata*	9–5			WC, N, (S)	L
Archer's Dart *Agrotis vestigialis*	9–6				L
Silver-striped Hawk-moth *Hippotion celerio*	10				Bm

Beeches *Fagus sylvatica* & *Nothofagus* spp.

Barred Sallow *Xanthia aurago*	4–6		B, F & L	S, C, (N)	
Common Quaker *Orthosia cerasi*	4–6				
Northern Winter Moth *Operophtera fagata*	4–6				
Pale November Moth *Epirrita christyi*	4–6			S, C, (N)	
Satellite *Eupsilia transversa*	4–6				
Scarce Umber *Agriopis aurantiaria*	4–6				
Sprawler *Asteroscopus sphinx*	4–6			S, C	
Yellow-line Quaker *Agrochola macilenta*	4–6				
August Thorn *Ennomos quercinaria*	5–7			S, C, (N)	L
Brindled Beauty *Lycia hirtaria*	5–7			S, C, (N)	
Brindled Pug *Eupithecia abbreviata*	5–7		F		
Marbled Pug *Eupithecia irriguata*	5–7			S, (C)	Nb
Nut-tree Tussock *Colocasia coryli*	5–7 & 9–10	7–9			
September Thorn *Ennomos erosaria*	5–7			S, C, (N)	
Barred Hook-tip *Watsonalla cultraria*	6–7 & 9			S, C	L
Coxcomb Prominent *Ptilodon capucina*	6–7 & 8–9	6–8			
Least Black Arches *Nola confusalis*	6–8			S, C, (N)	L
Small Engrailed *Ectropis crepuscularia*	6–8			S, C, (N)	L
Square Spot *Paradarisa consonaria*	6–8			S, C, SN	L
Clay Triple-lines *Cyclophora linearia*	7–8	+		S, C	L
Green Silver-lines *Pseudoips prasinana*	7–9	+			
Lobster Moth *Stauropus fagi*	7–9			S, (WC)	
Marbled Brown *Drymonia dodonaea*	7–9			S, C, (NW)	L
Peppered Moth *Biston betularia*	7–9				
Scorched Wing *Plagodis dolabraria*	7–9			S, (WC)	L
Buff-tip *Phalera bucephala*	7–10				
Fan-foot *Zanclognatha tarsipennalis*	7–10		DL	S, C, (N)	
Triangle *Heterogenea asella*	7–10			S, (EC)	RDB
Festoon *Apoda limacodes*	7–5			S, (C)	Nb
Clouded Magpie *Abraxas sylvata*	7–10			S, C, SN, (N)	L
Olive Crescent *Trisateles emortualis*	8–10		DL	SE	RDB
Leopard Moth *Zeuzera pyrina*	8–5	*	ISt	S, C	
Light Emerald *Campaea margaritata*	8–5	+			
Scarce Silver-lines *Bena bicolorana*	8–5			S, C	L
Yellow-legged Clearwing *Synanthedon vespiformis*	8–5		ISt	S, C	Nb
Scarce Vapourer *Orgyia recens*	8–6			EC	RDB
Yellow-tail *Euproctis similis*	8–6			S, C, (N)	
Broad-bordered Yellow Underwing *Noctua fimbriata*	9–4				
Large Emerald *Geometra papilionaria*	9–5				

Bellflowers *Campanula* spp.

Lime-speck Pug *Eupithecia centaureata*	5–10	+	F		
Campanula Pug *Eupithecia denotata*	8–10		F	S, (C)	Na

Betony *Stachys officinalis*

Speckled Yellow *Pseudopanthera macularia*	6–8			S, WC, N, (EC)	
Grey Pug *Eupithecia subfuscata*	6–10		F & L		

Bilberry *Vaccinium myrtillus*

Scalloped Oak *Crocallis elinguaria*	3–7				
Bilberry Pug *Pasiphila debiliata*	4–5		F	S, C	Nb
Early Moth *Theria primaria*	4–5			S, C, (N)	
Northern Dart *Xestia alpicola*	4–5	*		N	Na
Rannoch Looper *Itame brunneata*	4–5			N	Na
Small Autumnal Moth *Epirrita filigrammaria*	4–5			C, N	
Autumnal Moth *Epirrita autumnata*	4–6				
Dark Marbled Carpet *Chloroclysta citrata*	4–6				
Flounced Chestnut *Agrochola helvola*	4–6				
Hebrew Character *Orthosia gothica*	4–7				
Manchester Treble-bar *Carsia sororiata*	4–6		F & L	C, N	Nb
Northern Spinach *Eulithis populata*	4–6			SW, C, N	
November Moth *Epirrita dilutata*	4–6				
Pale Eggar *Trichiura crataegi*	4–6				
Twin-spot Carpet *Perizoma didymata*	4–6				
White-marked *Cerastis leucographa*	4–6			S, C	L
Golden-rod Brindle *Lithomoia solidaginis*	4–7			WC, N	L
July Highflyer *Hydriomena furcata*	5–6				
Red Chestnut *Cerastis rubricosa*	5–6				
Green Hairstreak *Callophrys rubi*	5–8		F & L		L
Rannoch Brindled Beauty *Lycia lapponaria*	5–8			N	Na
Vapourer *Orgyia antiqua*	5–8	+			
Common Pug *Eupithecia vulgata*	6–7 & 8–10	7–8			
Small Dark Yellow Underwing *Anarta cordigera*	6–7			N	Na
Glaucous Shears *Papestra biren*	6–8			WC, N, (SW)	L
Ringed Carpet *Cleora cinctaria*	6–8			S, WC, N	Na
Light Knot Grass *Acronicta menyanthidis*	6–9			C, N, (SE)	L
Scalloped Hazel *Odontopera bidentata*	6–9				
Fox Moth *Macrothylacia rubi*	6–4				
Broad-bordered White Underwing *Anarta melanopa*	7–8			N	RDB
Common Marbled Carpet *Chloroclysta truncata*	7–8 & 9–5	8–6			
Little Thorn *Cepphis advenaria*	7–8			S, (C)	Nb
Beautiful Snout *Hypena crassalis*	7–9			S, WC, (EC)	L
Fan-foot *Zanclognatha tarsipennalis*	7–10		DL	S, C, (N)	
Little Emerald *Jodis lactearia*	7–10			S, C, NW	
Saxon *Hyppa rectilinea*	7–10			N	Nb
Scallop Shell *Rheumaptera undulata*	7–10			S, C, (N)	L
Pale Shining Brown *Polia bombycina*	7–5			S	RDB
Scarce Silver Y *Syngrapha interrogationis*	7–6			W C, N	L
Beautiful Golden Y *Autographa pulchrina*	8–5				
Green Arches *Anaplectoides prasina*	8–5				
Mottled Beauty *Alcis repandata*	8–5				
Plain Wave *Idaea straminata*	8–5				L
Purple Clay *Diarsia brunnea*	8–5				
Scotch Burnet *Zygaena exulans*	8–5	*	L & S	N	RDB
Silurian *Eriopygodes imbecilla*	8–5			WC	RDB

Plant List | Foodplant List for the Caterpillars of Britain's Butterflies and Larger Moths

Smoky Wave *Scopula ternata*	8–5			W, N	L
Gold Spangle *Autographa bractea*	8–6			C, N	
Grey Mountain Carpet *Entephria caesiata*	8–6			C, N	
Barred Chestnut *Diarsia dahlii*	9–4			C, N, (S)	L
Ingrailed Clay *Diarsia mendica*	9–4				
Northern Deep-brown Dart *Aporophyla lueneburgensis*	9–5			WC, N	
Cousin German *Protolampra sobrina*	9–6			N	Na
Great Brocade *Eurois occulta*	9–6			N	Nb
Oak Eggar *Lasiocampa quercus*	All		*		
Speckled Footman *Coscinia cribraria*	9–6			SW	RDB

Bindweeds *Convolvulus* spp. & *Calystegia* spp.

Double-striped Pug *Gymnoscelis rufifasciata*	5–6 & 9–10	+	F		
Nutmeg *Discestra trifolii*	6–7 & 9–10	8–9		S, C, (N)	
Tawny Wave *Scopula rubiginata*	6–7 & 8–5			SE	RDB
Four-spotted *Tyta luctuosa*	7–8	+		S, C	Na
Bright-line Brown-eye *Lacanobia oleracea*	7–9	+			
Elephant Hawk-moth *Deilephila elpenor*	7–9	+		S, C, (N)	
Convolvulus Hawk-Moth *Agrius convolvuli*	7–11			(S)	Bm
Dot Moth *Melanchra persicariae*	8–10			S, C, (N)	
Small Scallop *Idaea emarginata*	8–5			S, C	L
Silver-striped Hawk-moth *Hippotion celerio*	10				Bm

Sea Bindweed *Calystegia soldanella*

White Colon *Sideridis albicolon*	6–7 & 9		F		Nb
Bordered Straw *Heliothis peltigera*	7–10		F		Bm
Sand Dart *Agrotis ripae*	8–10			S, C, NE	Nb
Portland Moth *Actebia praecox*	9–6			SW, C, N, (S)	Nb

Birches *Betula* spp.

Angle Shades *Phlogophora meticulosa*	All				
Scalloped Oak *Crocallis elinguaria*	3–7				
Svensson's Copper Underwing *Amphipyra berbera*	4–5			S, C	
Angle-striped Sallow *Enargia paleacea*	4–6			C, N	Nb
Autumnal Moth *Epirrita autumnata*	4–6				
Black Arches *Lymantria monacha*	4–6			S, C	L
Blue-bordered Carpet *Plemyria rubiginata*	4–6				
Common Quaker *Orthosia cerasi*	4–6				
Copper Underwing *Amphipyra pyramidea*	4–6			S, C, (N)	
Dark Chestnut *Conistra ligula*	4–6			S, C, (N)	
Dark Marbled Carpet *Chloroclysta citrata*	4–6				
December Moth *Poecilocampa populi*	4–6				
Dotted Border *Agriopis marginaria*	4–6				
Dun-bar *Cosmia trapezina*	4–6				
Engrailed *Ectropis bistortata*	4–6 & 7–9	5–7			
Feathered Thorn *Colotois pennaria*	4–6				
Flounced Chestnut *Agrochola helvola*	4–6				
Hebrew Character *Orthosia gothica*	4–7				
Lackey *Malacosoma neustria*	4–6			S, C, (N)	
Lesser Swallow Prominent *Pheosia gnoma*	4–6 & 7–8	5–8			
Mottled Umber *Erannis defoliaria*	4–6				
Northern Winter Moth *Operophtera fagata*	4–6				
November Moth *Epirrita dilutata*	4–6				
Orange Underwing *Archiearis parthenias*	4–6		F, L		L
Pale Brindled Beauty *Phigalia pilosaria*	4–6				

Species				
Pale Eggar *Trichiura crataegi*	4–6			
Pale November Moth *Epirrita christyi*	4–6		S, C, (N)	
Satellite *Eupsilia transversa*	4–6			
Scarce Umber *Agriopis aurantiaria*	4–6			
Small Brindled Beauty *Apocheima hispidaria*	4–6		S, (C, N)	L
Small Quaker *Orthosia cruda*	4–6			
Sprawler *Asteroscopus sphinx*	4–6		S, C	
Suspected *Parastichtis suspecta*	4–6			L
Winter Moth *Operophtera brumata*	4–6			
Golden-rod Brindle *Lithomoia solidaginis*	4–7		WC, N	L
Small Eggar *Eriogaster lanestris*	4–7	*	S, C	Nb
Blossom Underwing *Orthosia miniosa*	5–6		S, C	L
Chestnut *Conistra vaccinii*	5–6			
Chevron *Eulithis testata*	5–6			
Clouded Drab *Orthosia incerta*	4–6			
Early Thorn *Selenia dentaria*	5–6 & 8–9	6–8		
March Moth *Alsophila aescularia*	5–6			
Rannoch Sprawler *Brachionycha nubeculosa*	5–6		N	RDB
August Thorn *Ennomos quercinaria*	5–7		S, C, (N)	L
Brindled Beauty *Lycia hirtaria*	5–7		S, C, (N)	
Canary-shouldered Thorn *Ennomos alniaria*	5–7			
Dark Bordered Beauty *Epione vespertaria*	5–7		EC, NE	RDB
Early Tooth-striped *Trichopteryx carpinata*	5–7			
Netted Mountain Moth *Macaria carbonaria*	5–7		N	RDB
Northern Drab *Orthosia opima*	5–7			L
Nut-tree Tussock *Colocasia coryli*	5–7 & 9–10	7–9		
Oak Beauty *Biston strataria*	5–7		S, C, (N)	
Pale Pinion *Lithophane hepatica*	5–7		S, WC	L
Purple Thorn *Selenia tetralunaria*	5–7 & 8–9	6–7	S, C, (N)	
September Thorn *Ennomos erosaria*	5–7		S, C, (N)	
Scarce Prominent *Odontosia carmelita*	5–7		S, N, (C)	L
Yellow Horned *Achlya flavicornis*	5–7	*		
Emperor Moth *Saturnia pavonia*	5–8			
Grey Birch *Aethalura punctulata*	5–8			
Large Thorn *Ennomos autumnaria*	5–8		SE	Nb
Vapourer *Orgyia antiqua*	5–8	+		
Birch Mocha *Cyclophora albipunctata*	6–7 & 9–10	6–7		L
Common Wave *Cabera exanthemata*	6–7 & 8–9	7–8		
Coxcomb Prominent *Ptilodon capucina*	6–7 & 8–9	6–8		
False Mocha *Cyclophora porata*	6–7 & 9–10		S, C	Nb
Iron Prominent *Notodonta dromedarius*	6–7 & 9–10	8		
Maiden's Blush *Cyclophora punctaria*	6–7 & 8–9		S, C, (N)	L
Oak Hook-tip *Watsonalla binaria*	6–7 & 8–9		S, C	
Pebble Hook-tip *Drepana falcataria*	6–7 & 9	6–7		
Scalloped Hook-tip *Falcaria lacertinaria*	6–7 & 8–9	6–8		
Autumn Green Carpet *Chloroclysta miata*	6–8			L
Barred Umber *Plagodis pulveraria*	6–8			L
Kentish Glory *Endromis versicolora*	6–8		NE	Na
Least Black Arches *Nola confusalis*	6–8		S, C, (N)	L
Lunar Thorn *Selenia lunularia*	6–8			L
Peacock Moth *Macaria notata*	6–8	+	S, WC, NW	L
Red-green Carpet *Chloroclysta siterata*	6–8			
Ringed Carpet *Cleora cinctaria*	6–8		S, WC, N	Na
Small Engrailed *Ectropis crepuscularia*	6–8		S, C, (N)	L
Square Spot *Paradarisa consonaria*	6–8		S, C, SN	L

Alder Kitten *Furcula bicuspis*	6–9			S, C	L
Brindled White-spot *Parectropis similaria*	6–9			S, (C)	L
Common White Wave *Cabera pusaria*	6–10				
Light Knot Grass *Acronicta menyanthidis*	6–9			C, N, (SE)	L
Lime Hawk-moth *Mimas tiliae*	6–9			S, C	
Muslin Moth *Diaphora mendica*	6–9			S, C, (N)	
Scalloped Hazel *Odontopera bidentata*	6–9				
Sweet Gale Moth *Acronicta euphorbiae*	6–9			N	Na
Pale Tussock *Calliteara pudibunda*	6–10			S, C	
Alder Moth *Acronicta alni*	7–8			S, C, (N)	L
Clouded Silver *Lomographa temerata*	7–8			S, C, (N)	
Common Marbled Carpet *Chloroclysta truncata*	7–8 & 9~5	8~6			
Pale Oak Beauty *Hypomecis punctinalis*	7–8			S, (C)	
Small Grass Emerald *Chlorissa viridata*	7–8			S, (WC)	Na
Small White Wave *Asthena albulata*	7–8	+		S, C, (N)	
Argent & Sable *Rheumaptera hastata*	7–9				Nb
Broken-barred Carpet *Electrophaes corylata*	7–9				
Broom Moth *Melanchra pisi*	7–9				
Dark Dagger *Acronicta tridens*	7–9	+		S, C, (N)	
Green Silver-lines *Pseudoips prasinana*	7–9	+			
Grey Dagger *Acronicta psi*	7–9	+			
Lobster Moth *Stauropus fagi*	7–9			S, (WC)	
Pale-shouldered Brocade *Lacanobia thalassina*	7–9	+			
Peppered Moth *Biston betularia*	7–9				
Scorched Wing *Plagodis dolabraria*	7–9			S, (WC)	L
Small Angle Shades *Euplexia lucipara*	7–9	+			
Sycamore *Acronicta aceris*	7–9			S, (C)	L
Waved Carpet *Hydrelia sylvata*	7–9			S, W	Nb
Welsh Wave *Venusia cambrica*	7–9			W, N	L
Buff Ermine *Spilosoma luteum*	7–10				
Buff-tip *Phalera bucephala*	7–10				
Common Lutestring *Ochropacha duplaris*	7–10				
Little Emerald *Jodis lactearia*	7–10			S, C, NW	
Miller *Acronicta leporina*	7–10				
Small Fan-foot *Herminia grisealis*	7–10		L & DL		
Common Fan-foot *Pechipogo strigilata*	7~4		DL & F	S, C	Na
Large Red-belted Clearwing *Synanthedon culiciformis*	7~5	*	ISt		Nb
New Forest Burnet *Zygaena viciae*	7~6	*		NW	RDB
Willow Beauty *Peribatodes rhomboidaria*	7~6	+			
Beautiful Brocade *Lacanobia contigua*	8–9				L
Satin Lutestring *Tetheella fluctuosa*	8–9			SE, W	L
Common Emerald *Hemithea aestivaria*	8–5			S, C, (N)	
Double Dart *Graphiphora augur*	8–5				
Double Square-spot *Xestia triangulum*	8–5				
Goat Moth *Cossus cossus*	8–5	*	ISt		Nb
Great Oak Beauty *Hypomecis roboraria*	8–5			S, (C)	Nb
Grey Arches *Polia nebulosa*	8–5				
Light Emerald *Campaea margaritata*	8~5	+			
Mottled Beauty *Alcis repandata*	8~5				
Orange Moth *Angerona prunaria*	8~5			S, (C)	L
Purple Clay *Diarsia brunnea*	8–5				
Satin Beauty *Deileptenia ribeata*	8–5				
Scarce Silver-lines *Bena bicolorana*	8–5			S, C	L
Silvery Arches *Polia trimaculosa*	8–5				Nb
Treble Brown Spot *Idaea trigeminata*	8–5	+		S, (C)	L

Triple-spotted Clay *Xestia ditrapezium*	8~5		B		L
Welsh Clearwing *Synanthedon scoliaeformis*	8–5	*	ISt	WC, N	RDB
White-barred Clearwing *Synanthedon spheciformis*	8–5	*	ISt	S, C	Nb
Yellow-legged Clearwing *Synanthedon vespiformis*	8–5		ISt	S, C	Nb
Dark Tussock *Dicallomera fascelina*	8–6			S, WC, N	L
Scarce Vapourer *Orgyia recens*	8–6			EC	RDB
Yellow-tail *Euproctis similis*	8–6			S, C, (N)	
Barred Chestnut *Diarsia dahlii*	9–4			C, N, (S)	L
Broad-bordered Yellow Underwing *Noctua fimbriata*	9–4				
Lesser Broad-bordered Yellow Underwing *Noctua janthe*	9–4				
Dotted Clay *Xestia baja*	9–5				
Large Emerald *Geometra papilionaria*	9–5				
Old Lady *Mormo maura*	9–5			S, C, (N)	L
Square-spotted Clay *Xestia rhomboidea*	9–5			S, (WC, N)	Nb
Cousin German *Protolampra sobrina*	9–6			N	Na
Great Brocade *Eurois occulta*	9–6			N	Nb
Autumnal Rustic *Eugnorisma glareosa*	10~5				

Bird's-foot *Ornithopus perpusillus*

Chalkhill Blue *Lysandra coridon*	3–6			S	S
Silver-studded Blue *Plebejus argus*	4–6		F & L	S, WC	R
Common Blue *Polyommatus icarus*	6–7 & 8~4	8~5			

Birds-foot-trefoils *Lotus* spp.

Common Bird's-foot-trefoil *Lotus corniculatus*

Chalkhill Blue *Lysandra coridon*	3–6			S	S
Grass Eggar *Lasiocampa trifolii*	3–6			S, WC	Na
Silver-studded Blue *Plebejus argus*	4–6		F & L	S, WC	R
Belted Beauty *Lycia zonaria*	5–7			NW	Na
Silver Cloud *Egira conspicillaris*	5–7			SW, WC	Na
Green Hairstreak *Callophrys rubi*	5–8		F & L		L
Clouded Yellow *Colias croceus*	6–7 & 8–11				Bm
Common Blue *Polyommatus icarus*	6–7 & 8~4	8~5			
Wood White *Leptidea sinapis*	6–7 & 8–9	7–8		S	R
Ringed Carpet *Cleora cinctaria*	6–8			S, WC, N	Na
Yellow Belle *Semiaspilates ochrearia*	6–8 & 9–5			S, C	L
Five-spot Burnet *Zygaena trifolii*	6–5	*		S, WC	L
Burnet Companion *Euclidia glyphica*	7–8	+		S, C, (N)	
Mother Shipton *Callistege mi*	7–9				
Dingy Skipper *Erynnis tages*	7~4	+		S, C, N	L
Pale Clouded Yellow *Colias hyale*	7~4			S,C	Bm
Black-veined Moth *Siona lineata*	7–5			SE	RDB
Slender Scotch Burnet *Zygaena loti*	7–5	*		NW	
Narrow-bordered Five-spot Burnet *Zygaena lonicerae*	7–6			S, C, (N)	
Six-belted Clearwing *Bembecia ichneumoniformis*	7–6		R	S, C	Nb
Chalk Carpet *Scotopteryx bipunctaria*	8–6			S, C, (N)	Nb
Scarce Black Arches *Nola aerugula*	8–6				Bm
Shaded Broad-bar *Scotopteryx chenopodiata*	8–6				
Annulet *Charissa obscurata*	9–5				L
Northern Deep-brown Dart *Aporophyla lueneburgensis*	9–5			WC, N	
Bordered Grey *Selidosema brunnearia*	9–6				Na
Hoary Footman *Eilema caniola*	9–6			SW, (WC)	Nb
Portland Moth *Actebia praecox*	9–6			SW, C, N, (S)	Nb
Six-spot Burnet *Zygaena filipendulae*	9–6	*			
Straw Belle *Aspitates gilvaria*	9–6			SE	RDB

Greater Birds-foot-trefoil *Lotus pedunculatus*

Common Blue *Polyommatus icarus*	6–7 & 8~4	8~5		
Dingy Skipper *Erynnis tages*	6~4	+	S, C, N	L
Five-spot Burnet *Zygaena trifolii*	6–5	*	S, WC	L
Narrow-bordered Five-spot Burnet *Zygaena lonicerae*	7–6		S, C, (N)	
Six-spot Burnet *Zygaena filipendulae*	9–6	*		

Bistorts *Persicaria* spp.

Brown Rustic *Rusina ferruginea*	8~5			

Bitter-cresses *Cardamine* spp.

Large Bitter-cress *C. amara*

Green-veined White *Pieris napi*	5–6 & 7–8	6–8		
Orange-tip *Anthocharis cardamines*	5–7		S, B, F & L	

Hairy Bitter-cress *C. hirsuta*

Garden Carpet *Xanthorhoe fluctuata*	6–10			

Bitter-vetch *Lathyrus linifolius* see under Peas

Bittersweet *Solanum dulcamara*

Death's-head Hawk-moth *Acherontia atropos*	7–10			Bm

Black Horehound *Ballota nigra*

Wormwood Pug *Eupithecia absinthiata*	8–10		F	
Cream-spot Tiger *Arctia villica*	8~5		S	L

Black Medick *Medicago lupulina*

Clouded Yellow *Colias croceus*	6–7 & 8–11			Bm
Common Blue *Polyommatus icarus*	6–7 & 8~4	8~5		
Latticed Heath *Chiasmia clathrata*	6–7 & 8–9	7–8		
Burnet Companion *Euclidia glyphica*	7–8	+	S, C, (N)	
Mother Shipton *Callistege mi*	7–9			
Pale Clouded Yellow *Colias hyale*	7~4		S,C	Bm
Chalk Carpet *Scotopteryx bipunctaria*	8~6		S, C, (N)	Nb
Scarce Black Arches *Nola aerugula*	8~6			Bm
Straw Belle *Aspitates gilvaria*	9~6		SE	RDB

Blackthorn *Prunus spinosa*

Brimstone Moth *Opisthograptis luteolata*	All	7–9		
Sloe Pug *Pasiphila chloerata*	3–5		F	S, C
Dotted Chestnut *Conistra rubiginea*	3–6			S, (C)	Nb
Grass Eggar *Lasiocampa trifolii*	3–6			S, WC	Na
Scalloped Oak *Crocallis elinguaria*	3–7				
Black Hairstreak *Satyrium pruni*	4–5		F & L	SE, EC	R
Early Moth *Theria primaria*	4–5			S, C, (N)	
Green Pug *Pasiphila rectangulata*	4–5		F		
Blue-bordered Carpet *Plemyria rubiginata*	4–6				
Common Quaker *Orthosia cerasi*	4–6				
Copper Underwing *Amphipyra pyramidea*	4–6			S, C, (N)	
Dark Chestnut *Conistra ligula*	4–6			S, C, (N)	
December Moth *Poecilocampa populi*	4–6				
Dotted Border *Agriopis marginaria*	4–6				
Dun-bar *Cosmia trapezina*	4–6				
Feathered Thorn *Colotois pennaria*	4–6				

Species		Months			
Green-brindled Crescent *Allophyes oxyacanthae*	4–6				
Hebrew Character *Orthosia gothica*	4–7				
Lackey *Malacosoma neustria*	4–6			S, C, (N)	
Lunar-spotted Pinion *Cosmia pyralina*	4–6			S, (C)	L
Mottled Umber *Erannis defoliaria*	4–6				
November Moth *Epirrita dilutata*	4–6				
Pale Brindled Beauty *Phigalia pilosaria*	4–6				
Pale Eggar *Trichiura crataegi*	4–6				
Pale November Moth *Epirrita christyi*	4–6			S, C, (N)	
Satellite *Eupsilia transversa*	4–6				
Scarce Umber *Agriopis aurantiaria*	4–6				
Sprawler *Asteroscopus sphinx*	4–6			S, C	
Twin-spotted Quaker *Orthosia munda*	4–6			S, C, (N)	
Winter Moth *Operophtera brumata*	4–6				
Shoulder Stripe *Anticlea badiata*	4–7			S, C, (N)	
Small Eggar *Eriogaster lanestris*	4–7	*		S, C	Nb
Blossom Underwing *Orthosia miniosa*	5–6			S, C	L
Brown Hairstreak *Thecla betulae*	5–6			S, (C)	S
Chestnut *Conistra vaccinii*	5–6				
Clouded Drab *Orthosia incerta*	4–6				
Early Thorn *Selenia dentaria*	5–6 & 8–9	6–8			
March Moth *Alsophila aescularia*	5–6				
August Thorn *Ennomos quercinaria*	5–7			S, C, (N)	L
Figure of Eight *Diloba caeruleocephala*	5–7			S, C, (N)	
Nut-tree Tussock *Colocasia coryli*	5–7 & 9–10	7–9			
Powdered Quaker *Orthosia gracilis*	5–7				
Sloe Carpet *Aleucis distinctata*	5–7			SE	Nb
Streamer *Anticlea derivata*	5–7				
Emperor Moth *Saturnia pavonia*	5–8				
Large Thorn *Ennomos autumnaria*	5–8			SE	Nb
Vapourer *Orgyia antiqua*	5–8	+			
Ash Pug *Eupithecia fraxinata*	6–7 & 8–9				
Chinese Character *Cilix glaucata*	6–7 & 8–9			S, C, (N)	
Least Black Arches *Nola confusalis*	6–8			S, C, (N)	L
Lunar Thorn *Selenia lunularia*	6–8				L
Pinion-spotted Pug *Eupithecia insigniata*	6–8		F	S, EC	Nb
Red-green Carpet *Chloroclysta siterata*	6–8				
White–pinion Spotted *Lomographa bimaculata*	6–8			S, C	
Scalloped Hazel *Odontopera bidentata*	6–9				
Grey Pug *Eupithecia subfuscata*	6–10		F & L		
Mottled Pug *Eupithecia exiguata*	6–10			S, C, (N)	
Pale Tussock *Calliteara pudibunda*	6–10			S, C	
Sharp-angled Peacock *Macaria alternata*	7 & 9			S, (C)	L
Clouded Silver *Lomographa temerata*	7–8			S, C, (N)	
Broken-barred Carpet *Electrophaes corylata*	7–9				
Dark Dagger *Acronicta tridens*	7–9	+		S, C, (N)	
Grey Dagger *Acronicta psi*	7–9	+			
Lobster Moth *Stauropus fagi*	7–9			S, (WC)	
Pale-shouldered Brocade *Lacanobia thalassina*	7–9	+			
Peppered Moth *Biston betularia*	7–9				
Little Emerald *Jodis lactearia*	7–10			S, C, NW	
Gothic *Naenia typica*	8–3				L
Common Emerald *Hemithea aestivaria*	8–5			S, C, (N)	
Double Dart *Graphiphora augur*	8–5				
Double Square-spot *Xestia triangulum*	8–5				

Grass Wave *Perconia strigillaria*	8–5			S, C, (N)	L
Grey Arches *Polia nebulosa*	8–5				
Lappet *Gastropacha quercifolia*	8–5			S, EC	
Leopard Moth *Zeuzera pyrina*	8–5	★	lSt	S, C	
Light Emerald *Campaea margaritata*	8–5	+			
Mottled Beauty *Alcis repandata*	8–5				
Orange Moth *Angerona prunaria*	8–5			S, (C)	L
Purple Clay *Diarsia brunnea*	8–5				
Scarlet Tiger *Callimorpha dominula*	8–5			S, (WC)	L
Short-cloaked Moth *Nola cucullatella*	8–5			S, C	
Triple-spotted Clay *Xestia ditrapezium*	8–5		B		L
Lesser Yellow Underwing *Noctua comes*	8–6				
Scarce Vapourer *Orgyia recens*	8–6			EC	RDB
Swallow-tailed Moth *Ourapteryx sambucaria*	8–6				
Yellow-tail *Euproctis similis*	8–6			S, C, (N)	
Broad-bordered Yellow Underwing *Noctua fimbriata*	9–4				
Ingrailed Clay *Diarsia mendica*	9–4				
Lesser Broad-bordered Yellow Underwing *Noctua janthe*	9–4				
Dotted Clay *Xestia baja*	9–5				
Old Lady *Mormo maura*	9–5			S, C, (N)	L
Brown-tail *Euproctis chrysorrhoea*	9–6			S, (EC)	L
Great Brocade *Eurois occulta*	9–6			N	Nb
Magpie *Abraxas grossulariata*	9–6				
Oak Eggar *Lasiocampa quercus*	All	★			
Feathered Brindle *Aporophyla australis*	10–5			S	Nb
Deep-brown Dart *Aporophyla lutulenta*	10–6			S, EC	

Bladder-senna *Colutea arborescens*

Long-tailed Blue *Lampides boeticus*	9–11		F&S	S	Bm

Bluebell *Hyacinthoides non-scripta*

Six-striped Rustic *Xestia sexstrigata*	9–4				
Autumnal Rustic *Eugnorisma glareosa*	10–5				

Bog Asphodel *Narthecium ossifragum*

Shoulder-striped Clover *Heliothis maritima*	8–9		F & S	S	RDB

Bogbean *Menyanthes trifoliata*

Light Knot Grass *Acronicta menyanthidis*	6–9			C, N, (SE)	L
Elephant Hawk-moth *Deilephila elpenor*	7–9	+		S, C, (N)	

Bog-myrtle *Myrica gale*

Winter Moth *Operophtera brumata*	4–6				
Golden-rod Brindle *Lithomoia solidaginis*	4–7			WC, N	L
Early Thorn *Selenia dentaria*	5–6 & 8–9	6–8			
Powdered Quaker *Orthosia gracilis*	5–7				
Red Sword-grass *Xylena vetusta*	5–7				L
Sword-grass *Xylena exsoleta*	5–7			C, N	Nb
Rannoch Brindled Beauty *Lycia lapponaria*	5–8			N	Na
Vapourer *Orgyia antiqua*	5–8	+			
Glaucous Shears *Papestra biren*	6–8			WC, N, (SW)	L
Ringed Carpet *Cleora cinctaria*	6–8			S, WC, N	Na
Common Heath *Ematurga atomaria*	6–9	+			
Dark Brocade *Blepharita adusta*	6–9				
Light Knot Grass *Acronicta menyanthidis*	6–9			C, N, (SE)	L
Sweet Gale Moth *Acronicta euphorbiae*	6–9			N	Na

Fox Moth *Macrothylacia rubi*	6~4				
Argent & Sable *Rheumaptera hastata*	7–9				Nb
Clouded Buff *Diacrisia sannio*	7~5				L
Beautiful Brocade *Lacanobia contigua*	8–9				L
Silvery Arches *Polia trimaculosa*	8~5				Nb
Dotted Clay *Xestia baja*	9~5				
Great Brocade *Eurois occulta*	9~6			N	Nb
Rosy Marsh Moth *Coenophila subrosea*	9–6			WC	RDB

Bog-rosemary *Andromeda polifolia*

Rosy Marsh Moth *Coenophila subrosea*	9–6			WC	RDB

Borage *Borago officinalis*

Angle Shades *Phlogophora meticulosa*	All				
Jersey Tiger *Euplagia quadripunctaria*	9~6			SW	Nb

Box *Buxus sempervirens*

Satin Beauty *Deileptenia ribeata*	8–5				

Bracken *Pteridium aquilinum*

Angle Shades *Phlogophora meticulosa*	All				
Brown Silver-line *Petrophora chlorosata*	6–9				
Broom Moth *Melanchra pisi*	7–9				
Grey Dagger *Acronicta psi*	7–9	+			
Small Angle Shades *Euplexia lucipara*	7–9	+			
Map-winged Swift *Hepialus fusconebulosa*	7~5	*	St & R		L
Gold Swift *Hepialus hecta*	7~6	*	R		L
Beautiful Brocade *Lacanobia contigua*	8–9				L
Dot Moth *Melanchra persicariae*	8–10			S, C, (N)	
Orange Swift *Hepialus sylvina*	9~5	*	R		

Bramble *Rubus fruticosus* agg.

Angle Shades *Phlogophora meticulosa*	All				
Grass Eggar *Lasiocampa trifolii*	3–6			S, SW	Na
Brown-spot Pinion *Agrochola litura*	4–6				
Lackey *Malacosoma neustria*	4–6			S, C, (N)	
Pale Eggar *Trichiura crataegi*	4–6				
Blossom Underwing *Orthosia miniosa*	5–6			S, C	L
Double-striped Pug *Gymnoscelis rufifasciata*	5–6 & 9–10		F		
Early Thorn *Selenia dentaria*	5–6 & 8–9	6–8			
Holly Blue *Celastrina argiolus*	5–7 & 8–9		B, F & S	S, C, (SN)	
Pale Pinion *Lithophane hepatica*	5–7			S, WC	L
Powdered Quaker *Orthosia gracilis*	5–7				
Emperor Moth *Saturnia pavonia*	5–8				
Green Hairstreak *Callophrys rubi*	5–8		F & L		L
Chinese Character *Cilix glaucata*	6–7 & 8–9			S, C, (N)	
Common Pug *Eupithecia vulgata*	6–7 & 8–10	7–8			
V-Pug *Chloroclystis v-ata*	5–7 & 8–10	7–9	F	S, C, (N)	
Rosy Marbled *Elaphria venustula*	6–8		F	SE	Nb
Light Knot Grass *Acronicta menyanthidis*	6–9			C, N, (SE)	L
Sweet Gale Moth *Acronicta euphorbiae*	6–9			N	Na
Grey Pug *Eupithecia subfuscata*	6–10	+	F & L		
Fox Moth *Macrothylacia rubi*	6~4				
Common Marbled Carpet *Chloroclysta truncata*	7–8 & 9~5	8~6			
Light Brocade *Lacanobia w-latinum*	7–8			S, C, (N)	L
Little Thorn *Cepphis advenaria*	7–8			S, (C)	Nb

Species	Months			
Small Grass Emerald *Chlorissa viridata*	7–8		S, (WC)	Na
Beautiful Carpet *Mesoleuca albicillata*	7–9			
Broom Moth *Melanchra pisi*	7–9			
Grizzled Skipper *Pyrgus malvae*	7–9	+	S, C	S
Knot Grass *Acronicta rumicis*	7–9	+		
Peach Blossom *Thyatira batis*	7–9	+		
Peppered Moth *Biston betularia*	7–9			
Buff Arches *Habrosyne pyritoides*	7–10		S, C	
Fan-foot *Zanclognatha tarsipennalis*	7–10	DL	S, C, (N)	
Saxon *Hyppa rectilinea*	7–10		N	Nb
Small Fan-foot *Herminia grisealis*	7–10	L & DL		
Shaded Fan-foot *Herminia tarsicrinalis*	8~4	DL	SE	RDB
Brown Rustic *Rusina ferruginea*	8~5			
Double Square-spot *Xestia triangulum*	8~5			
Green Arches *Anaplectoides prasina*	8~5			
Grey Arches *Polia nebulosa*	8~5			
Mottled Beauty *Alcis repandata*	8~5			
Purple Clay *Diarsia brunnea*	8~5			
Scarlet Tiger *Callimorpha dominula*	8~5		S, (WC)	L
Silvery Arches *Polia trimaculosa*	8~5			Nb
Small Fan-footed Wave *Idaea biselata*	8–5			
Triple-spotted Clay *Xestia ditrapezium*	8~5	B		L
Dark Tussock *Dicallomera fascelina*	8~6		S, WC, N	L
Garden Tiger *Arctia caja*	8~6			
Kent Black Arches *Meganola albula*	8~6		SE	Nb
Lesser Yellow Underwing *Noctua comes*	8~6			
Scarce Footman *Eilema complana*	8~6		S, C	L
Scarce Vapourer *Orgyia recens*	8~6		EC	RDB
Barred Chestnut *Diarsia dahlii*	9~4		C, N, (S)	L
Broad-bordered Yellow Underwing *Noctua fimbriata*	9~4			
Ingrailed Clay *Diarsia mendica*	9~4			
Lesser Broad-bordered Yellow Underwing *Noctua janthe*	9~4			
Six-striped Rustic *Xestia sexstrigata*	9~4			
Dotted Clay *Xestia baja*	9–5			
Square-spotted Clay *Xestia rhomboidea*	9–5		S, (WC, N)	Nb
Brown-tail *Euproctis chrysorrhoea*	9–6		S, (EC)	L
Great Brocade *Eurois occulta*	9–6		N	Nb
Jersey Tiger *Euplagia quadripunctaria*	9–6		SW	Nb
Oak Eggar *Lasiocampa quercus*	All	*		
Feathered Brindle *Aporophyla australis*	10–5		S	Nb

Broom *Cytisus scoparius*

Species	Months			
Grass Eggar *Lasiocampa trifolii*	3–6		S, WC	Na
Engrailed *Ectropis bistortata*	4–6 & 7–9	5–7		
Silver-studded Blue *Plebejus argus*	4–6	F & L	S, WC	R
Streak *Chesias legatella*	4–6			
Double-striped Pug *Gymnoscelis rufifasciata*	5–6 & 9–10	F		
Holly Blue *Celastrina argiolus*	5–7 & 8–9	B, F & S	S, C, (SN)	
Ruby Tiger *Phragmatobia fuliginosa*	5–7 & 7~4	7–5		
Green Hairstreak *Callophrys rubi*	5–8	F & L		L
Scalloped Hazel *Odontopera bidentata*	6–9			
Light Brocade *Lacanobia w-latinum*	7–8		S, C, (N)	L
Broom Moth *Melanchra pisi*	7–9			
Broom-tip *Chesias rufata*	7–9			Nb
Pale-shouldered Brocade *Lacanobia thalassina*	7–9	+		

Peppered Moth *Biston betularia*	7–9				
Little Emerald *Jodis lactearia*	7–10				
Pale Shining Brown *Polia bombycina*	7~5			S	RDB
Willow Beauty *Peribatodes rhomboidaria*	7~6	+			
Lead Belle *Scotopteryx mucronata*	8–3			W, N	L
Grass Wave *Perconia strigillaria*	8–5			S, C, (N)	L
Light Emerald *Campaea margaritata*	8~5	+			
Mottled Beauty *Alcis repandata*	8~5				
Orange Moth *Angerona prunaria*	8~5			S, (C)	L
Small Scallop *Idaea emarginata*	8–5			S, C	L
Dark Tussock *Dicallomera fascelina*	8~6			S, WC, N	L
Lesser Yellow Underwing *Noctua comes*	8–6				
Beautiful Brocade *Lacanobia contigua*	8–9				L
Long-tailed Blue *Lampides boeticus*	9–11		F&S	S	Bm
Large Emerald *Geometra papilionaria*	9–5				
Bordered Grey *Selidosema brunnearia*	9–6				Na
Grass Emerald *Pseudoterpna pruinata*	9~6				
Scotch Annulet *Gnophos obfuscatus*	9~6			N	Nb
Autumnal Rustic *Eugnorisma glareosa*	10~5				
Deep-brown Dart *Aporophyla lutulenta*	10~6			S, EC	

Buckthorns *Rhamnus & Frangula* spp.

Buckthorn *R. cathartica*

Engrailed *Ectropis bistortata*	4–6 & 7–9	5–7			
Brown Scallop *Philereme vetulata*	5–6			S, C	L
Dark Umber *Philereme transversata*	5–6			S, C	L
Brimstone *Gonepteryx rhamni*	5–7			S, C	
Tissue *Triphosa dubitata*	5–7			S, C, (N)	L
Emperor Moth *Saturnia pavonia*	5–8				
Green Hairstreak *Callophrys rubi*	5–8		F & L		L
Least Black Arches *Nola confusalis*	6–8			S, C, (N)	L
Dark Dagger *Acronicta tridens*	7–9	+		S, C, (N)	
Willow Beauty *Peribatodes rhomboidaria*	7~6	+			
Lappet *Gastropacha quercifolia*	8~5			S, EC	

Alder Buckthorn *F. alnus*

Pale Brindled Beauty *Phigalia pilosaria*	4–6				
Dark Umber *Philereme transversata*	5–6			S, C	L
Brimstone *Gonepteryx rhamni*	5–7			S, C	
Holly Blue *Celastrina argiolus*	5–7 & 8–9		B, F & S	S, C, (SN)	
Tissue *Triphosa dubitata*	5–7			S, C, (N)	L
Emperor Moth *Saturnia pavonia*	5–8				
Yellow-barred Brindle *Acasis viretata*	6–7	+	F, S & L	S, C, (NW)	L
Lappet *Gastropacha quercifolia*	8~5			S, EC	
Scarce Vapourer *Orgyia recens*	8~6			EC	RDB

Buckwheats *Fagopyrum* spp.

White-line Dart *Euxoa tritici*	3–7				
Striped Hawk-moth *Hyles livornica*	6–7 & 9–10				Bm

Buddleias *Buddleia* spp.

Double-striped Pug *Gymnoscelis rufifasciata*	5–6 & 9–10		F		
Mullein *Shargacucullia verbasci*	5–7			S, C	
Gothic *Naenia typica*	8–3				L

Bullace *Prunus domestica* ssp. *insititia*

Dotted Chestnut *Conistra rubiginea*	3–6		S, (C)	Nb
Dark Chestnut *Conistra ligula*	4–6		S, C, (N)	
Lunar-spotted Pinion *Cosmia pyralina*	4–6		S, (C)	L

Burdocks *Arctium* spp.

Frosted Orange *Gortyna flavago*	4–8		ISt & R	
Setaceous Hebrew Character *Xestia c-nigrum*	5–7 & 9~4	9~5		
Rosy Rustic *Hydraecia micacea*	5–8		ISt & R	
Burnished Brass *Diachrysia chrysitis*	6–8 & 9~5	8~6		
Ghost Moth *Hepialus humuli*	7–5	*	R	
Beautiful Golden Y *Autographa pulchrina*	8~5			
Garden Tiger *Arctia caja*	8~6			

Burnet Rose *Rosa pimpinellifolia* see Roses

Burnet-saxifrages *Pimpinella* spp.

Lime-speck Pug *Eupithecia centaureata*	5–10	+	F	
Grey Pug *Eupithecia subfuscata*	6–10		F & L	
Transparent Burnet *Zygaena purpuralis*	7–5	*		NW	Na
Shaded Pug *Eupithecia subumbrata*	7–9		F	S, (C)	L
Pimpinel Pug *Eupithecia pimpinellata*	8–10		F & S	S, C	L
Triple-spotted Pug *Eupithecia trisignaria*	8–10		F & S	S, C, (N)	L
Single-dotted Wave *Idaea dimidiata*	8–5		F & L	S, C, NW	

Bur-reeds *Sparganium* spp.

Bulrush Wainscot *Nonagria typhae*	4–7		ISt		
Rush Wainscot *Archanara algae*	6–8		ISt	SE, EC	RDB
Webb's Wainscot *Archanara sparganii*	6–8		ISt	S, (EC)	Nb
Gold Spot *Plusia festucae*	9~5 & 7–8	9~5			

Butterbur *Petasites hybridus*

Ear Moth *Amphipoea oculea*	4–6		St & R		
Butterbur *Hydraecia petasitis*	4–7		ISt & R	S, C, SN	L

Buttercups *Ranunculus* spp.

Beaded Chestnut *Agrochola lychnidis*	3–6			S, C, (N)	
Slender-striped Rufous *Coenocalpe lapidata*	4–8			N	Na
Fern *Horisme tersata*	7–9			S, (C)	
Lunar Yellow Underwing *Noctua orbona*	9–5				Nb

Cabbage family *Brassica* spp.

Cabbage Moth *Mamestra brassicae*	5–10	+			
Silver Y *Autographa gamma*	5–10	+			Bm
Small White *Pieris rapae*	5–10				
Large White *Pieris brassicae*	5–12				
Flame Carpet *Xanthorhoe designata*	6–7 & 8–9	7–8			
Garden Carpet *Xanthorhoe fluctuata*	6–10				
Pearly Underwing *Peridroma saucia*	7–10				Bm
Turnip Moth *Agrotis segetum*	7–4	+	St & R		
Dotted Rustic *Rhyacia simulans*	9–5				
Large Yellow Underwing *Noctua pronuba*	9–5				
Feathered Ranunculus *Polymixis lichenea*	10–5			S, C, (N)	L

Californian Poppy *Eschscholzia californica*

Mouse *Amphipyra tragopoginis*	4–6		L & F		

Campions *Silene* spp.

Bladder Campion *S. vulgaris*

Brown-spot Pinion *Agrochola litura*	4–6				
Marbled Coronet *Hadena confusa*	5–8	+	S		L
Campion *Hadena rivularis*	6–7 & 8–9	7–9	S		
Common Pug *Eupithecia vulgata*	6–7 & 8–10	7–8			
Netted Pug *Eupithecia venosata*	6–8		S		L
Lychnis *Hadena bicruris*	6–8 & 9	7–8	S		
Dark Brocade *Blepharita adusta*	6–9				
The Grey *Hadena caesia*	6–9		S, R & L	NW	RDB
Tawny Shears *Hadena perplexa*	7–8	+	S		
Barrett's Marbled Coronet *Hadena luteago*	7–9		ISt & R	SW	Nb
Sandy Carpet *Perizoma flavofasciata*	7–9		F & S		
Varied Coronet *Hadena compta*	7–9		S	S, C	
Marbled Clover *Heliothis viriplaca*	8–9	+	F & S	SE, (S)	RDB

Moss Campion *S. acaulis*

Netted Pug *Eupithecia venosata*	6–8		S		L

Night-flowering Catchfly *S. noctiflora*

Campion *Hadena rivularis*	6–7 & 8–9	7–9	S		
Lychnis *Hadena bicruris*	6–8 & 9	7–8	S		
Tawny Shears *Hadena perplexa*	7–8	+	S		

Nottingham Catchfly *S. nutans*

Marbled Coronet *Hadena confusa*	5–8	+	S		L
Campion *Hadena rivularis*	6–7 & 8–9	7–9	S		
Netted Pug *Eupithecia venosata*	6–7		S		L
Lychnis *Hadena bicruris*	6–8 & 9	7–8	S		
Tawny Shears *Hadena perplexa*	7–8	+	S		
White Spot *Hadena albimacula*	7–8		S	S	RDB

Red Campion *S. dioica*

Twin-spot Carpet *Perizoma didymata*	4–6				
Marbled Coronet *Hadena confusa*	5–8	+	S		L
Campion *Hadena rivularis*	6–7 & 8–9	7–9	S		
Netted Pug *Eupithecia venosata*	6–7		S		L
Lychnis *Hadena bicruris*	6–8 & 9	7–8	S		
Sweet Gale Moth *Acronicta euphorbiae*	6–9			N	Na
Tawny Shears *Hadena perplexa*	7–8	+	S		
Rivulet *Perizoma affinitata*	7–9		F & S		
Sandy Carpet *Perizoma flavofasciata*	7–9		F & S		

Sea Campion *S. uniflora*

Black-banded *Polymixis xanthomista*	3–7		F & S	SW, WC	Na
Twin-spot Carpet *Perizoma didymata*	4–6				
Ground Lackey *Malacosoma castrensis*	4–7			SE, (SW)	Na
Marbled Coronet *Hadena confusa*	5–8	+	S		L
Campion *Hadena rivularis*	6–7 & 8–9	7–9	S		
Netted Pug *Eupithecia venosata*	6–8		S		L
Lychnis *Hadena bicruris*	6–8 & 9	7–8	S		
The Grey *Hadena caesia*	6–9		S & L	NW	RDB
Tawny Shears *Hadena perplexa*	7–8	+	S		
Barrett's Marbled Coronet *Hadena luteago*	7–9		ISt & R	SW	Nb
Annulet *Charissa obscurata*	9–5				L
Feathered Brindle *Aporophyla australis*	10–5			S	Nb

Spanish Catchfly *S. otites*

Yellow Belle *Semiaspilates ochrearia*	6–8 & 9–5			S, C	L
Shaded Pug *Eupithecia subumbrata*	7–9		F	S, (C)	L
Marbled Clover *Heliothis viriplaca*	8–9	+	F & S	SE, (S)	RDB

White Campion *S. latifolia*

Marbled Coronet *Hadena confusa*	5–8	+	S		L
Campion *Hadena rivularis*	6–7 & 8–9	7–9	S		
Lychnis *Hadena bicruris*	6–8 & 9	7–8	S		
Tawny Shears *Hadena perplexa*	7–8	+	S		
Rivulet *Perizoma affinitata*	7–9		F & S		
Sandy Carpet *Perizoma flavofasciata*	7–9		F & S		
Marbled Clover *Heliothis viriplaca*	8–9	+	F & S	SE, (S)	RDB

Candytufts *Iberis* spp.

Garden Carpet *Xanthorhoe fluctuata*	6–10				

Carrots *Daucus* spp.

Ground Lackey *Malacosoma castrensis*	4–7			SE, (SW)	Na
Swallowtail *Papilio machaon*	6–8	+		SE	R
Yellow Belle *Semiaspilates ochrearia*	6–8 & 9–5			S, C	L
White-spotted Pug *Eupithecia tripunctaria*	6–9		F & S	S, C, (N)	L
Red Twin-spot Carpet *Xanthorhoe spadicearia*	7 & 9	6–8			
Marbled Clover *Heliothis viriplaca*	8–9	+	F & S	SE, (S)	RDB
Heart and Club *Agrotis clavis*	8–5		L & R		
Sussex Emerald *Thalera fimbrialis*	8–6			SE	RDB

Cedars *Cedrus* spp.

Spruce Carpet *Thera britannica*	6–7 & 9–5			S, C, (N)	
Tawny-barred Angle *Macaria liturata*	6–8 & 9–10	7–8			
Pine Hawk-moth *Hyloicus pinastri*	6–9			S, EC	L
Dwarf Pug *Eupithecia tantillaria*	7–8				
Grey Pine Carpet *Thera obeliscata*	7–8 & 9–6				
Mottled Beauty *Alcis repandata*	8–5				

Cereals, Wheat, Barley, Oats, etc. *Triticum, Hordeum* & *Avena* spp. See also Wild-oat

Brighton Wainscot *Oria musculosa*	4–6		lSt & S	S	RDB
Dusky Sallow *Eremobia ochroleuca*	5–7		F & S	S, EC, (SW)	
Rosy Rustic *Hydraecia micacea*	5–8		lSt		
Pale Mottled Willow *Paradrina clavipalpis*	6–8 & 9–4		S		
Rustic Shoulder-knot *Apamea sordens*	7–3		S		
Large Nutmeg *Apamea anceps*	8–4		L & S	S, (C)	L
Common Rustic *Mesapamea secalis*	9–5		lSt		
White-speck *Mythimna unipuncta*	9–5				Bm
Flounced Rustic *Luperina testacea*	9–6		St & R		
Rosy Minor *Mesoligia literosa*	9–6		lSt & R		

Chamomiles *Anthemis* & *Chamaemelum* spp.

Chamomile Shark *Cucullia chamomillae*	5–7		F	S, C, (N)	L

Charlock *Sinapis arvensis*

Clouded Yellow *Colias croceus*	6–7 & 8–11			S, C, (N)	Bm
Orange-tip *Anthocharis cardamines*	5–7		S, B, F & L		
Small White *Pieris rapae*	5–10				

Cherrys *Prunus* spp.

Green Pug *Pasiphila rectangulata*	4–5		F		
Blue-bordered Carpet *Plemyria rubiginata*	4–6				
Green-brindled Crescent *Allophyes oxyacanthae*	4–6				
Lackey *Malacosoma neustria*	4–6			S, C, (N)	
Northern Winter Moth *Operophtera fagata*	4–6				
Sprawler *Asteroscopus sphinx*	4–6			S, C	
March Moth *Alsophila aescularia*	5–6				
Figure of Eight *Diloba caeruleocephala*	5–7			S, C, (N)	
Purple Thorn *Selenia tetralunaria*	5–7 & 8–9	6–7		S, C, (N)	
Tissue *Triphosa dubitata*	5–7			S, C, (N)	L
Large Thorn *Ennomos autumnaria*	5–8			SE	Nb
Barred Umber *Plagodis pulveraria*	6–8				L
Red-green Carpet *Chloroclysta siterata*	6–8				
White-pinion Spotted *Lomographa bimaculata*	6–8			S, C	
Clouded Silver *Lomographa temerata*	7–8			S, C, (N)	
Small Fan-foot *Herminia grisealis*	7–10		L & DL		
Red-belted Clearwing *Synanthedon myopaeformis*	7–5	*	lSt	S, (C)	Nb
Grey Arches *Polia nebulosa*	8~5				
Leopard Moth *Zeuzera pyrina*	8~5	*	lSt	S, C	
Yellow-legged Clearwing *Synanthedon vespiformis*	8~5		lSt	S, C	Nb
Dotted Clay *Xestia baja*	9~5				
Brown-tail *Euproctis chrysorrhoea*	9~6			S, (EC)	L

Chervils *Chaerophyllum* spp.

Chimney Sweeper *Odezia atrata*	4–6		F	C, N, (S)	
Twin-spot Carpet *Perizoma didymata*	4–6				
Double-striped Pug *Gymnoscelis rufifasciata*	5–6 & 9–10		F		
Beautiful Golden Y *Autographa pulchrina*	8~5				
Plain Golden Y *Autographa jota*	8~5				
Single-dotted Wave *Idaea dimidiata*	8~5		F & L	S, C, NW	
Gold Spangle *Autographa bractea*	8~6			C, N	

Chestnut *Aesculus hippocastanum* or *Castanea sativa* see under Horse or Sweet Chestnut

Chickweeds *Stellaria* spp.

Angle Shades *Phlogophora meticulosa*	All				
Beaded Chestnut *Agrochola lychnidis*	3–6			S, C, (N)	
White-line Dart *Euxoa tritici*	3–7				
Brown-spot Pinion *Agrochola litura*	4–6				
Twin-spot Carpet *Perizoma didymata*	4–6				
White-marked *Cerastis leucographa*	4–6			S, C	L
Red Chestnut *Cerastis rubricosa*	5–6				
Pale Pinion *Lithophane hepatica*	5–7			S, WC	L
Ruby Tiger *Phragmatobia fuliginosa*	5–7 & 7~4	7–5			
Setaceous Hebrew Character *Xestia c-nigrum*	5–7 & 9~4	9–5			
Dark-barred Twin-spot Carpet *Xanthorhoe ferrugata*	6–7 & 9	6–8		S, C, (N)	
Flame Shoulder *Ochropleura plecta*	6–7 & 9–10	8–9			
Small Square-spot *Diarsia rubi*	6–7 & 9~4	8~5			
Small Yellow Underwing *Panemeria tenebrata*	6–7		F & S	S, C, (N)	L
White Colon *Sideridis albicolon*	6–7 & 9		F		Nb
Pale Mottled Willow *Paradrina clavipalpis*	6–8 & 9~4				
Muslin Moth *Diaphora mendica*	6–9			S, C, (N)	
Blood-vein *Timandra comae*	7 & 9~4			S, C, (N)	
Red Twin-spot Carpet *Xanthorhoe spadicearia*	7 & 9	6–8			

Shears *Hada plebeja*	7–8	+			
Sharp-angled Carpet *Euphyia unangulata*	7–9			S, (C)	L
Heart and Dart *Agrotis exclamationis*	7–3	+			
Uncertain *Hoplodrina alsines*	7–4			S, C, (N)	
Clouded Buff *Diacrisia sannio*	7–5				L
Riband Wave *Idaea aversata*	7–5	+			
Rustic *Hoplodrina blanda*	7–5				
Silver-ground Carpet *Xanthorhoe montanata*	7–5				
Yellow Shell *Camptogramma bilineata*	7–5				
Cloaked Carpet *Euphyia biangulata*	8–9			S, W	Nb
Mottled Rustic *Caradrina morpheus*	8–11				
Clouded Brindle *Apamea epomidion*	8–3			S, C, (N)	
Cream-spot Tiger *Arctia villica*	8–5			S	L
Double Square-spot *Xestia triangulum*	8–5				
Large Twin-spot Carpet *Xanthorhoe quadrifasiata*	8–5			S, C	L
Plain Wave *Idaea straminata*	8–5				L
Red Carpet *Xanthorhoe decoloraria*	8–5			C, N	
Satin Wave *Idaea subsericeata*	8–5	+		S, (C, NW)	
Triple-spotted Clay *Xestia ditrapezium*	8–5		B		L
Lesser Yellow Underwing *Noctua comes*	8–6				
Lesser Broad-bordered Yellow Underwing *Noctua janthe*	9–4				
Lunar Yellow Underwing *Noctua orbona*	9–5				Nb
Square-spot Rustic *Xestia xanthographa*	9–4				
Vine's Rustic *Hoplodrina ambigua*	9–4 & 7–8			S, (C)	L
Clay *Mythimna ferrago*	9–5				
Dotted Clay *Xestia baja*	9–5				
Old Lady *Mormo maura*	9–5			S, C, (N)	L
Square-spotted Clay *Xestia rhomboidea*	9–5			S, (WC, N)	Nb
Stout Dart *Spaelotis ravida*	9–5			S, EC, (WC, N)	L
Archer's Dart *Agrotis vestigialis*	9–6				L
Portland Moth *Actebia praecox*	9–6			SW, C, N, (S)	Nb
Autumnal Rustic *Eugnorisma glareosa*	10–5				
Black Rustic *Aporophyla nigra*	10–5				
Feathered Brindle *Aporophyla australis*	10–5			S	Nb
Feathered Ranunculus *Polymixis lichenea*	10–5			S, C, (N)	L
Northern Rustic *Standfussiana lucernea*	10–5			SW, WC, N	L
Deep-brown Dart *Aporophyla lutulenta*	10–6			S, EC	

Chicory *Cichorium intybus*

Marbled Clover *Heliothis viriplaca*	8–9	+	F & S	SE, (S)	RDB
Feathered Brindle *Aporophyla australis*	10–5			S	Nb

China Aster *Callistephus chinensis*

Star-wort *Cucullia asteris*	7–9		F	S, C	Nb

Cinquefoils *Potentilla* spp.

Sword-grass *Xylena exsoleta*	5–7			C, N	Nb
Rosy Marbled *Elaphria venustula*	6–8		F	SE	Nb
Mullein Wave *Scopula marginepunctata*	7 & 9–5	9–5		S, C, (N)	L
Grizzled Skipper *Pyrgus malvae*	7–9	+		S, C	S
Common Emerald *Hemithea aestivaria*	8–5			S, C, (N)	
Kent Black Arches *Meganola albula*	8–6			SE	Nb
Lunar Yellow Underwing *Noctua orbona*	9–5				Nb
Annulet *Charissa obscurata*	9–5				L
Least Yellow Underwing *Noctua interjecta*	9–5			S, C, (SN)	

Straw Belle *Aspitates gilvaria*	9–6			SE	RDB
Deep-brown Dart *Aporophyla lutulenta*	10~6			S, EC	

Clarys *Salvia* spp.

Grey Chi *Antitype chi*	4–6			C, N, (S)	

Cleavers *Galium aparine* see under Bedstraw (Goosegrass)

Clematis (Garden) *Clematis* spp.

Small Emerald *Hemistola chrysoprasaria*	8–6			S, (C)	L

Clovers *Trifolium* spp.

Unspecified

Beaded Chestnut *Agrochola lychnidis*	3–6			S, C, (N)	
Hebrew Character *Orthosia gothica*	4–7				
Belted Beauty *Lycia zonaria*	5–7			NW	Na
Silver Y *Autographa gamma*	5–10	+			Bm
Latticed Heath *Chiasmia clathrata*	6–7 & 8–9	7–8			
Common Heath *Ematurga atomaria*	6–9	+			
Five-spot Burnet *Zygaena trifolii*	6–5			S, WC	L
Narrow-bordered Five-spot Burnet *Zygaena lonicerae*	7–6			S, C, (N)	
Common Emerald *Hemithea aestivaria*	8~5			S, C, (N)	
Lesser Yellow Underwing *Noctua comes*	8–6				
Scarce Black Arches *Nola aerugula*	8~6				Bm
Bordered Grey *Selidosema brunnearia*	9–6				Na
Six-spot Burnet *Zygaena filipendulae*	9–6	*			
Black Rustic *Aporophyla nigra*	10–5				

Hare's-foot Clover *T. arvense*

Yellow Belle *Semiaspilates ochrearia*	6–8 & 9–5			S, C	L
Mother Shipton *Callistege mi*	7–9				
Bright Wave *Idaea ochrata*	8–5			SE	RDB

Red Clover *T. pratense*

Garden Dart *Euxoa nigricans*	2–6				
Grass Eggar *Lasiocampa trifolii*	3–6			S, WC	Na
Clouded Yellow *Colias croceus*	6–7 & 8–11				Bm
Common Blue *Polyommatus icarus*	6–7 & 8–4	8~5			
Burnet Companion *Euclidia glyphica*	7–8	+		S, C, (N)	
Shears *Hada plebeja*	7–8	+			
Mother Shipton *Callistege mi*	7–9				
Pearly Underwing *Peridroma saucia*	7–10				Bm
Pale Clouded Yellow *Colias hyale*	7–4			S,C	Bm
Narrow-bordered Five-spot Burnet *Zygaena lonicerae*	7–6			S, C, (N)	
Marbled Clover *Heliothis viriplaca*	8–9	+	F & S	SE, (S)	RDB
Chalk Carpet *Scotopteryx bipunctaria*	8–6			S, C, (N)	Nb
Scarce Black Arches *Nola aerugula*	8~6				Bm

White Clover *T. repens*

Garden Dart *Euxoa nigricans*	2–6				
Clouded Yellow *Colias croceus*	6–7 & 8–11				Bm
Common Blue *Polyommatus icarus*	6–7 & 8~4	8~5			
Latticed Heath *Chiasmia clathrata*	6–7 & 8–9	7–8			
Burnet Companion *Euclidia glyphica*	7–8	+		S, C, (N)	
Shears *Hada plebeja*	7–8	+			
Mother Shipton *Callistege mi*	7–9				

Pale Clouded Yellow *Colias hyale*	7~4			S,C	Bm
Narrow-bordered Five-spot Burnet *Zygaena lonicerae*	7–6			S, C, (N)	
Dot Moth *Melanchra persicariae*	8–10			S, C, (N)	
Heart and Club *Agrotis clavis*	8–5		L & R		
Chalk Carpet *Scotopteryx bipunctaria*	8–6			S, C, (N)	Nb
Scarce Black Arches *Nola aerugula*	8–6				Bm
Shaded Broad-bar *Scotopteryx chenopodiata*	8–6				
Hoary Footman *Eilema caniola*	9–6			SW, (WC)	Nb

Colt's-foot *Tussilago farfara*

Belted Beauty *Lycia zonaria*	5–7			NW	Na
Glaucous Shears *Papestra biren*	6–8			WC, N, (SW)	L
Cinnabar *Tyria jacobaeae*	7–9			S, C, (N)	
Bright Wave *Idaea ochrata*	8–5			SE	RDB

Columbine *Aquilegia vulgaris*

Grey Chi *Antitype chi*	4–6			C, N, (S)	

Comfrey *Symphytum officinale*

Gothic *Naenia typica*	8–3				L
Scarlet Tiger *Callimorpha dominula*	8–5			S, (WC)	L

Cotoneasters *Cotoneaster* spp.

Green-brindled Crescent *Allophyes oxyacanthae*	4–6				
Figure of Eight *Diloba caeruleocephala*	5–7			S, C, (N)	
Vapourer *Orgyia antiqua*	5–8	+			
Dark Dagger *Acronicta tridens*	7–9	+		S, C, (N)	

Cottongrasses *Eriophorum* spp.

Antler Moth *Cerapteryx graminis*	3–6				
Haworth's Minor *Celaena haworthii*	4–7		lSt	C, N, (S)	L
Large Ear *Amphipoea lucens*	5–7		lSt & R	SW, WC, N	L
Large Heath *Coenonympha tullia*	7–5			WC, N, (EC)	S
Small Wainscot *Chortodes pygmina*	9–7		lSt		

Cowbane *Cicuta virosa*

Lime-speck Pug *Eupithecia centaureata*	5–10	+		F	
Rush Wainscot *Archanara algae*	6–8		lSt	SE, EC	RDB

Cowberry *Vaccinium vitis-idaea*

Northern Dart *Xestia alpicola*	4–5	*		N	Na
Rannoch Looper *Itame brunneata*	4–5			N	Na
Manchester Treble-bar *Carsia sororiata*	4–6		F & L	C, N	Nb
Northern Spinach *Eulithis populata*	4–6			SW, C, N	
Golden-rod Brindle *Lithomoia solidaginis*	4–7			WC, N	L
Green Hairstreak *Callophrys rubi*	5–8		F & L		L
Small Dark Yellow Underwing *Anarta cordigera*	6–7			N	Na
Broad-bordered White Underwing *Anarta melanopa*	7–8			N	RDB
Saxon *Hyppa rectilinea*	7–10			N	Nb
Black Mountain Moth *Glacies coracina*	8–5	*		N	Na
Scotch Burnet *Zygaena exulans*	8–5	*	L & S	N	RDB
Grey Mountain Carpet *Entephria caesiata*	8–6			C, N	

Cow Parsley *Anthriscus sylvestris*

Garden Dart *Euxoa nigricans*	2–6				
Twin-spot Carpet *Perizoma didymata*	4–6				

White-spotted Pug *Eupithecia tripunctaria*	6–7 & 9–10	F & S	S, C, (N)	L
Double Square-spot *Xestia triangulum*	8~5			
Single-dotted Wave *Idaea dimidiata*	8–5	F & L	S, C, NW	

Cowslip *Primula veris*

Duke of Burgundy *Hamearis lucina*	6–8		S, (C, N)	S
Lunar Yellow Underwing *Noctua orbona*	9–5			Nb
Plain Clay *Eugnorisma depuncta*	9~5		SW, WC, N	Nb
Northern Rustic *Standfussiana lucernea*	10–5		SW, WC, N	L

Cow-wheats *Melampyrum* spp.

Lead-coloured Pug *Eupithecia plumbeolata*	7–8	F	S, C, (N)	Nb
Heath Fritillary *Melitaea athalia*	7~6		SW, SE	R

Cranberry *Vaccinium oxycoccos*

Manchester Treble-bar *Carsia sororiata*	4–6	F & L	C, N	Nb

Crane's-bills *Geranium* spp.

Brown Argus *Aricia agestis*	6–7 & 8~4		S, C	L
Satyr Pug *Eupithecia satyrata*	6–9	F		L
Fox Moth *Macrothylacia rubi*	6~4			
Annulet *Charissa obscurata*	9~5			L

Crowberry *Empetrum nigrum*

Northern Dart *Xestia alpicola*	4–5	*	N	Na
Northern Spinach *Eulithis populata*	4–6		SW, C, N	
Green Hairstreak *Callophrys rubi*	5–8	F & L		L
Broad-bordered White Underwing *Anarta melanopa*	7–8		N	RDB
Black Mountain Moth *Glacies coracina*	8–5	*	N	Na
Scotch Burnet *Zygaena exulans*	8–5	*	L & S	N	RDB
Weaver's Wave *Idaea contiguaria*	8–5		WC	Na
Grey Mountain Carpet *Entephria caesiata*	8–6		C, N	

Cuckooflower *Cardamine pratensis*

Green-veined White *Pieris napi*	5–6 & 7–8	6–8	
Orange-tip *Anthocharis cardamines*	5–7		

Cuckoo-pint *Arum maculatum*

Lesser Broad-bordered Yellow Underwing *Noctua janthe*	9–4

Cudweed *Filago vulgaris*

Painted Lady *Vanessa cardui*	5–10	Bm

Currants *Ribes* spp.

Unspecified

Copper Underwing *Amphipyra pyramidea*	4–6		S, C, (N)	
Large Ranunculus *Polymixis flavicincta*	4–7		S, (C)	L
March Moth *Alsophila aescularia*	5–6			
Waved Umber *Menophra abruptaria*	6–9		S, C	
Garden Carpet *Xanthorhoe fluctuata*	6–10			
Mottled Pug *Eupithecia exiguata*	6–10		S, C, (N)	
Small Angle Shades *Euplexia lucipara*	7–9	+		
Common Emerald *Hemithea aestivaria*	8~5		S, C, (N)	
Magpie *Abraxas grossulariata*	9–6			

Black Currant *R. nigrum*

Spinach *Eulithis mellinata*	4–5			S, C, (N)	
Phoenix *Eulithis prunata*	4–6				
V-Moth *Macaria wauaria*	4–6				L
Comma *Polygonia c-album*	5–6 & 7–8	F		S, C, (SN)	
Currant Pug *Eupithecia assimilata*	6–7 & 8–10				
Peppered Moth *Biston betularia*	7–9				
Dot Moth *Melanchra persicariae*	8–10			S, C, (N)	
Currant Clearwing *Synanthedon tipuliformis*	8–5	*	ISt	S, C, (N)	Nb
Leopard Moth *Zeuzera pyrina*	8–5	*	ISt	S, C	
Swallow-tailed Moth *Ourapteryx sambucaria*	8–6				
Magpie *Abraxas grossulariata*	9–6				

Flowering Currant *R. sanguineum*

Magpie *Abraxas grossulariata*	9–6				

Mountain Currant *R. alpinum*

Magpie *Abraxas grossulariata*	9–6				

Red Currant *R. rubrum*

Spinach *Eulithis mellinata*	4–5			S, C, (N)	
Phoenix *Eulithis prunata*	4–6				
V-Moth *Macaria wauaria*	4–6				L
Comma *Polygonia c-album*	5–6 & 7–8	F		S, C, (SN)	
Currant Pug *Eupithecia assimilata*	6–7 & 8–10				
Currant Clearwing *Synanthedon tipuliformis*	8–5	*	ISt	S, C, (N)	Nb
Magpie *Abraxas grossulariata*	9–6				

Cypress *Cupressus, Cupressocyparis leylandii* & *Chamaecyparis* spp.

Unspecified

Blair's Shoulder-knot *Lithophane leautieri*	3–7	S, C, (N)	
Juniper Pug *Eupithecia pusillata*	4–6		
Ochreous Pug *Eupithecia indigata*	6–9		
Freyer's Pug *Eupithecia intricata arceuthata*	8–9		L
Mere's Pug *Eupithecia intricata hibernica*	8–9		L
Cypress Pug *Eupithecia phoeniceata*	10–6	S	UC

Lawson's Cypress *Chamaecyparis lawsoniana*

Blair's Shoulder-knot *Lithophane leautieri*	3–7	S, C, (N)	
Spruce Carpet *Thera britannica*	6–7 & 9–5	S, C, (N)	
Scalloped Hazel *Odontopera bidentata*	6–9		
Dwarf Pug *Eupithecia tantillaria*	7–8		
Grey Pine Carpet *Thera obeliscata*	7–8 & 9–6		
Cypress Carpet *Thera cupressata*	7–9 & 10–5	S	UC
Freyer's Pug *Eupithecia intricata arceuthata*	8–9		L
Mere's Pug *Eupithecia intricata hibernica*	8–9		L
Mottled Beauty *Alcis repandata*	8–5		
Cypress Pug *Eupithecia phoeniceata*	10–6	S	UC

Monterey Cypress *Cupressus macrocarpa*

Blair's Shoulder-knot *Lithophane leautieri*	3–7	S, C, (N)	
Scalloped Hazel *Odontopera bidentata*	6–9		
Grey Pine Carpet *Thera obeliscata*	7–8 & 9–6		
Cypress Carpet *Thera cupressata*	7–9 & 10–5	S	UC
Freyer's Pug *Eupithecia intricata arceuthata*	8–9		L

Mere's Pug *Eupithecia intricata hibernica*	8–9				L
Willow Beauty *Peribatodes rhomboidaria*	7~6	+			
Cypress Pug *Eupithecia phoeniceata*	10–6			S	UC

Daisy *Bellis perennis*

Large Ranunculus *Polymixis flavicincta*	4–7			S, (C)	L
Bright Wave *Idaea ochrata*	8–5			SE	RDB
Red Carpet *Xanthorhoe decoloraria*	9~5			C, N	

Dame's-violet *Hesperis matronalis*

Green-veined White *Pieris napi*	5–6 & 7–8	6–8			
Orange-tip *Anthocharis cardamines*	5–7		S, B, F & L		

Dandelions *Taraxacum* spp.

Garden Dart *Euxoa nigricans*	2–6				
Beaded Chestnut *Agrochola lychnidis*	3–6			S, C, (N)	
Sallow *Xanthia icteritia*	3–6				
White-line Dart *Euxoa tritici*	3–7				
Dark Chestnut *Conistra ligula*	4–6			S, C, (N)	
Grey Chi *Antitype chi*	4–6			C, N, (S)	
Hebrew Character *Orthosia gothica*	4–7				
Large Ranunculus *Polymixis flavicincta*	4–7			S, (C)	L
Slender-striped Rufous *Coenocalpe lapidata*	4–8			N	Na
Chestnut *Conistra vaccinii*	5–6				
Red Chestnut *Cerastis rubricosa*	5–6				
Belted Beauty *Lycia zonaria*	5–7			NW	Na
Ruby Tiger *Phragmatobia fuliginosa*	5–7 & 7~4	7–5			
Setaceous Hebrew Character *Xestia c-nigrum*	5–7 & 9~4	9–5			
Silver Y *Autographa gamma*	5–10	+			Bm
Common Pug *Eupithecia vulgata*	6–7 & 8–10	7–8			
Dark-barred Twin-spot Carpet *Xanthorhoe ferrugata*	6–7 & 9	6–8		S, C, (N)	
Dog's Tooth *Lacanobia suasa*	6–7 & 8–9	7–8		S, C, (N)	L
Flame Shoulder *Ochropleura plecta*	6–7 & 9–10	8–9			
Nutmeg *Discestra trifolii*	6–7 & 9–10	8–9		S, C, (N)	
Small Square-spot *Diarsia rubi*	6–7 & 9~4	8~5			
Muslin Moth *Diaphora mendica*	6–9			S, C, (N)	
Shuttle-shaped Dart *Agrotis puta*	6–4	+		S, C, (N)	
Treble Lines *Charanyca trigrammica*	6–4			S, C	
Red Twin-spot Carpet *Xanthorhoe spadicearia*	7 & 9	6–8			
Shears *Hada plebeja*	7–8	+			
Bright-line Brown-eye *Lacanobia oleracea*	7–9	+			
Pearly Underwing *Peridroma saucia*	7–10				Bm
Cream Wave *Scopula floslactata*	7~4				L
Uncertain *Hoplodrina alsines*	7~4			S, C, (N)	
Clouded Buff *Diacrisia sannio*	7~5				L
Ghost Moth *Hepialus humuli*	7~5	*	R		
Pale Shining Brown *Polia bombycina*	7~5			S	RDB
Riband Wave *Idaea aversata*	7~5	+			
Rustic *Hoplodrina blanda*	7~5				
Yellow Shell *Camptogramma bilineata*	7~5				
Dot Moth *Melanchra persicariae*	8–10			S, C, (N)	
Mottled Rustic *Caradrina morpheus*	8–11				
Gothic *Naenia typica*	8–3				L
Bright Wave *Idaea ochrata*	8–5			SE	RDB
Brown Rustic *Rusina ferruginea*	8–5				

Common Emerald *Hemithea aestivaria*	8~5			S, C, (N)	
Double Square-spot *Xestia triangulum*	8~5				
Dwarf Cream Wave *Idaea fuscovenosa*	8~5			S, C	L
Heart and Club *Agrotis clavis*	8~5		L & R		
Plain Golden Y *Autographa jota*	8~5				
Plain Wave *Idaea straminata*	8~5				L
Satin Wave *Idaea subsericeata*	8~5	+		S, (C, NW)	
Small Fan-footed Wave *Idaea biselata*	8~5				
Sub-angled Wave *Scopula nigropunctata*	8~5			SE	RDB
Triple-spotted Clay *Xestia ditrapezium*	8~5		B		L
Wood Tiger *Parasemia plantaginis*	8~5				L
Garden Tiger *Arctia caja*	8~6				
Gold Spangle *Autographa bractea*	8~6			C, N	
Barred Chestnut *Diarsia dahlii*	9~4			C, N, (S)	L
Vine's Rustic *Hoplodrina ambigua*	9~4 & 7~8			S, (C)	L
Clay *Mythimna ferrago*	9~5				
Dotted Clay *Xestia baja*	9~5				
Dotted Rustic *Rhyacia simulans*	9~5				L
Orange Swift *Hepialus sylvina*	9~5	*	R		
Square-spotted Clay *Xestia rhomboidea*	9~5			S, (WC, N)	Nb
Stout Dart *Spaelotis ravida*	9~5			S, EC, (WC, N)	L
Great Brocade *Eurois occulta*	9~6			N	Nb
Jersey Tiger *Euplagia quadripunctaria*	9~6			SW	Nb
Speckled Footman *Coscinia cribraria*	9~6			SW	RDB
Black Rustic *Aporophyla nigra*	10–5				
Feathered Ranunculus *Polymixis lichenea*	10 5			S, C, (N)	L

Dead-nettles *Lamium* spp.

Brown-spot Pinion *Agrochola litura*	4–6				
Setaceous Hebrew Character *Xestia c-nigrum*	5–7 & 9~4	9–5			
Green Carpet *Colostygia pectinataria*	6–7 & 9~5	8~5			
Burnished Brass *Diachrysia chrysitis*	6–8 & 9~5	8~6			
Speckled Yellow *Pseudopanthera macularia*	6–8			S, WC, N, (EC)	
Muslin Moth *Diaphora mendica*	6–9			S, C, (N)	
Flame *Axylia putris*	7–9			S, C, (N)	
Uncertain *Hoplodrina alsines*	7–4			S, C, (N)	
Beautiful Golden Y *Autographa pulchrina*	8~5				
Cream-spot Tiger *Arctia villica*	8~5			S	L
Large Twin-spot Carpet *Xanthorhoe quadrifasiata*	8~5			S, C	L
Plain Golden Y *Autographa jota*	8~5				
Gold Spangle *Autographa bractea*	8~6			C, N	
Broad-bordered Yellow Underwing *Noctua fimbriata*	9~4				
Lesser Broad-bordered Yellow Underwing *Noctua janthe*	9~4				
Plain Clay *Eugnorisma depuncta*	9~5			SW, WC, N	Nb
Jersey Tiger *Euplagia quadripunctaria*	9~6			SW	Nb

Deergrass *Trichophorum cespitosum*

Antler Moth *Cerapteryx graminis*	3–6				
Slender Brindle *Apamea scolopacina*	9–5		lSt & L	S, C	
Confused *Apamea furva*	9–6		St & R	C, N, (SE, SW)	L

Delphiniums *Consolida* spp.

Golden Plusia *Polychrysia moneta*	9~6		B, L & S	S, C, (N)	

Dewberry *Rubus caesius*

Beautiful Carpet *Mesoleuca albicillata*	7–9			
Buff Arches *Habrosyne pyritoides*	7–10		S, C	
Kent Black Arches *Meganola albula*	8~6		SE	Nb

Docks *Rumex* spp.

Angle Shades *Phlogophora meticulosa*	All			
Garden Dart *Euxoa nigricans*	2–6			
Beaded Chestnut *Agrochola lychnidis*	3–6		S, C, (N)	
Pink-barred Sallow *Xanthia togata*	3–6	F		
Sallow *Xanthia icteritia*	3–6			
Brown-spot Pinion *Agrochola litura*	4–6			
Dark Chestnut *Conistra ligula*	4–6		S, C, (N)	
Grey Chi *Antitype chi*	4–6		C, N, (S)	
Hebrew Character *Orthosia gothica*	4–7			
Twin-spot Carpet *Perizoma didymata*	4–6			
White-marked *Cerastis leucographa*	4–6		S, C	L
Large Ranunculus *Polymixis flavicincta*	4–7		S, (C)	L
Chestnut *Conistra vaccinii*	5–6			
Red Chestnut *Cerastis rubricosa*	5–6			
Belted Beauty *Lycia zonaria*	5–7		NW	Na
Pale Pinion *Lithophane hepatica*	5–7		S, WC	L
Red Sword-grass *Xylena vetusta*	5–7			L
Ruby Tiger *Phragmatobia fuliginosa*	5–7 & 7~4	7–5		
Setaceous Hebrew Character *Xestia c-nigrum*	5–7 & 9~4	9–5		
Sword-grass *Xylena exsoleta*	5–7		C, N	Nb
Rosy Rustic *Hydraecia micacea*	5–8	IR		
Silver Y *Autographa gamma*	5–10	+		Bm
Small Copper *Lycaena phlaeas*	5~4	+		
Dark-barred Twin-spot Carpet *Xanthorhoe ferrugata*	6–7 & 9	6–8	S, C, (N)	
Dog's Tooth *Lacanobia suasa*	6–7 & 8–9	7–8	S, C, (N)	L
Flame Shoulder *Ochropleura plecta*	6–7 & 9–10	8–9		
Nutmeg *Discestra trifolii*	6–7 & 9–10	8–9	S, C, (N)	
Reed Dagger *Simyra albovenosa*	6–7 & 8–9		SE	Nb
Small Square-spot *Diarsia rubi*	6–7 & 9~4	8~5		
Striped Hawk-moth *Hyles livornica*	6–7 & 9–10			Bm
White Colon *Sideridis albicolon*	6–7 & 9	F		Nb
Muslin Moth *Diaphora mendica*	6–9		S, C, (N)	
Shuttle-shaped Dart *Agrotis puta*	6–4	+	S, C, (N)	
Blood-vein *Timandra comae*	7 & 9–4		S, C, (N)	
Bird's Wing *Dypterygia scabriuscula*	7–8	+	S, C	L
Common Marbled Carpet *Chloroclysta truncata*	7–8 & 9~5	8~6		
Light Brocade *Lacanobia w-latinum*	7–8		S, C, (N)	L
Bright-line Brown-eye *Lacanobia oleracea*	7–9	+		
Broom Moth *Melanchra pisi*	7–9			
Flame *Axylia putris*	7–9		S, C, (N)	
Knot Grass *Acronicta rumicis*	7–9	+		
Pale-shouldered Brocade *Lacanobia thalassina*	7–9	+		
White Ermine *Spilosoma lubricipeda*	7–9			
Pearly Underwing *Peridroma saucia*	7–10			Bm
Cream Wave *Scopula floslactata*	7~4			L
Uncertain *Hoplodrina alsines*	7~4		S, C, (N)	
Clouded Buff *Diacrisia sannio*	7~5			L
Common Swift *Hepialus lupulinus*	7~5	*	R	

Riband Wave *Idaea aversata*	7–5	+				
Rustic *Hoplodrina blanda*	7–5					
Silver-ground Carpet *Xanthorhoe montanata*	7–5					
Yellow Shell *Camptogramma bilineata*	7–5					
Beautiful Brocade *Lacanobia contigua*	8–9					L
Dot Moth *Melanchra persicariae*	8–10				S, C, (N)	
Mottled Rustic *Caradrina morpheus*	8–11					
Clouded Brindle *Apamea epomidion*	8–3				S, C, (N)	
Gothic *Naenia typica*	8–3					L
Brown Rustic *Rusina ferruginea*	8–5					
Double Dart *Graphiphora augur*	8–5					
Double Square-spot *Xestia triangulum*	8–5					
Fiery Clearwing *Pyropteron chrysidiformis*	8–5	*	R		SE	RDB
Ghost Moth *Hepialus humuli*	8–5	*	R			
Green Arches *Anaplectoides prasina*	8–5					
Grey Arches *Polia nebulosa*	8–5					
Heart and Club *Agrotis clavis*	8–5			L & R		
Large Twin-spot Carpet *Xanthorhoe quadrifasiata*	8–5				S, C	L
Plain Wave *Idaea straminata*	8–5					L
Purple Clay *Diarsia brunnea*	8–5					
Silvery Arches *Polia trimaculosa*	8–5					Nb
Triple-spotted Clay *Xestia ditrapezium*	8–5			B		L
Wood Tiger *Parasemia plantaginis*	8–5					L
Garden Tiger *Arctia caja*	8–6					
Lesser Yellow Underwing *Noctua comes*	8–6					
Barred Chestnut *Diarsia dahlii*	9–4				C, N, (S)	L
Broad-bordered Yellow Underwing *Noctua fimbriata*	9–4					
Ingrailed Clay *Diarsia mendica*	9–4					
Lesser Broad-bordered Yellow Underwing *Noctua janthe*	9–4					
Six-striped Rustic *Xestia sexstrigata*	9–4					
Square-spot Rustic *Xestia xanthographa*	9–4					
Vine's Rustic *Hoplodrina ambigua*	9–4 & 7–8				S, (C)	L
Dotted Clay *Xestia baja*	9–5					
Dotted Rustic *Rhyacia simulans*	9–5					L
Large Yellow Underwing *Noctua pronuba*	9–5					
Least Yellow Underwing *Noctua interjecta*	9–5				S, C, (SN)	
Old Lady *Mormo maura*	9–5				S, C, (N)	L
Orange Swift *Hepialus sylvina*	9–5	*	R			
Plain Clay *Eugnorisma depuncta*	9–5				SW, WC, N	Nb
Square-spotted Clay *Xestia rhomboidea*	9–5				S, (WC, N)	Nb
Stout Dart *Spaelotis ravida*	9–5				S, EC, (WC, N)	L
Bordered Grey *Selidosema brunnearia*	9–6			F		Na
Great Brocade *Eurois occulta*	9–6				N	Nb
Autumnal Rustic *Eugnorisma glareosa*	10–5					
Black Rustic *Aporophyla nigra*	10–5					
Feathered Ranunculus *Polymixis lichenea*	10–5				S, C, (N)	L
Deep-brown Dart *Aporophyla lutulenta*	10–6				S, EC	

Water Dock *R. hydrolapathum*

Water Ermine *Spilosoma urticae*	7–9				SE, (SW)	Nb
Fiery Clearwing *Pyropteron chrysidiformis*	8–5	*	R		SE	RDB
Scarce Vapourer *Orgyia recens*	8–6				EC	RDB

Dog's Mercury *Mercurialis perennis*

Square-spotted Clay *Xestia rhomboidea*	9–5				S, (WC, N)	Nb

Dogwoods *Cornus* spp.

Holly Blue *Celastrina argiolus*	5–7 & 8–9		B, F & S	S, C, (SN)	
Green Hairstreak *Callophrys rubi*	5–8		F & L		L
Yellow-barred Brindle *Acasis viretata*	6–7	+	F, S & L	S, C, (NW)	L
Mottled Pug *Eupithecia exiguata*	6–10			S, C, (N)	
Little Thorn *Cepphis advenaria*	7–8			S, (C)	Nb
Privet Hawk-moth *Sphinx ligustri*	7–9			S, (C)	
Little Emerald *Jodis lactearia*	7–10			S, C, NW	
Cream-spot Tiger *Arctia villica*	8~5			S	L
Triple-spotted Clay *Xestia ditrapezium*	8~5		B		L
Broad-bordered Yellow Underwing *Noctua fimbriata*	9~4				
Oak Eggar *Lasiocampa quercus*	All	*			

Dyer's Greenweed *Genista tinctoria*

Northern Drab *Orthosia opima*	5–7				L
Powdered Quaker *Orthosia gracilis*	5–7				
Green Hairstreak *Callophrys rubi*	5–8		F & L		L
Light Brocade *Lacanobia w-latinum*	7–8			S, C, (N)	L
Black-veined Moth *Siona lineata*	7~5			SE	RDB
Beautiful Brocade *Lacanobia contigua*	8–9				L
Lead Belle *Scotopteryx mucronata*	8–3			W, N	L
July Belle *Scotopteryx luridata*	9–4				
Scotch Annulet *Gnophos obfuscatus*	9~6			N	Nb

Elders *Sambucus* spp.

Frosted Orange *Gortyna flavago*	4–8		lSt & R		
Ash Pug *Eupithecia fraxinata*	6–7 & 8–9				
V-Pug *Chloroclystis v-ata*	5–7 & 8–10	7–9	F	S, C, (N)	
White-spotted Pug *Eupithecia tripunctaria*	6–9		F & S	S, C, (N)	L
Dot Moth *Melanchra persicariae*	8–10			S, C, (N)	
Swallow-tailed Moth *Ourapteryx sambucaria*	8~6				

Elms *Ulmus* spp.

Orange Sallow *Xanthia citrago*	3–6		B & L		
Sallow *Xanthia icteritia*	3–6				
Autumnal Moth *Epirrita autumnata*	4–6				
Black Arches *Lymantria monacha*	4–6			S, C	L
Brick *Agrochola circellaris*	4–6		F, S & L		
Common Quaker *Orthosia cerasi*	4–6				
Copper Underwing *Amphipyra pyramidea*	4–6			S, C, (N)	
Dark Chestnut *Conistra ligula*	4–6			S, C, (N)	
December Moth *Poecilocampa populi*	4–6				
Dotted Border *Agriopis marginaria*	4–6				
Dun-bar *Cosmia trapezina*	4–6				
Dusky-lemon Sallow *Xanthia gilvago*	4–6		F & S	S, C, (N)	L
Feathered Thorn *Colotois pennaria*	4–6				
Flounced Chestnut *Agrochola helvola*	4–6				
Lackey *Malacosoma neustria*	4–6			S, C, (N)	
Lesser-spotted Pinion *Cosmia affinis*	4–6			S, (C)	L
Lunar-spotted Pinion *Cosmia pyralina*	4–6			S, (C)	L
Mottled Umber *Erannis defoliaria*	4–6				
November Moth *Epirrita dilutata*	4–6				
Pale Brindled Beauty *Phigalia pilosaria*	4–6				
Pale November Moth *Epirrita christyi*	4–6			S, C, (N)	
Satellite *Eupsilia transversa*	4–6				

Scarce Umber *Agriopis aurantiaria*	4–6				
Small Brindled Beauty *Apocheima hispidaria*	4–6			S, (C, N)	L
Sprawler *Asteroscopus sphinx*	4–6			S, C	
Twin-spotted Quaker *Orthosia munda*	4–6			S, C, (N)	
White-letter Hairstreak *Satyrium w-album*	4–6			S, C, (N)	L
White-spotted pinion *Cosmia diffinis*	4–6			S, (C)	RDB
Winter Moth *Operophtera brumata*	4–6				
Chestnut *Conistra vaccinii*	5–6				
Clouded Drab *Orthosia incerta*	4–6				
Comma *Polygonia c-album*	5–6 & 7–8			S, C, (SN)	
August Thorn *Ennomos quercinaria*	5–7			S, C, (N)	L
Brindled Beauty *Lycia hirtaria*	5–7			S, C, (N)	
Canary-shouldered Thorn *Ennomos alniaria*	5–7				
Oak Beauty *Biston strataria*	5–7			S, C, (N)	
Emperor Moth *Saturnia pavonia*	5–8				
White-spotted Pug *Eupithecia tripunctaria*	6–7 & 9–10		F & S	S, C, (N)	L
Lunar Thorn *Selenia lunularia*	6–8				L
Lime Hawk-moth *Mimas tiliae*	6–9			S, C	
Pale Tussock *Calliteara pudibunda*	6–10			S, C	
Alder Moth *Acronicta alni*	7–8			S, C, (N)	L
Clouded Silver *Lomographa temerata*	7–8			S, C, (N)	
Blomer's Rivulet *Discoloxia blomeri*	7–9			S, C, (SN)	Nb
Bright-line Brown-eye *Lacanobia oleracea*	7–9	+			
Broom Moth *Melanchra pisi*	7–9				
Green Silver-lines *Pseudoips prasinana*	7–9	+			
Grey Dagger *Acronicta psi*	7–9				
Peppered Moth *Biston betularia*	7–9				
Buff-tip *Phalera bucephala*	7–10				
Clouded Magpie *Abraxas sylvata*	7–10			S, C, SN, (N)	L
Double Dart *Graphiphora augur*	8–5				
Goat Moth *Cossus cossus*	8–5	∗	ISt		Nb
Mottled Beauty *Alcis repandata*	8–5				
Leopard Moth *Zeuzera pyrina*	8–5	∗	ISt	S, C	
Light Emerald *Campaea margaritata*	8–5	+			
Yellow-legged Clearwing *Synanthedon vespiformis*	8–5		ISt	S, C	Nb
Scarce Vapourer *Orgyia recens*	8–6			EC	RDB
Yellow-tail *Euproctis similis*	8–6			S, C, (N)	
Lesser Broad-bordered Yellow Underwing *Noctua janthe*	9–4				
Old Lady *Mormo maura*	9–5			S, C, (N)	L
Magpie *Abraxas grossulariata*	9–6				

Enchanter's-nightshade *Circaea lutetiana*

Small Phoenix *Ecliptopera silaceata*	6–7	+			
Elephant Hawk-moth *Deilephila elpenor*	7–9	+		S, C, (N)	

Evening-primroses *Oenothera* spp.

Elephant Hawk-moth *Deilephila elpenor*	7–9	+		S, C, (N)	

Eyebrights *Euphrasia* spp.

Heath Rivulet *Perizoma minorata*	8–9		S	N, (C)	Nb
Pretty Pinion *Perizoma blandiata*	8–9		F & S	W, N	L
Barred Rivulet *Perizoma bifaciata*	8–10		S	S, C, (N)	L

Fairy Flax *Linum catharticum*

Straw Belle *Aspitates gilvaria*	9–6			SE	RDB

Fat-hens *Chenopodium* spp. see under Goosefoot

Fennel *Foeniculum vulgare*
Mouse *Amphipyra tragopoginis*	4–6		L & F

Feverfew *Tanacetum parthenium*
Chamomile Shark *Cucullia chamomillae*	5–7	F	S, C, (N)	L
Tawny Speckled Pug *Eupithecia icterata*	8–10	F & L		

Field Gromwell *Lithospermum arvense*
Deep-brown Dart *Aporophyla lutulenta*	10~6		S, EC

Field Maple *Acer campestre*
Barred Sallow *Xanthia aurago*	4–6	B, F & L	S, C, (N)	
Dotted Border *Agriopis marginaria*	4–6			
Dun-bar *Cosmia trapezina*	4–6			
Mottled Umber *Erannis defoliaria*	4–6			
Pale November Moth *Epirrita christyi*	4–6		S, C, (N)	
Plumed Prominent *Ptilophora plumigera*	4–6		S	Na
Small Quaker *Orthosia cruda*	4–6			
Twin-spotted Quaker *Orthosia munda*	4–6		S, C, (N)	
Maple Pug *Eupithecia inturbata*	5–6	F	S, C	L
March Moth *Alsophila aescularia*	5–6			
Satellite *Eupsilia transversa*	5–6			
Nut-tree Tussock *Colocasia coryli*	5–7 & 9–10	7–9		
Emperor Moth *Saturnia pavonia*	5–8			
Maple Prominent *Ptilodon cucullina*	6–9		SE, (SW)	L
Mottled Pug *Eupithecia exiguata*	6–10		S, C, (N)	
Mocha *Cyclophora annularia*	7 & 8–9		S, (C)	Nb
Small Yellow Wave *Hydrelia flammeolaria*	7–9		S, C, (N)	
Sycamore *Acronicta aceris*	7–9		S, (C)	L
Treble Brown Spot *Idaea trigeminata*	8~5	+	S, (C)	L

Figworts *Scrophularia* spp.
Frosted Orange *Gortyna flavago*	4–8	ISt & R		
Mullein *Shargacucullia verbasci*	5–7		S, C	
Star-wort *Cucullia asteris*	7–9	F	S, C	Nb
Striped Lychnis *Shargacucullia lychnitis*	7–9	F & S	S	Na
Purple Clay *Diarsia brunnea*	8~5			
Six-striped Rustic *Xestia sexstrigata*	9~4			

Firethorns *Pyracantha* spp.
Holly Blue *Celastrina argiolus*	5–7 & 8–9	B, F & S	S, C, (SN)	
Vapourer *Orgyia antiqua*	5–8	+		
Grey Dagger *Acronicta psi*	7–9	+		

Firs *Abies* spp. & *Pseudotsuga*

Unspecified
Dwarf Pug *Eupithecia tantillaria*	7–8
Willow Beauty *Peribatodes rhomboidaria*	7~6 +

Douglas Fir *P. menziesii*
Spruce Carpet *Thera britannica*	6–7 & 9–5		S, C, (N)	
Cloaked Pug *Eupithecia abietaria*	6–9	S	C, N, (S)	UC
Dwarf Pug *Eupithecia tantillaria*	7–8			

Grey Pine Carpet *Thera obeliscata*	7–8 & 9–6				
Satin Beauty *Deileptenia ribeata*	8–5				
Barred Red *Hylaea fasciaria*	9~5				

Noble Fir *A. procera*

Cloaked Pug *Eupithecia abietaria*	6–9			S, C, NE	UC

Silver Fir *A. alba*

Pine Beauty *Panolis flammea*	5–7				
Spruce Carpet *Thera britannica*	6–7 & 9–5			S, C, (N)	
Cloaked Pug *Eupithecia abietaria*	6–9			C, N, (S)	UC
Bordered White *Bupalus piniaria*	6–10				
Satin Beauty *Deileptenia ribeata*	8–5				

Fleabane *Pulicaria dysenterica*

Powdered Quaker *Orthosia gracilis*	5–7				
Small Marbled *Eublemma parva*	7–9		F	S, C, (N)	Bm

Flixweed *Descurainia sophia*

White Colon *Sideridis albicolon*	6–7 & 9		F		Nb
Grey Carpet *Lithostege griseata*	6–8		S	SE	RDB
Cinnabar *Tyria jacobaeae*	7–9			S, C, (N)	
Shaded Pug *Eupithecia subumbrata*	7–9		F	S, (C)	L

Foxgloves *Digitalis* spp.

Frosted Orange *Gortyna flavago*	4–8		ISt & R		
Small Square-spot *Diarsia rubi*	6–7 & 9~4	8~5			
Foxglove Pug *Eupithecia pulchellata*	6–8		F		
Small Angle Shades *Euplexia lucipara*	7–9	+			
Heath Fritillary *Melitaea athalia*	7~6			SW, SE	R
Purple Clay *Diarsia brunnea*	8~5				
Ashworth's Rustic *Xestia ashworthii*	8~6			WC	Na
Lesser Yellow Underwing *Noctua comes*	8–6				
Large Yellow Underwing *Noctua pronuba*	9–5				
Feathered Ranunculus *Polymixis lichenea*	10–5			S, C, (N)	L

Fuchsias *Fuchsia* spp.

Striped Hawk-moth *Hyles livornica*	6–7 & 9–10				Bm
Bedstraw Hawk-moth *Hyles gallii*	7–9				Bm
Elephant Hawk-moth *Deilephila elpenor*	7–9	+		S, C, (N)	
Silver-striped Hawk-moth *Hippotion celerio*	10				Bm

Fungi

Waved Black *Parascotia fuliginaria*	8–6			S, C	Nb

Galingale *Cyperus longus*

Rosy Rustic *Hydraecia micacea*	5–8		ISt & R		
Dotted Fan-foot *Macrochilo cribrumalis*	8–5		DL, ISt	SE, (EC)	Nb

Galls

Blossom Underwing *Orthosia miniosa*	5–6			S, C	L

Garlic Mustard *Alliaria petiolata*

Green-veined White *Pieris napi*	5–6 & 7–8	6–8			
Orange-tip *Anthocharis cardamines*	5–7		S, B, F & L		
Small White *Pieris rapae*	5–10				
Garden Carpet *Xanthorhoe fluctuata*	6–10				

Gentians *Gentiana* spp.

Satyr Pug *Eupithecia satyrata*	6–9		F	L
Shaded Pug *Eupithecia subumbrata*	7–9		F	S, (C)	L

Geraniums (Garden) *Pelargonium* spp.

Scarce Bordered Straw *Helicoverpa armigera*	?				Bm

Globeflower *Trollius europaeus*

Golden Plusia *Polychrysia moneta*	9–6		B, L & S	S, C, (N)

Godetia *Clarkia amoena*

Bedstraw Hawk-moth *Hyles gallii*	7–9				Bm
Elephant Hawk-moth *Deilephila elpenor*	7–9	+		S, C, (N)

Goldenrods *Solidago* spp.

Phoenix *Eulithis prunata*	4–6				
Lime-speck Pug *Eupithecia centaureata*	5–10	+	F		
Common Pug *Eupithecia vulgata*	6–7 & 8–10	7–8			
Flame Shoulder *Ochropleura plecta*	6–7 & 9–10	8–9			
Golden-rod Pug *Eupithecia virgaureata*	6–7 & 9–10		F		L
Ruby Tiger *Phragmatobia fuliginosa*	5–7 & 7–4	7–5			
V-Pug *Chloroclystis v-ata*	5–7 & 8–10	7–9	F	S, C, (N)	
White-spotted Pug *Eupithecia tripunctaria*	6–7 & 9–10		F & S	S, C, (N)	L
Grey Pug *Eupithecia subfuscata*	6–10		F & L		
Peppered Moth *Biston betularia*	7–9				
Shaded Pug *Eupithecia subumbrata*	7–9		F	S, (C)	L
Star-wort *Cucullia asteris*	7–9		F	S, C	Nb
Beautiful Brocade *Lacanobia contigua*	8–9				L
Wormwood Pug *Eupithecia absinthiata*	8–10		F		
Bright Wave *Idaea ochrata*	8–5			SE	RDB
Currant Clearwing *Synanthedon tipuliformis*	8–5	*	lSt	S, C, (N)	Nb
Satin Wave *Idaea subsericeata*	8–5	+		S, (C, NW)	
Ashworth's Rustic *Xestia ashworthii*	8–6			WC	Na
Swallow-tailed Moth *Ourapteryx sambucaria*	8–6				
Bleached Pug *Eupithecia expallidata*	9–10		F & S	S, C, (NW)	Nb
Magpie *Abraxas grossulariata*	9–6				

Golden Samphire *Inula crithmoides*

Ground Lackey *Malacosoma castrensis*	4–7			SE, (SW)	Na

Good-King-Henry *Chenopodium bonus-henricus*

Nutmeg *Discestra trifolii*	6–7 & 9–10	8–9		S, C, (N)	
Plain Pug *Eupithecia simpliciata*	8–9		F & S	S, C	L
Dark Spinach *Pelurga comitata*	9–10			S, C, (N)	

Gooseberry *Ribes uva-crispa*

Phoenix *Eulithis prunata*	4–6				
V-Moth *Macaria wauaria*	4–6				L
Comma *Polygonia c-album*	5–6 & 7–8		F	S, C, (SN)	
Currant Clearwing *Synanthedon tipuliformis*	8–5	*	lSt	S, C, (N)	Nb
Magpie *Abraxas grossulariata*	9–6				

Goosefoots *Chenopodium* spp.

Dog's Tooth *Lacanobia suasa*	6–7 & 8–9	7–8		S, C, (N)	L
Nutmeg *Discestra trifolii*	6–7 & 9–10	8–9		S, C, (N)	
White Colon *Sideridis albicolon*	6–7 & 9		F		Nb

Dark Sword-grass *Agrotis ipsilon*	7–8		L & R	Bm
Bright-line Brown-eye *Lacanobia oleracea*	7–9	+		
Flame *Axylia putris*	7–9		S, C, (N)	
Heart and Dart *Agrotis exclamationis*	7~3	+		
Plain Pug *Eupithecia simpliciata*	8–9		F & S	S, C	L
Sand Dart *Agrotis ripae*	8–10			S, C, NE	Nb
Wormwood Pug *Eupithecia absinthiata*	8–10		F	
Mottled Rustic *Caradrina morpheus*	8–11			
Heart and Club *Agrotis clavis*	8~5		L & R	
Dark Spinach *Pelurga comitata*	9–10			S, C, (N)

Goosegrass *Galium aparine* see under Bedstraws

Gorse *Ulex europaeus*

Grass Eggar *Lasiocampa trifolii*	3–6		S, WC	Na
Silver-studded Blue *Plebejus argus*	4–6	F & L	S, WC	R
Double-striped Pug *Gymnoscelis rufifasciata*	5–6 & 9–10	F		
Holly Blue *Celastrina argiolus*	5–7 & 8–9	B, F & S	S, C, (SN)	
Green Hairstreak *Callophrys rubi*	5–8	F & L		L
Small Grass Emerald *Chlorissa viridata*	7–8		S, (WC)	Na
Willow Beauty *Peribatodes rhomboidaria*	7~6	+		
Beautiful Brocade *Lacanobia contigua*	8–9	F		L
Lead Belle *Scotopteryx mucronata*	8–3		W, N	L
Grass Wave *Perconia strigillaria*	8–5	F	S, C, (N)	L
Dark Tussock *Dicallomera fascelina*	8~6	F	S, WC, NE	L
July Belle *Scotopteryx luridata*	9–4			
Grass Emerald *Pseudoterpna pruinata*	9~5			

Grape-vines *Vitis* spp.

Striped Hawk-moth *Hyles livornica*	6–7 & 9–10			Bm
Bedstraw Hawk-moth *Hyles gallii*	7–9			Bm
Elephant Hawk-moth *Deilephila elpenor*	7–9	+	S, C, (N)	
Silver-striped Hawk-moth *Hippotion celerio*	10			Bm

Grasses

COASTAL:

Unspecified

Saltern Ear *Amphipoea fucosa*	5–7	St & R		L
Devonshire Wainscot *Mythimna putrescens*	9–2		SW	Na
Archer's Dart *Agrotis vestigialis*	9–6			L
Crescent Striped *Apamea oblonga*	9–6	St & R	S, C, (N)	Nb

Hard-grasses *Parapholis* spp.

Sandhill Rustic *Luperina nickerlii*	9–7	St & R	SE, SW, WC	Na

Lyme Grass *Leymus arenarius*

Lyme Grass *Chortodes elymi*	3–6	lSt	E, NE	Nb
Rosy Minor *Mesoligia literosa*	9–6	lSt & R		

Marram *Ammophila arenaria*

Grass Eggar *Lasiocampa trifolii*	3–6		S, WC	Na
L-album Wainscot *Mythimna l-album*	8 & 10~5		S	Nb
Shore Wainscot *Mythimna litoralis*	8–5		S, C, (N)	Nb
Grayling *Hipparchia semele*	8–6			L
Portland Moth *Actebia praecox*	9–6		SW, C, N, (S)	Nb
Rosy Minor *Mesoligia literosa*	9–6	lSt & R		

Rush-leaved Fescue *Festuca arenaria*

Portland Moth *Actebia praecox*	9–6			SW, C, N, (S)	Nb

Saltmarsh-grasses *Puccinellia* spp.

Ear Moth *Amphipoea oculea*	4–6		St & R		
Mathew's Wainscot *Mythimna favicolor*	8–5			S	Nb
Crescent Striped *Apamea oblonga*	9–6		St & R	S, C, (N)	Nb
Sandhill Rustic *Luperina nickerlii*	9–7		St & R	SE, SW, WC	Na

Sand Couch *Elytrigia juncea*

Coast Dart *Euxoa cursoria*	3–7			E, WC, N	Nb
Sandhill Rustic *Luperina nickerlii*	9–7		St & R	SE, SW, WC	Na

GENERAL:

Unspecified

Beaded Chestnut *Agrochola lychnidis*	3–6			S, C, (N)	
Brighton Wainscot *Oria musculosa*	4–6		lSt & S	S	RDB
Twin-spot Carpet *Perizoma didymata*	4–6				
Belted Beauty *Lycia zonaria*	5–7			NW	Na
Saltern Ear *Amphipoea fucosa*	5–7		St & R		L
Small Square-spot *Diarsia rubi*	6–7 & 9–4	8–5			
Dark Brocade *Blepharita adusta*	6–9				
Marbled White Spot *Protodeltote pygarga*	7–9			S, C	
Mother Shipton *Callistege mi*	7–9				
Common Swift *Hepialus lupulinus*	7–5	*	R		
Yellow Shell *Camptogramma bilineata*	7–5				
Gold Swift *Hepialus hecta*	7–6	*	R		L
Dotted Fan-foot *Macrochilo cribrumalis*	8–5		DL, lSt	SE, (EC)	Nb
Ghost Moth *Hepialus humuli*	8–5	*	R		
Light Arches *Apamea lithoxylaea*	8–5		St & R		
Reddish Light Arches *Apamea sublustris*	8–5		St & R	S, (C)	L
Striped Wainscot *Mythimna pudorina*	8–5			S, (C)	L
Devonshire Wainscot *Mythimna putrescens*	9–2			SW	Na
Pale Mottled Willow *Paradrina clavipalpis*	9–4 & 6–8		S		
Dotted Rustic *Rhyacia simulans*	9–5				L
Large Yellow Underwing *Noctua pronuba*	9–5				
Least Yellow Underwing *Noctua interjecta*	9–5			S, C, (SN)	
Northern Deep-brown Dart *Aporophyla lueneburgensis*	9–5			WC, N	
White-speck *Mythimna unipuncta*	9–5				Bm
Flounced Rustic *Luperina testacea*	9–6		St & R		
Small Wainscot *Chortodes pygmina*	9–7		lSt		
Autumnal Rustic *Eugnorisma glareosa*	10–5				
Black Rustic *Aporophyla nigra*	10–5				
Deep-brown Dart *Aporophyla lutulenta*	10–6			S, EC	

Annual Meadow-grass *P. annua* see under Meadow-grass

Bents *Agrostis* spp.

Antler Moth *Cerapteryx graminis*	3–6				
Small Heath *Coenonympha pamphilus*	6–4	+			
Meadow Brown *Maniola jurtina*	7–6				
Double Line *Mythimna turca*	8–5			S, (WC)	Nb
Gatekeeper *Pyronia tithonus*	8–6			S, C	
Grayling *Hipparchia semele*	8–6				L

Bristle Bent *A. curtisii*

Speckled Footman *Coscinia cribraria*	9~6		SW	RDB

Blue Moor-grass *Sesleria caerulea*

Scotch Argus *Erebia aethiops*	8~6		N	S

Bromes *Bromus, Bromopsis, Anisantha* spp.

Chequered Skipper *Carterocephalus palaemon*	6~4		NW	R
Marbled White *Melanargia galathea*	8~6		S, C	L
Shaded Broad-bar *Scotopteryx chenopodiata*	8~6			

Cat's-tails *Phleum* spp.

Essex Skipper *Thymelicus lineola*	3–6		S, EC	L
Large Skipper *Ochlodes faunus*	7~5		S, C, (SN)	
Meadow Brown *Maniola jurtina*	7~6			
Marbled White *Melanargia galathea*	8~6		S, C	L

Cock's-foot *Dactylis glomerata*

Dusky Sallow *Eremobia ochroleuca*	5–7	F & S	S, EC, (SW)	
Speckled Wood *Pararge aegeria*	5~3		S, C, (N)	
Nutmeg *Discestra trifolii*	6–7 & 9–10	8–9	S, C, (N)	
Wall *Lasiommata megera*	6–7 & 9~5		S, C	
Common Wainscot *Mythimna pallens*	6–8 & 9~5	8~6		
Mother Shipton *Callistege mi*	7–9			
Rustic Shoulder-knot *Apamea sordens*	7–3			
Shoulder-striped Wainscot *Mythimna comma*	7~4		S, C, (N)	
Large Skipper *Ochlodes faunus*	7~5		S, C, (SN)	
Smoky Wainscot *Mythimna impura*	7–5			
Meadow Brown *Maniola jurtina*	7–6			
Ringlet *Aphantopus hyperantus*	7–6			
L-album Wainscot *Mythimna l-album*	8 & 10~5		S	Nb
Clouded Brindle *Apamea epomidion*	8–3	S & L	S, C, (N)	
Clouded-bordered Brindle *Apamea crenata*	8–4	F & S		
Large Nutmeg *Apamea anceps*	8–4	L & S	S, (C)	L
Rufous Minor *Oligia versicolor*	8–4	lSt	S, C, (N)	L
Brown-line Bright-eye *Mythimna conigera*	8–5			
Double Line *Mythimna turca*	8–5		S, (WC)	Nb
Striped Wainscot *Mythimna pudorina*	8~5		S, (C)	L
Dark Arches *Apamea monoglypha*	8–6	St & R		
Drinker *Euthrix potatoria*	8–6		S, C, NW	
Gatekeeper *Pyronia tithonus*	8–6		S, C	
Marbled White *Melanargia galathea*	8–6		S, C	L
Small Skipper *Thymelicus sylvestris*	8–6		S, C, NE	
Lunar Yellow Underwing *Noctua orbona*	9–5			Nb
White-point *Mythimna albipuncta*	9–4		S	Bm
Clay *Mythimna ferrago*	9~5			
Common Rustic *Mesapamea secalis*	9–5		lSt	
Marbled Minor *Oligia strigilis*	9–5	lSt		
Tawny Marbled Minor *Oligia latruncula*	9–5	lSt	S, C, (N)	
White-speck *Mythimna unipuncta*	9–5			Bm
Essex Skipper *Thymelicus lineola*	9–6		S, EC	L
Rosy Minor *Mesoligia literosa*	9–6	lSt & R		
Lesser Common Rustic *Mesapamea didyma*	10–5	lSt		

Couches *Elytrigia* spp.

Dusky Sallow *Eremobia ochroleuca*	5–7	F & S	S, EC, (SW)	

Speckled Wood *Pararge aegeria*	5~3		S, C, (N)	
Wall *Lasiommata megera*	6–7 & 9~5		S, C	
Common Wainscot *Mythimna pallens*	6–8 & 9~5	8~6		
Rustic Shoulder-knot *Apamea sordens*	7–3	S		
Small Clouded Brindle *Apamea unaminis*	7–3		S, C, (N)	
Large Skipper *Ochlodes faunus*	7~5		S, C, (SN)	
Meadow Brown *Maniola jurtina*	7–6			
Ringlet *Aphantopus hyperantus*	7–6			
Large Nutmeg *Apamea anceps*	8–4	L & S	S, (C)	L
Brown-line Bright-eye *Mythimna conigera*	8–5			
Dark Arches *Apamea monoglypha*	8–6	St & R		
Drinker *Euthrix potatoria*	8–6		S, C, NW	
Gatekeeper *Pyronia tithonus*	8–6		S, C	
Grayling *Hipparchia semele*	8–6			L
Dusky Brocade *Apamea remissa*	9–4	F, S & L		
Lunar Yellow Underwing *Noctua orbona*	9–5			Nb
White-point *Mythimna albipuncta*	9–4		S	Bm
Common Rustic *Mesapamea secalis*	9–5	lSt		
Marbled Minor *Oligia strigilis*	9–5	lSt		
Slender Brindle *Apamea scolopacina*	9–5	lSt & L	S, C	
White-speck *Mythimna unipuncta*	9–5			Bm
Essex Skipper *Thymelicus lineola*	9–6		S, EC	L
Flounced Rustic *Luperina testacea*	9–6	St & R		
Beautiful Gothic *Leucochlaena oditis*	10–3		S	RDB

Creeping Soft-grass *Holcus mollis*

Large Skipper *Ochlodes faunus*	7~5		S, C, (SN)	
Small Skipper *Thymelicus sylvestris*	8~6		S, C, NE	
Common Rustic *Mesapamea secalis*	9–5	lSt		
Essex Skipper *Thymelicus lineola*	9–6		S, EC	L

Crested Dog's-tail *Cynosurus cristatus*

Small Heath *Coenonympha pamphilus*	6–4	+		

Downy Oat-grass *Helictotrichon pubescens*

Beaded Chestnut *Agrochola lychnidis*	3–6		S, C, (N)	
Dusky Sallow *Eremobia ochroleuca*	5–7	F & S	S, EC, (SW)	
Meadow Brown *Maniola jurtina*	7–6			
Least Minor *Photedes captiuncula*	8~5	lSt	SN	RDB

Early Hair-grass *Aira praecox*

Coast Dart *Euxoa cursoria*	3–7		E, WC, N	Nb
Grayling *Hipparchia semele*	8~6			L

False Oat-grass *Arrhenatherum elatius*

Grass Eggar *Lasiocampa trifolii*	3–6		S, WC	Na
Dusky Sallow *Eremobia ochroleuca*	5–7	F & S	S, EC, (SW)	
Cloaked Minor *Mesoligia furuncula*	8–6	lSt		

False-brome *Brachypodium sylvaticum*

Speckled Wood *Pararge aegeria*	5~3		S, C, (N)	
Chequered Skipper *Carterocephalus palaemon*	6–4		NW	R
Wall *Lasiommata megera*	6–7 & 9~5		S, C	
Straw Dot *Rivula sericealis*	7 & 8~5	8~5	S, C, NW, (NE)	
Marbled White Spot *Protodeltote pygarga*	7–9		S, C	
Large Skipper *Ochlodes faunus*	7~5		S, C, (SN)	
Meadow Brown *Maniola jurtina*	7–6			

Ringlet *Aphantopus hyperantus*	7–6			
Grayling *Hipparchia semele*	8–6			L
Small Skipper *Thymelicus sylvestris*	8–6		S, C, NE	
Slender Brindle *Apamea scolopacina*	9–5	ISt & L	S, C	
Essex Skipper *Thymelicus lineola*	9–6		S, EC	L

Heath False-brome *B. pinnatum* see under Tor Grass

Fescues *Festuca* spp.

Unspecified

Small Heath *Coenonympha pamphilus*	6–4	+		
Meadow Brown *Maniola jurtina*	7–6			
Brown-line Bright-eye *Mythimna conigera*	8–5			
Gatekeeper *Pyronia tithonus*	8–6		S, C	
Scotch Argus *Erebia aethiops*	8–6		N	S
Flounced Rustic *Luperina testacea*	9–6	St & R		
Lesser Common Rustic *Mesapamea didyma*	10–5	ISt		

Meadow Fescue *F. pratensis*

Large Heath *Coenonympha tullia*	7–5		WC, N, (EC)	S
L-album Wainscot *Mythimna l-album*	8 & 10–5		S	Nb
Cloaked Minor *Mesoligia furuncula*	8–6	ISt		
Common Rustic *Mesapamea secalis*	9–5	ISt		

Red Fescue *F. rubra*

Map-winged Swift *Hepialus fusconebulosa*	7–5	*	St & R	L
Grayling *Hipparchia semele*	8–6			L
Marbled White *Melanargia galathea*	8–6		S, C	L
Crescent Striped *Apamea oblonga*	9–6	St & R	S, C, (N)	Nb
Sandhill Rustic *Luperina nickerlii*	9–7	St & R	SE, SW, WC	Na

Sheep's-fescue *F. ovina*

Antler Moth *Cerapteryx graminis*	3–6			
Feathered Gothic *Tholera decimalis*	3–7	L & St	S, C, (N)	
Silver-spotted Skipper *Hesperia comma*	3–7		SE	R
Small Heath *Coenonympha pamphilus*	6–4	+		
Large Heath *Coenonympha tullia*	7–5		WC, N, (EC)	S
Meadow Brown *Maniola jurtina*	7–6			
Brown-line Bright-eye *Mythimna conigera*	8–5			
Cloaked Minor *Mesoligia furuncula*	8–6	ISt		
Grayling *Hipparchia semele*	8–6			L
Marbled White *Melanargia galathea*	8–6		S, C	L
Lunar Yellow Underwing *Noctua orbona*	9–5			Nb
Common Rustic *Mesapamea secalis*	9–5	ISt		
Northern Rustic *Standfussiana lucernea*	10–5		SW, WC, N	L

Tall Fescue *F. arundinacea*

L-album Wainscot *Mythimna l-album*	8 & 10–5		S	Nb
Cloaked Minor *Mesoligia furuncula*	8–6	ISt		
Morris's Wainscot *Chortodes morrisii*	8–6	ISt	SW	RDB
Common Rustic *Mesapamea secalis*	9–5	ISt		

Hair-grasses *Koeleria* spp.

Grayling *Hipparchia semele*	8–6			L
Straw Underwing *Thalpophila matura*	9–5		S, C, (N)	
Confused *Apamea furva*	9–6	St & R	C, N, (SE, SW)	L

Mat Grass *Nardus stricta*

Antler Moth *Cerapteryx graminis*	3–6			
Feathered Gothic *Tholera decimalis*	3–7		L & St	S, C, (N)
Hedge Rustic *Tholera cespitis*	3–7			
Small Heath *Coenonympha pamphilus*	6–4	+		
Mountain Ringlet *Erebia epiphron*	8–5			NW	R
Straw Underwing *Thalpophila matura*	9–5			S, C, (N)

Meadow Foxtail *Alopecurus pratensis*

Small Skipper *Thymelicus sylvestris*	8–6			S, C, NE
Essex Skipper *Thymelicus lineola*	9–6			S, EC	L

Meadow-grasses *Poa* spp.

Alpine Meadow-grass *P. alpina*

Northern Arches (Exile) *Apamea zeta*	9–6		lSt & R	N	Na

Annual Meadow-grass *P. annua*

Feathered Gothic *Tholera decimalis*	3–7		L & St	S, C, (N)
Ear Moth *Amphipoea oculea*	4–6		St & R	
Saltern Ear *Amphipoea fucosa*	5–7		St & R		L
Speckled Wood *Pararge aegeria*	5–3			S, C, (N)
Wall *Lasiommata megera*	6–7 & 9–5			S, C
Common Wainscot *Mythimna pallens*	6–8 & 9–5	8–6		
Small Heath *Coenonympha pamphilus*	6–4	+		
Silver Barred *Deltote bankiana*	7–8			SE	RDB
Small Clouded Brindle *Apamea unaminis*	7–3			S, C, (N)
Smoky Wainscot *Mythimna impura*	7–5			
Yellow Shell *Camptogramma bilineata*	7–5			
Meadow Brown *Maniola jurtina*	7–6			
Ringlet *Aphantopus hyperantus*	7–6			
Clouded Brindle *Apamea epomidion*	8–3		S & L	S, C, (N)
Large Nutmeg *Apamea anceps*	8–4		L & S	S, (C)	L
Brown-line Bright-eye *Mythimna conigera*	8–5			
Light Arches *Apamea lithoxylaea*	8–5		St & R	
Dark Arches *Apamea monoglypha*	8–6		St & R	
Drinker *Euthrix potatoria*	8–6			S, C, NW
Gatekeeper *Pyronia tithonus*	8–6			S, C
Grayling *Hipparchia semele*	8–6				L
Marbled White *Melanargia galathea*	8–6	+		S, EC	L
Devonshire Wainscot *Mythimna putrescens*	9–2			SW	Na
Dusky Brocade *Apamea remissa*	9–4			
Square-spot Rustic *Xestia xanthographa*	9–4			
Clay *Mythimna ferrago*	9–5			
Gold Spot *Plusia festucae*	9–5 & 7–8	9–5		
Large Yellow Underwing *Noctua pronuba*	9–5			
Straw Underwing *Thalpophila matura*	9–5			S, C, (N)
Confused *Apamea furva*	9–6		St & R	C, N, (SE, SW)	L
Speckled Footman *Coscinia cribraria*	9–6			SW	RDB
Beautiful Gothic *Leucochlaena oditis*	10–3			S	RDB
Anomalous *Stilbia anomala*	10–4				L
Feathered Brindle *Aporophyla australis*	10–5			S	Nb
Lunar Underwing *Omphaloscelis lunosa*	10–5			S, C, (N)
Deep-brown Dart *Aporophyla lutulenta*	10–6			S, EC

Bulbous Meadow-grass *P. bulbosa*

Crescent Striped *Apamea oblonga*	9–6	St & R	S, C, (N)	Nb
Sandhill Rustic *Luperina nickerlii*	9–7	St & R	SE, SW, WC	Na

Rough Meadow-grass *P. trivialis*

Antler Moth *Cerapteryx graminis*	3–6			
Speckled Wood *Pararge aegeria*	5~3		S, C, (N)	
Meadow Brown *Maniola jurtina*	7–6			
Gatekeeper *Pyronia tithonus*	8–6		S, C	
Southern Wainscot *Mythimna straminea*	8~6		S, C	L
Confused *Apamea furva*	9–6	St & R	C, N, (SE, SW)	L

Smooth Meadow-grass *P. pratensis*

Silver Barred *Deltote bankiana*	7–8		SE	RDB
Shaded Broad-bar *Scotopteryx chenopodiata*	8~6			

Wood Meadow-grass *P. nemoralis*

Speckled Wood *Pararge aegeria*	5~3		S, C, (N)	
Small Heath *Coenonympha pamphilus*	6–4	+		
Meadow Brown *Maniola jurtina*	7–6			
Double Line *Mythimna turca*	8~5		S, (WC)	Nb
Clay *Mythimna ferrago*	9~5			
Slender Brindle *Apamea scolopacina*	9–5	lSt & L	S, C	
Confused *Apamea furva*	9–6	St & R	C, N, (SE, SW)	L

Pampas-grass *Cortaderia selloana*

Double Lobed *Apamea ophiogramma*	8~6	lSt	S, C, (N)	L

Purple Moor-grass *Molinia caerulea*

Antler Moth *Cerapteryx graminis*	3–6			
Crescent *Celaena leucostigma*	3–7	lSt		L
Large Ear *Amphipoea lucens*	5–7	lSt & R	SW, WC, N	L
Chequered Skipper *Carterocephalus palaemon*	6–4		NW	R
Straw Dot *Rivula sericealis*	7 & 8~5	8~5	S, C, NW, (NE)	
Silver Barred *Deltote bankiana*	7–8		SE	RDB
Marbled White Spot *Protodeltote pygarga*	7–9		S, C	
Large Heath *Coenonympha tullia*	7~5		WC, N, (EC)	S
Large Skipper *Ochlodes faunus*	7~5		S, C, (SN)	
Striped Wainscot *Mythimna pudorina*	8~5		S, (C)	L
Drinker *Euthrix potatoria*	8~6		S, C, (N)	
Scotch Argus *Erebia aethiops*	8~6		N	S

Quaking-grasses *Briza* spp.

Slender Brindle *Apamea scolopacina*	9–5	lSt & L	S, C	

Reed Canary-grass *Phalaris arundinacea*

Small Clouded Brindle *Apamea unaminis*	7–3		S, C, (N)	
Striped Wainscot *Mythimna pudorina*	8~5		S, (C)	L
Double Lobed *Apamea ophiogramma*	8~6	lSt	S, C, (N)	L
Drinker *Euthrix potatoria*	8~6		S, C, NW	
Southern Wainscot *Mythimna straminea*	8~6		S, C	L
Dusky Brocade *Apamea remissa*	9–4	F, S & L		
Lunar Yellow Underwing *Noctua orbona*	9–5			Nb
Marbled Minor *Oligia strigilis*	9–5	lSt		

Reed Sweet-grass *Glyceria maxima*

Double Lobed *Apamea ophiogramma*	8~6	lSt	S, C, (N)	L

Ryegrasses *Lolium* spp.

Gatekeeper *Pyronia tithonus*	8~6		S, C	

Timothy *Phleum pratense*

Small Skipper *Thymelicus sylvestris*	8~6		S, C, NE	
Essex Skipper *Thymelicus lineola*	9~6		S, EC	L

Tor-grass *Brachypodium pinnatum*

Essex Skipper *Thymelicus lineola*	9~6		S, EC	L
Wall *Lasiommata megera*	6–7 & 9~5		S, C	
Chequered Skipper *Carterocephalus palaemon*	6–4		NW	R
Straw Dot *Rivula sericealis*	7 & 8~5	8~5	S, C, NW, (NE)	
Marbled White *Melanargia galathea*	8~6		S, C	L
Lulworth Skipper *Thymelicus acteon*	8~6		SW	R
Small Skipper *Thymelicus sylvestris*	8~6		S, C, NE	

Tufted Hair-grass *Deschampsia cespitosa*

Antler Moth *Cerapteryx graminis*	3–6			
Hedge Rustic *Tholera cespitis*	3–7			
Ear Moth *Amphipoea oculea*	4–6	St & R		
Wall *Lasiommata megera*	6–7 & 9~5		S, C	
Common Wainscot *Mythimna pallens*	6–8 & 9~5	8~6		
Silver Hook *Deltote uncula*	7–9		S, C, NW	L
Smoky Wainscot *Mythimna impura*	7–5			
Ringlet *Aphantopus hyperantus*	7–6			
Clouded Brindle *Apamea epomidion*	8–3	S & L	S, C, (N)	
Middle-barred Minor *Oligia fasciuncula*	8–5			
Cloaked Minor *Mesoligia furuncula*	8–6	lSt		
Dark Arches *Apamea monoglypha*	8–6	St & R		
Grayling *Hipparchia semele*	8–6			L
Scotch Argus *Erebia aethiops*	8–6		N	S
Small Dotted Buff *Photedes minima*	8–6	lSt & R		
Common Rustic *Mesapamea secalis*	9–5	lSt		
Speckled Footman *Coscinia cribraria*	9–6		SW	RDB
Anomalous *Stilbia anomala*	10–4			L
Black Rustic *Aporophyla nigra*	10–5			
Deep-brown Dart *Aporophyla lutulenta*	10~6		S, EC	

Wavy Hair-grass *D. flexuosa*

Hedge Rustic *Tholera cespitis*	3–7			
Wall *Lasiommata megera*	6–7 & 9~5		S, C	
Small Clouded Brindle *Apamea unaminis*	7–3		S, C, (N)	
Large Heath *Coenonympha tullia*	7–5		WC, N, (EC)	S
Lunar Yellow Underwing *Noctua orbona*	9–5			Nb
Anomalous *Stilbia anomala*	10–4			L

Whorl-grass *Catabrosa aquatica*

Reed Dagger *Simyra albovenosa*	6–7 & 8–9		SE	Nb

Wood Melick *Melica uniflora*

Slender Brindle *Apamea scolopacina*	9–5	lSt & L	S, C	

Wood Millet *Milium effusum*

Ringlet *Aphantopus hyperantus*	7–6

Yorkshire-fog *Holcus lanatus*

Antler Moth *Cerapteryx graminis*	3–6

Speckled Wood *Pararge aegeria*	5~3			S, C, (N)	
Wall *Lasiommata megera*	6–7 & 9~5			S, C	
Large Skipper *Ochlodes faunus*	7~5			S, C, (SN)	
Lempke's Gold Spot *Plusia putnami*	8–5			C, (S, N)	L
Marbled White *Melanargia galathea*	8~6			S, C	L
Small Skipper *Thymelicus sylvestris*	8~6			S, C, NE	
Lunar Underwing *Omphaloscelis lunosa*	10–5			S, C, (N)	

Ground-ivy *Glechoma hederacea*

Dark-barred Twin-spot Carpet *Xanthorhoe ferrugata*	6–7 & 9	6–8		S, C, (N)	
Mullein Wave *Scopula marginepunctata*	7 & 9~5	9–5		S, C, (N)	L
Red Twin-spot Carpet *Xanthorhoe spadicearia*	7 & 9	6–8			
Gold Spangle *Autographa bractea*	8~6			C, N	
Jersey Tiger *Euplagia quadripunctaria*	9~6			SW	Nb

Groundsels *Senecio* spp. See also Ragwort

Scarce Bordered Straw *Helicoverpa armigera*	?				Bm
Angle Shades *Phlogophora meticulosa*	All				
Beaded Chestnut *Agrochola lychnidis*	3–6			S, C, (N)	
Grey Chi *Antitype chi*	4–6			C, N, (S)	
Large Ranunculus *Polymixis flavicincta*	4–7			S, (C)	L
Red Chestnut *Cerastis rubricosa*	5–6				
Setaceous Hebrew Character *Xestia c-nigrum*	5–7 & 9~4	9–5			
Sword-grass *Xylena exsoleta*	5–7			C, N	Nb
Lime-speck Pug *Eupithecia centaureata*	5–10	+	F		
Dark-barred Twin-spot Carpet *Xanthorhoe ferrugata*	6–7 & 9	6–8		S, C, (N)	
Flame Shoulder *Ochropleura plecta*	6–7 & 9–10	8–9			
Red Twin-spot Carpet *Xanthorhoe spadicearia*	7 & 9	6–8			
Cinnabar *Tyria jacobaeae*	7–9			S, C, (N)	
Grey Dagger *Acronicta psi*	7–9	+			
Pale-shouldered Brocade *Lacanobia thalassina*	7–9	+			
Bordered Straw *Heliothis peltigera*	7–10		F		Bm
Silver-ground Carpet *Xanthorhoe montanata*	7~5				
Marbled Clover *Heliothis viriplaca*	8–9	+	F & S	SE, (S)	RDB
Dot Moth *Melanchra persicariae*	8–10			S, C, (N)	
Beautiful Golden Y *Autographa pulchrina*	8–5				
Brown Rustic *Rusina ferruginea*	8–5				
Large Twin-spot Carpet *Xanthorhoe quadrifasiata*	8–5			S, C	L
Least Carpet *Idaea rusticata*	8–5			SE	L
Plain Golden Y *Autographa jota*	8–5				
Scarlet Tiger *Callimorpha dominula*	8–5			S, (WC)	L
Wood Tiger *Parasemia plantaginis*	8–5				L
Gold Spangle *Autographa bractea*	8–6			C, N	
Vine's Rustic *Hoplodrina ambigua*	9–4 & 7–8			S, (C)	L
Dotted Rustic *Rhyacia simulans*	9–5				L
Red Carpet *Xanthorhoe decoloraria*	9~5			C, N	
Jersey Tiger *Euplagia quadripunctaria*	9~6			SW	Nb
Feathered Ranunculus *Polymixis lichenea*	10–5			S, C, (N)	L
Deep-brown Dart *Aporophyla lutulenta*	10~6			S, EC	

Guelder-rose *Viburnum opulus*

Yellow-barred Brindle *Acasis viretata*	6–7	+	F, S & L	S, C, (NW)	L
Privet Hawk-moth *Sphinx ligustri*	7–9			S, (C)	
Orange-tailed Clearwing *Synanthedon andrenaeformis*	7–5	*	ISt	S	Nb

Hairy Rock-cress *Arabis hirsuta*
Orange-tip *Anthocharis cardamines*	5–7		S, B, F & L		

Harebell *Campanula rotundifolia*
Black-banded *Polymixis xanthomista*	3–7		F & S	SW, WC	Na
Ashworth's Rustic *Xestia ashworthii*	8~6			WC	Na
Northern Rustic *Standfussiana lucernea*	10–5			SW, WC, N	L

Hawkbits *Leontodon* spp.
Shaded Pug *Eupithecia subumbrata*	7–9		F	S, (C)	L
Stout Dart *Spaelotis ravida*	9–5			S, EC, (WC, N)	L

Hawk's-beards *Crepis* spp.
Yellow Belle *Semiaspilates ochrearia*	6–8 & 9–5			S, C	L
Shears *Hada plebeja*	7–8	+			
Shaded Pug *Eupithecia subumbrata*	7–9		F	S, (C)	L
Shark *Cucullia umbratica*	7–9				
Broad-barred White *Hecatera bicolorata*	8–9		F & S	S, C, (N)	
Marbled Clover *Heliothis viriplaca*	8–9	+	F & S	SE, (S)	RDB
Bright Wave *Idaea ochrata*	8–5			SE	RDB

Hawkweeds *Hieracium* spp.
Satyr Pug *Eupithecia satyrata*	6–9		F		L
Shears *Hada plebeja*	7–8	+			
Shark *Cucullia umbratica*	7–9				
Clouded Buff *Diacrisia sannio*	7~5				L
Broad-barred White *Hecatera bicolorata*	8–9		F & S	S, C, (N)	
Marbled Clover *Heliothis viriplaca*	8–9	+	F & S	SE, (S)	RDB
Cream-spot Tiger *Arctia villica*	8~5			S	L
Ashworth's Rustic *Xestia ashworthii*	8~6			WC	Na
Gold Spangle *Autographa bractea*	8~6			C, N	
Autumnal Rustic *Eugnorisma glareosa*	10~5				

Hawthorns *Crataegus* spp.
Brimstone Moth *Opisthograptis luteolata*	All	7–9		
Beaded Chestnut *Agrochola lychnidis*	3–6			S, C, (N)
Brindled Green *Dryobotodes eremita*	3–6			
Grass Eggar *Lasiocampa trifolii*	3–6			S, WC	Na
Scalloped Oak *Crocallis elinguaria*	3–7			
Early Moth *Theria primaria*	4–5			S, C, (N)
Green Pug *Pasiphila rectangulata*	4–5		F	
Autumnal Moth *Epirrita autumnata*	4–6			
Black Arches *Lymantria monacha*	4–6			S, C	L
Blue-bordered Carpet *Plemyria rubiginata*	4–6			
Brown-spot Pinion *Agrochola litura*	4–6			
Common Quaker *Orthosia cerasi*	4–6			
Copper Underwing *Amphipyra pyramidea*	4–6			S, C, (N)
Dark Chestnut *Conistra ligula*	4–6			S, C, (N)
December Moth *Poecilocampa populi*	4–6			
Dotted Border *Agriopis marginaria*	4–6			
Dun-bar *Cosmia trapezina*	4–6			
Engrailed *Ectropis bistortata*	4–6 & 7–9	5–7		
Feathered Thorn *Colotois pennaria*	4–6			
Flounced Chestnut *Agrochola helvola*	4–6			
Green-brindled Crescent *Allophyes oxyacanthae*	4–6			

Species		Months			
Grey Chi *Antitype chi*	4–6			C, N, (S)	
Hebrew Character *Orthosia gothica*	4–7				
Lackey *Malacosoma neustria*	4–6			S, C, (N)	
Lunar-spotted Pinion *Cosmia pyralina*	4–6			S, C	L
Minor Shoulder-knot *Brachylomia viminalis*	4–6				
Mottled Umber *Erannis defoliaria*	4–6				
Mouse *Amphipyra tragopoginis*	4–6		L & F		
Pale Brindled Beauty *Phigalia pilosaria*	4–6				
Pale Eggar *Trichiura crataegi*	4–6				
Pale November Moth *Epirrita christyi*	4–6			S, C, (N)	
November Moth *Epirrita dilutata*	4–6				
Satellite *Eupsilia transversa*	4–6				
Scarce Umber *Agriopis aurantiaria*	4–6				
Small Brindled Beauty *Apocheima hispidaria*	4–6			S, (C, N)	L
Small Quaker *Orthosia cruda*	4–6				
Sprawler *Asteroscopus sphinx*	4–6			S, C	
Winter Moth *Operophtera brumata*	4–6				
Yellow-line Quaker *Agrochola macilenta*	4–6				
Golden-rod Brindle *Lithomoia solidaginis*	4–7			WC, N	L
Small Eggar *Eriogaster lanestris*	4–7	*		S, C	Nb
Blossom Underwing *Orthosia miniosa*	5–6			S, C	L
Chestnut *Conistra vaccinii*	5–6				
Clouded Drab *Orthosia incerta*	4–6				
Double-striped Pug *Gymnoscelis rufifasciata*	5–6 & 9–10		F		
Early Thorn *Selenia dentaria*	5–6 & 8–9	6–8			
March Moth *Alsophila aescularia*	5–6				
August Thorn *Ennomos quercinaria*	5–7			S, C, (N)	L
Brindled Beauty *Lycia hirtaria*	5–7			S, C, (N)	
Brindled Pug *Eupithecia abbreviata*	5–7		F		
Figure of Eight *Diloba caeruleocephala*	5–7			S, C, (N)	
Purple Thorn *Selenia tetralunaria*	5–7 & 8–9	6–7		S, C, (N)	
Streamer *Anticlea derivata*	5–7				
Emperor Moth *Saturnia pavonia*	5–8				
Large Thorn *Ennomos autumnaria*	5–8			SE	Nb
Vapourer *Orgyia antiqua*	5–8	+			
Ash Pug *Eupithecia fraxinata*	6–7 & 8–9				
Chinese Character *Cilix glaucata*	6–7 & 8–9			S, C, (N)	
Common Pug *Eupithecia vulgata*	6–7 & 8–10	7–8			
Coxcomb Prominent *Ptilodon capucina*	6–7 & 8–9	6–8			
V-Pug *Chloroclystis v-ata*	5–7 & 8–10	7–9	F	S, C, (N)	
Yellow-barred Brindle *Acasis viretata*	6–7	+	F, S & L	S, C, (NW)	L
Barred Umber *Plagodis pulveraria*	6–8				L
Oak-tree Pug *Eupithecia dodoneata*	6–8		S	S, C	
Pinion-spotted Pug *Eupithecia insigniata*	6–8		F	S, EC	Nb
White-pinion Spotted *Lomographa bimaculata*	6–8			S, C	
Brindled White-spot *Parectropis similaria*	6–9			S, (C)	L
Dark Brocade *Blepharita adusta*	6–9				
Scalloped Hazel *Odontopera bidentata*	6–9				
Grey Pug *Eupithecia subfuscata*	6–10		F & L		
Mottled Pug *Eupithecia exiguata*	6–10			S, C, (N)	
Pale Tussock *Calliteara pudibunda*	6–10			S, C	
Alder Moth *Acronicta alni*	7–8			S, C, (N)	L
Clouded Silver *Lomographa temerata*	7–8			S, C, (N)	
Common Marbled Carpet *Chloroclysta truncata*	7–8 & 9–5	8–6			
Broken-barred Carpet *Electrophaes corylata*	7–9				

Dark Dagger *Acronicta tridens*	7–9	+		S, C, (N)	
Grey Dagger *Acronicta psi*	7–9	+			
Knot Grass *Acronicta rumicis*	7–9	+			
Lobster Moth *Stauropus fagi*	7–9			S, (WC)	
Pale-shouldered Brocade *Lacanobia thalassina*	7–9	+			
Peppered Moth *Biston betularia*	7–9				
Little Emerald *Jodis lactearia*	7–10			S, C, NW	
Small Fan-foot *Herminia grisealis*	7–10		L & DL		
Red-belted Clearwing *Synanthedon myopaeformis*	7–5	*	ISt	S, (C)	Nb
Willow Beauty *Peribatodes rhomboidaria*	7–6	+			
Common Emerald *Hemithea aestivaria*	8–5			S, C, (N)	
Double Dart *Graphiphora augur*	8–5				
Double Square-spot *Xestia triangulum*	8–5				
Grey Arches *Polia nebulosa*	8–5				
Lappet *Gastropacha quercifolia*	8–5			S, EC	
Leopard Moth *Zeuzera pyrina*	8–5	*	ISt	S, C	
Light Emerald *Campaea margaritata*	8–5	+			
Mottled Beauty *Alcis repandata*	8–5				
Orange Moth *Angerona prunaria*	8–5			S, (C)	L
Plain Golden Y *Autographa jota*	8–5				
Short-cloaked Moth *Nola cucullatella*	8–5			S, C	
Silvery Arches *Polia trimaculosa*	8–5				Nb
Triple-spotted Clay *Xestia ditrapezium*	8–5		B		L
Dark Tussock *Dicallomera fascelina*	8–6			S, WC, N	L
Lesser Yellow Underwing *Noctua comes*	8–6				
Scarce Vapourer *Orgyia recens*	8–6			EC	RDB
Swallow-tailed Moth *Ourapteryx sambucaria*	8–6				
Yellow-tail *Euproctis similis*	8–6			S, C, (N)	
Broad-bordered Yellow Underwing *Noctua fimbriata*	9–4				
Ingrailed Clay *Diarsia mendica*	9–4				
Lesser Broad-bordered Yellow Underwing *Noctua janthe*	9–4				
Square-spot Rustic *Xestia xanthographa*	9–4				
Dotted Clay *Xestia baja*	9–5				
Least Yellow Underwing *Noctua interjecta*	9–5			S, C, (SN)	
Old Lady *Mormo maura*	9–5			S, C, (N)	L
Brown-tail *Euproctis chrysorrhoea*	9–6			S, (EC)	L
Magpie *Abraxas grossulariata*	9–6				
Oak Eggar *Lasiocampa quercus*	All	*			
Deep-brown Dart *Aporophyla lutulenta*	10–6			S, EC	

Hazel *Corylus avellana*

Angle Shades *Phlogophora meticulosa*	All				
Brimstone Moth *Opisthograptis luteolata*	All	7–9			
Brindled Green *Dryobotodes eremita*	3–6		B & L		
Autumnal Moth *Epirrita autumnata*	4–6				
Common Quaker *Orthosia cerasi*	4–6				
Copper Underwing *Amphipyra pyramidea*	4–6			S, C, (N)	
Dotted Border *Agriopis marginaria*	4–6				
Dun-bar *Cosmia trapezina*	4–6				
Engrailed *Ectropis bistortata*	4–6 & 7–9	5–7			
Feathered Thorn *Colotois pennaria*	4–6				
Mottled Umber *Erannis defoliaria*	4–6				
November Moth *Epirrita dilutata*	4–6				
Pale Brindled Beauty *Phigalia pilosaria*	4–6				
Pale Eggar *Trichiura crataegi*	4–6				

Pale November Moth *Epirrita christyi*	4–6			S, C, (N)	
Satellite *Eupsilia transversa*	4–6				
Scarce Umber *Agriopis aurantiaria*	4–6				
Small Brindled Beauty *Apocheima hispidaria*	4–6			S, (C, N)	L
Small Quaker *Orthosia cruda*	4–6				
Sprawler *Asteroscopus sphinx*	4–6			S, C	
Winter Moth *Operophtera brumata*	4–6				
Blossom Underwing *Orthosia miniosa*	5–6			S, C	L
Chevron *Eulithis testata*	5–6				
Clouded Drab *Orthosia incerta*	4–6				
Early Thorn *Selenia dentaria*	5–6 & 8–9	6–8			
July Highflyer *Hydriomena furcata*	5–6				
Bordered Beauty *Epione repandaria*	5–7				
Nut-tree Tussock *Colocasia coryli*	5–7 & 9–10	7–9			
Oak Beauty *Biston strataria*	5–7			S, C, (N)	
Purple Thorn *Selenia tetralunaria*	5–7 & 8–9	6–7		S, C, (N)	
Sword-grass *Xylena exsoleta*	5–7			C, N	Nb
Emperor Moth *Saturnia pavonia*	5–8				
Large Thorn *Ennomos autumnaria*	5–8			SE	Nb
Vapourer *Orgyia antiqua*	5–8	+			
Coxcomb Prominent *Ptilodon capucina*	6–7 & 8–9	6–8			
Iron Prominent *Notodonta dromedarius*	6–7 & 9–10	8			
Barred Umber *Plagodis pulveraria*	6–8				L
Cream-bordered Green Pea *Earias clorana*	6–8 & 9–10			S, EC	Nb
Brindled White-spot *Parectropis similaria*	6–9			S, (C)	L
Common White Wave *Cabera pusaria*	6–10				
Lime Hawk-moth *Mimas tiliae*	6–9			S, C	
Mottled Pug *Eupithecia exiguata*	6–10			S, C, (N)	
Pale Tussock *Calliteara pudibunda*	6–10			S, C	
Bordered Sallow *Pyrrhia umbra*	7–8			S, C, NE	L
Pale Oak Beauty *Hypomecis punctinalis*	7–8			S, (C)	
Small White Wave *Asthena albulata*	7–8	+		S, C, (N)	
Beautiful Carpet *Mesoleuca albicillata*	7–9				
Bright-line Brown-eye *Lacanobia oleracea*	7–9	+			
Clouded Border *Lomaspilis marginata*	7–9				
Green Silver-lines *Pseudoips prasinana*	7–9	+			
Knot Grass *Acronicta rumicis*	7–9	+			
Lobster Moth *Stauropus fagi*	7–9			S, (WC)	
Buff-tip *Phalera bucephala*	7–10				
Common Lutestring *Ochropacha duplaris*	7–10				
Little Emerald *Jodis lactearia*	7–10			S, C, NW	
Small Fan-foot *Herminia grisealis*	7–10		L & DL		
Beautiful Brocade *Lacanobia contigua*	8–9				L
Coronet *Craniophora ligustri*	8–9				L
Clouded Magpie *Abraxas sylvata*	7–10			S, C, SN, (N)	L
Common Emerald *Hemithea aestivaria*	8–5			S, C, (N)	
Grey Arches *Polia nebulosa*	8–5				
Mottled Beauty *Alcis repandata*	8–5				
Triple-spotted Clay *Xestia ditrapezium*	8–5		B		L
Clay Fan-foot *Paracolax tristalis*	8–6		DL	SE	Na
Scarce Vapourer *Orgyia recens*	8–6			EC	RDB
Yellow–tail *Euproctis similis*	8–6			S, C, (N)	
Dot Moth *Melanchra persicariae*	8–10			S, C, (N)	
Broad-bordered Yellow Underwing *Noctua fimbriata*	9–4				
Ingrailed Clay *Diarsia mendica*	9–4				

Large Emerald *Geometra papilionaria*	9–5				
Magpie *Abraxas grossulariata*	9–6				
Oak Eggar *Lasiocampa quercus*	All	*			

Heartsease *Viola tricolor* see Violets

Heathers *Calluna vulgaris* & *Erica* spp.

Grass Eggar *Lasiocampa trifolii*	3–6			S, WC	Na
Scalloped Oak *Crocallis elinguaria*	3–7				
Northern Dart *Xestia alpicola*	4–5	*		N	Na
Small Autumnal Moth *Epirrita filigrammaria*	4–5			C, N	
Autumnal Moth *Epirrita autumnata*	4–6				
Dark Marbled Carpet *Chloroclysta citrata*	4–6				
Dotted Border *Agriopis marginaria*	4–6				
Flounced Chestnut *Agrochola helvola*	4–6				
Pale Eggar *Trichiura crataegi*	4–6				
Silver-studded Blue *Plebejus argus*	4–6		F & L	S, WC	R
Twin-spot Carpet *Perizoma didymata*	4–6				
Winter Moth *Operophtera brumata*	4–6				
Yellow-line Quaker *Agrochola macilenta*	4–6				
Golden-rod Brindle *Lithomoia solidaginis*	4–7			WC, N	L
Southern Chestnut *Agrochola haematidea*	4–7			S	RDB
Beautiful Yellow Underwing *Anarta myrtilli*	4–10	7–9			
Chevron *Eulithis testata*	5–6				
Double-striped Pug *Gymnoscelis rufifasciata*	5–6 & 9–10		F		
July Highflyer *Hydriomena furcata*	5–6				
Holly Blue *Celastrina argiolus*	5–7 & 8–9		B, F & S	S, C, (SN)	
Horse Chestnut *Pachycnemia hippocastanaria*	5–7 & 9			S, (EC)	Nb
Red Sword-grass *Xylena vetusta*	5–7				L
Emperor Moth *Saturnia pavonia*	5–8				
Green Hairstreak *Callophrys rubi*	5–8		F & L		L
Rannoch Brindled Beauty *Lycia lapponaria*	5–8			N	Na
Ruby Tiger *Phragmatobia fuliginosa*	5–7 & 7–4	7–5			
Small Square-spot *Diarsia rubi*	6–7 & 9–4	8–5			
Glaucous Shears *Papestra biren*	6–8			WC, N, (SW)	L
Ringed Carpet *Cleora cinctaria*	6–8			S, WC, N	Na
Common Heath *Ematurga atomaria*	6–9	+			
Dark Brocade *Blepharita adusta*	6–9				
Light Knot Grass *Acronicta menyanthidis*	6–9			C, N, (SE)	L
Narrow-winged Pug *Eupithecia nanata*	6–10	+			
Ruddy Highflyer *Hydriomena ruberata*	6–9			W, N, (S, E)	L
Satyr Pug *Eupithecia satyrata*	6–9		F		L
Sweet Gale Moth *Acronicta euphorbiae*	6–9			N	Na
Grey Pug *Eupithecia subfuscata*	6–10		F & L		
Fox Moth *Macrothylacia rubi*	6–4				
Common Marbled Carpet *Chloroclysta truncata*	7–8 & 9–5	8–6			
Small Grass Emerald *Chlorissa viridata*	7–8			S, (WC)	Na
Beautiful Snout *Hypena crassalis*	7–9			S, WC, (EC)	L
Broom Moth *Melanchra pisi*	7–9				
Knot Grass *Acronicta rumicis*	7–9	+			
Clouded Buff *Diacrisia sannio*	7–5				L
Grey Scalloped Bar *Dyscia fagaria*	7–5				L
Scarce Silver Y *Syngrapha interrogationis*	7–6			W C, N	L
Beautiful Brocade *Lacanobia contigua*	8–9				L
Shoulder-striped Clover *Heliothis maritima*	8–9		F	S	RDB

Wormwood Pug *Eupithecia absinthiata*	8–10		F		
Black Mountain Moth *Glacies coracina*	8–5	*		N	Na
Grass Wave *Perconia strigillaria*	8–5			S, C, (N)	L
Mottled Beauty *Alcis repandata*	8–5				
Orange Moth *Angerona prunaria*	8–5			S, (C)	L
Purple Clay *Diarsia brunnea*	8–5				
Scotch Burnet *Zygaena exulans*	8–5	*	L & S	N	RDB
Smoky Wave *Scopula ternata*	8–5			W, N	L
True Lover's Knot *Lycophotia porphyrea*	8–5				
Weaver's Wave *Idaea contiguaria*	8–5			WC	Na
Wood Tiger *Parasemia plantaginis*	8–5				L
Ashworth's Rustic *Xestia ashworthii*	8–6			WC	Na
Dark Tussock *Dicallomera fascelina*	8–6			S, WC, N	L
Grey Mountain Carpet *Entephria caesiata*	8–6			C, N	
Lesser Yellow Underwing *Noctua comes*	8–6				
Scarce Vapourer *Orgyia recens*	8–6			EC	RDB
Ingrailed Clay *Diarsia mendica*	9–4				
Annulet *Charissa obscurata*	9–5				L
Northern Deep-brown Dart *Aporophyla lueneburgensis*	9–5			WC, N	
White-line Snout *Schrankia taenialis*	9–5			S	Nb
Bordered Grey *Selidosema brunnearia*	9–6				Na
Cousin German *Protolampra sobrina*	9–6			N	Na
Great Brocade *Eurois occulta*	9–6			N	Nb
Heath Rustic *Xestia agathina*	9–6				L
Magpie *Abraxas grossulariata*	9–6				
Oak Eggar *Lasiocampa quercus*	All	*			
Scotch Annulet *Gnophos obfuscatus*	9–6			N	Nb
Speckled Footman *Coscinia cribraria*	9–6			SW	RDB
Autumnal Rustic *Eugnorisma glareosa*	10–5				
Black Rustic *Aporophyla nigra*	10–5				
Neglected Rustic *Xestia castanea*	10–5				L
Deep-brown Dart *Aporophyla lutulenta*	10–6			S, EC	

Hedge Mustard *Sisymbrium officinale*

Green-veined White *Pieris napi*	5–6 & 7–8	6–8			
Orange-tip *Anthocharis cardamines*	5–7		S, B, F & L		
Small White *Pieris rapae*	5–10				
Garden Carpet *Xanthorhoe fluctuata*	6–10				

Hemp-agrimony *Eupatorium cannabinum*

Frosted Orange *Gortyna flavago*	4–8		lSt & R		
Double-striped Pug *Gymnoscelis rufifasciata*	5–6 & 9–10		F		
V-Pug *Chloroclystis v-ata*	5–7 & 8–10	7–9	F	S, C, (N)	
Lime-speck Pug *Eupithecia centaureata*	5–10	+	F		
Wormwood Pug *Eupithecia absinthiata*	8–10		F		
Scarlet Tiger *Callimorpha dominula*	8–5			S, (WC)	L
Gold Spangle *Autographa bractea*	8–6			C, N	
Kent Black Arches *Meganola albula*	8–6			SE	Nb
Jersey Tiger *Euplagia quadripunctaria*	9–6			SW	Nb
Scarce Burnished Brass *Diachrysia chryson*	9–6			S, WC	Na

Hemp-nettles *Galeopsis* spp.

Burnished Brass *Diachrysia chrysitis*	6–8 & 9–5	8–6			
Satyr Pug *Eupithecia satyrata*	6–9		F		L
Small Rivulet *Perizoma alchemillata*	7–9		F & S		

Henbane *Hyoscyamus niger*

Scarce Bordered Straw *Helicoverpa armigera*	?			Bm
Bordered Sallow *Pyrrhia umbra*	7–8	F & S	S, C, NE	L
Bordered Straw *Heliothis peltigera*	7–10	F		Bm

Hoary Cress *Lepidium draba*

Small White *Pieris rapae*	5–10			
Feathered Ranunculus *Polymixis lichenea*	10–5		S, C, (N)	L

Hog's Fennel *Peucedanum officinale*

Fisher's Estuarine Moth *Gortyna borelii*	6–8	ISt & R	SE	RDB

Hogweed *Heracleum sphondylium*

Brindled Ochre *Dasypolia templi*	4–8	F, ISt & R	SW, C, N	L
Common Pug *Eupithecia vulgata*	6–7 & 8–10	7–8		
White-spotted Pug *Eupithecia tripunctaria*	6–7 & 9–10	F & S	S, C, (N)	L
Triple-spotted Pug *Eupithecia trisignaria*	8–9	F & S	S, C, (N)	L
Plain Golden Y *Autographa jota*	8~5			

Holly *Ilex aquifolium*

Double-striped Pug *Gymnoscelis rufifasciata*	5–6 & 9–10	F		
Holly Blue *Celastrina argiolus*	5–7 & 8–9	B, F & S	S, C, (SN)	
Yellow-barred Brindle *Acasis viretata*	6–7	+	F, S & L	S, C, (NW)	L
Privet Hawk-moth *Sphinx ligustri*	7–9		S, (C)	

Hollyhock *Althaea rosea*

Mallow *Larentia clavaria*	4–6		S, C, (SN)

Honesty *Lunaria annua*

Orange-tip *Anthocharis cardamines*	5–7

Honeysuckles *Lonicera* spp.

Scalloped Oak *Crocallis elinguaria*	3–7			
Barred Tooth-striped *Trichopteryx polycommata*	4–6		S, N, (C)	Na
Copper Underwing *Amphipyra pyramidea*	4–6		S, C, (N)	
Dark Chestnut *Conistra ligula*	4–6		S, C, (N)	
Early Grey *Xylocampa areola*	4–6			
Mottled Umber *Erannis defoliaria*	4–6			
Twin-spotted Quaker *Orthosia munda*	4–6		S, C, (N)	
Early Thorn *Selenia dentaria*	5–6 & 8–9	6–8		
Early Tooth-striped *Trichopteryx carpinata*	5–7			
Marsh Fritillary *Euphydryas aurinia*	7–5		W, NW	S
Willow Beauty *Peribatodes rhomboidaria*	7–6	+		
Broad-bordered Bee Hawk-moth *Hemaris fuciformis*	7–8		S, C	Nb
Pale-shouldered Brocade *Lacanobia thalassina*	7–9	+		
Privet Hawk-moth *Sphinx ligustri*	7–9		S, (C)	
Buff Ermine *Spilosoma luteum*	7–10			
Gothic *Naenia typica*	8–3			L
Beautiful Golden Y *Autographa pulchrina*	8~5			
Common Emerald *Hemithea aestivaria*	8~5		S, C, (N)	
Green Arches *Anaplectoides prasina*	8–5			
Grey Arches *Polia nebulosa*	8~5			
Leopard Moth *Zeuzera pyrina*	8–5	*	ISt	S, C
Orange Moth *Angerona prunaria*	8–5		S, (C)	L
Plain Golden Y *Autographa jota*	8~5			
Silvery Arches *Polia trimaculosa*	8–5			Nb

Scarlet Tiger *Callimorpha dominula*	8–5			S, (WC)	L
Triple-spotted Clay *Xestia ditrapezium*	8–5		B		L
Gold Spangle *Autographa bractea*	8–6			C, N	
White Admiral *Limenitis camilla*	8–6			S, EC	S
Ingrailed Clay *Diarsia mendica*	9–4				
Lilac Beauty *Apeira syringaria*	9–5			S, C, (N)	L
Small Blood-vein *Scopula imitaria*	9–5			S, C	
Silver-striped Hawk-moth *Hippotion celerio*	10				Bm

Hop *Humulus lupulus*

Angle Shades *Phlogophora meticulosa*	All				
Twin-spotted Quaker *Orthosia munda*	4–6			S, C, (N)	
Clouded Drab *Orthosia incerta*	4–6				
Comma *Polygonia c-album*	5–6 & 7–8			S, C, (SN)	
Peacock *Inachis io*	5–7			S, C, (N)	
Sword-grass *Xylena exsoleta*	5–7			C, N	Nb
Rosy Rustic *Hydraecia micacea*	5–8		ISt & R		
Currant Pug *Eupithecia assimilata*	6–7 & 8–10				
Buttoned Snout *Hypena rostralis*	6–8			S, (C)	Nb
Pale Tussock *Calliteara pudibunda*	6–10			S, C	
Red Admiral *Vanessa atalanta*	6–5				Bm
Bright-line Brown-eye *Lacanobia oleracea*	7–9	+			
Dark Spectacle *Abrostola triplasia*	7–9	+			
Knot Grass *Acronicta rumicis*	7–9	+			
Peppered Moth *Biston betularia*	7–9				
Privet Hawk-moth *Sphinx ligustri*	7–9			S, (C)	
Buff Ermine *Spilosoma luteum*	7–10				
Dot Moth *Melanchra persicariae*	8–10			S, C, (N)	
Mottled Rustic *Caradrina morpheus*	8–11				
Ghost Moth *Hepialus humuli*	8–5	*	R		
Brown-tail *Euproctis chrysorrhoea*	9–6			S, (EC)	L

Hornbeam *Carpinus betulus*

Svensson's Copper Underwing *Amphipyra berbera*	4–5			S, C	
Barred Sallow *Xanthia aurago*	4–6		B, F & L	S, C, (N)	
Black Arches *Lymantria monacha*	4–6			S, C	L
Dotted Border *Agriopis marginaria*	4–6				
Engrailed *Ectropis bistortata*	4–6 & 7–9	5–7			
Mottled Umber *Erannis defoliaria*	4–6				
November Moth *Epirrita dilutata*	4–6				
Pale November Moth *Epirrita christyi*	4–6			S, C, (N)	
Scarce Umber *Agriopis aurantiaria*	4–6				
Small Brindled Beauty *Apocheima hispidaria*	4–6			S, (C, N)	L
Nut-tree Tussock *Colocasia coryli*	5–7 & 9–10	7–9			
Emperor Moth *Saturnia pavonia*	5–8				
Coxcomb Prominent *Ptilodon capucina*	6–7 & 8–9	6–8			
Red-green Carpet *Chloroclysta siterata*	6–8				
Square Spot *Paradarisa consonaria*	6–8			S, C, SN	L
Mocha *Cyclophora annularia*	7 & 8–9			S, (C)	Nb
Small White Wave *Asthena albulata*	7–8	+		S, C, (N)	
Buff-tip *Phalera bucephala*	7–10				
Little Emerald *Jodis lactearia*	7–10			S, C, NW	
Light Emerald *Campaea margaritata*	8–5	+			
Purple Clay *Diarsia brunnea*	8–5				
Dotted Clay *Xestia baja*	9–5				

Horse-chestnut *Aesculus hippocastanum*

Pale Pinion *Lithophane hepatica*	5–7		S, WC	L
Sycamore *Acronicta aceris*	7–9		S, (C)	L
Light Emerald *Campaea margaritata*	8~5	+		
Swallow-tailed Moth *Ourapteryx sambucaria*	8~6			

Horse-radish *Armoracia rusticana*

Green-veined White *Pieris napi*	5–6 & 7–8	6–8		
Orange-tip *Anthocharis cardamines*	5–7		S, B, F & L	
Garden Carpet *Xanthorhoe fluctuata*	6–10			

Horsetails *Equisetum* spp.

Rosy Rustic *Hydraecia micacea*	5–8		ISt & R	

Hound's-tongue *Cynoglossum officinale*

Coast Dart *Euxoa cursoria*	3–7		E, WC, N	Nb
Flame *Axylia putris*	7–9		S, C, (N)	
Scarlet Tiger *Callimorpha dominula*	8~5		S, (WC)	L
Garden Tiger *Arctia caja*	8~6			
Feathered Ranunculus *Polymixis lichenea*	10–5		S, C, (N)	L

Ivys *Hedera* spp.

Double-striped Pug *Gymnoscelis rufifasciata*	5–6 & 9–10		F	
Holly Blue *Celastrina argiolus*	5–7 & 8–9		B, F & S	S, C, (SN)
Rosy Rustic *Hydraecia micacea*	5–8		ISt & R	
Dark-barred Twin-spot Carpet *Xanthorhoe ferrugata*	6–7 & 9	6–8		S, C, (N)
Small Dusty Wave *Idaea seriata*	6–7 & 9–5	8–9		S, C, NE
Yellow-barred Brindle *Acasis viretata*	6–7	+	F, S & L	S, C, (NW)	L
Red Twin-spot Carpet *Xanthorhoe spadicearia*	7 & 9	6–8		
Small Angle Shades *Euplexia lucipara*	7–9	+	B	
Fan-foot *Zanclognatha tarsipennalis*	7–10		DL	S, C, (N)
Willow Beauty *Peribatodes rhomboidaria*	7–6	+		
Dot Moth *Melanchra persicariae*	8–10			S, C, (N)
Least Carpet *Idaea rusticata*	8~5			SE	L
Treble Brown Spot *Idaea trigeminata*	8~5	+		S, (C)	L
Swallow-tailed Moth *Ourapteryx sambucaria*	8~6			
Old Lady *Mormo maura*	9~5			S, C, (N)	L
Magpie *Abraxas grossulariata*	9–6			
Rosy Minor *Mesoligia literosa*	9–6		ISt & R	

Jack-by-the-Hedge *Alliaria petiolata* see under Garlic Mustard

Jasmines *Jasminum* spp.

Mottled Umber *Erannis defoliaria*	4–6			
Common Emerald *Hemithea aestivaria*	8~5		S, C, (N)	

Juniper, Common *Juniperus communis*

Blair's Shoulder-knot *Lithophane leautieri*	3–7		S, C, (N)	
Juniper Pug *Eupithecia pusillata*	4–6			
Ochreous Pug *Eupithecia indigata*	6–9			
Scalloped Hazel *Odontopera bidentata*	6–9			
Juniper Carpet *Thera juniperata*	7–9		S, C,	
Edinburgh Pug *Eupithecia intricata millieraria*	8–9			L
Freyer's Pug *Eupithecia intricata arceuthata*	8–9			L
Mere's Pug *Eupithecia intricata hibernica*	8–9			L
Mottled Beauty *Alcis repandata*	8~5			

Chestnut-coloured Carpet *Thera cognata*	9–6			C, N	Nb
Cypress Pug *Eupithecia phoeniceata*	10–6			S	UC

Knapweeds *Centaurea* spp.

Belted Beauty *Lycia zonaria*	5–7			NW	Na
Lime-speck Pug *Eupithecia centaureata*	5–10	+	F		
Satyr Pug *Eupithecia satyrata*	6–9		F		L
Grey Pug *Eupithecia subfuscata*	6–10		F & L		
Treble Lines *Charanyca trigrammica*	6–4			S, C	
Black-veined Moth *Siona lineata*	7–5			SE	RDB
Scarce Forester *Jordanita globulariae*	7–5			S	Na
Marbled Clover *Heliothis viriplaca*	8–9	+	F & S	SE, (S)	RDB

Knotgrass *Polygonum aviculare*

Belted Beauty *Lycia zonaria*	5–7			NW	Na
Red Sword-grass *Xylena vetusta*	5–7				L
Silver Cloud *Egira conspicillaris*	5–7			SW, WC	Na
Dark-barred Twin-spot Carpet *Xanthorhoe ferrugata*	6–7 & 9	6–8		S, C, (N)	
Dog's Tooth *Lacanobia suasa*	6–7 & 8–9	7–8		S, C, (N)	L
Flame Shoulder *Ochropleura plecta*	6–7 & 9–10	8–9			
Nutmeg *Discestra trifolii*	6–7 & 9–10	8–9		S, C, (N)	
Striped Hawk-moth *Hyles livornica*	6–7 & 9–10				Bm
White Colon *Sideridis albicolon*	6–7 & 9		F		Nb
Glaucous Shears *Papestra biren*	6–8			WC, N, (SW)	L
Dark Brocade *Blepharita adusta*	6–9				
Fox Moth *Macrothylacia rubi*	6–4				
Shuttle-shaped Dart *Agrotis puta*	6–4	+		S, C, (N)	
Treble Lines *Charanyca trigrammica*	6–4			S, C	
Blood-vein *Timandra comae*	7 & 9–4			S, C, (N)	
Mullein Wave *Scopula marginepunctata*	7 & 9–5	9–5		S, C, (N)	L
Red Twin-spot Carpet *Xanthorhoe spadicearia*	7 & 9	6–8			
Bird's Wing *Dypterygia scabriuscula*	7–8	+		S, C	L
Light Brocade *Lacanobia w-latinum*	7–8			S, C, (N)	L
Shears *Hada plebeja*	7–8	+			
Bordered Gothic *Heliophobus reticulata*	7–9		F	S, C	RDB
Bright-line Brown-eye *Lacanobia oleracea*	7–9	+			
Flame *Axylia putris*	7–9			S, C, (N)	
Knot Grass *Acronicta rumicis*	7–9	+			
Fan-foot *Zanclognatha tarsipennalis*	7–10		DL	S, C, (N)	
Cream Wave *Scopula floslactata*	7–4				L
Pale Shining Brown *Polia bombycina*	7–5			S	RDB
Riband Wave *Idaea aversata*	7–5	+			
Rustic *Hoplodrina blanda*	7–5				
Beautiful Brocade *Lacanobia contigua*	8–9				L
Mottled Rustic *Caradrina morpheus*	8–11				
Common Emerald *Hemithea aestivaria*	8–5			S, C, (N)	
Green Arches *Anaplectoides prasina*	8–5				
Heart and Club *Agrotis clavis*	8–5		L & R		
Plain Wave *Idaea straminata*	8–5				L
Satin Wave *Idaea subsericeata*	8–5	+		S, (C, NW)	
Silvery Arches *Polia trimaculosa*	8–5				Nb
Small Fan-footed Wave *Idaea biselata*	8–5				
Small Scallop *Idaea emarginata*	8–5			S, C	L
Treble Brown Spot *Idaea trigeminata*	8–5	+		S, (C)	L

Ingrailed Clay *Diarsia mendica*	9~4				
Vine's Rustic *Hoplodrina ambigua*	9~4 & 7–8			S, (C)	L
Straw Belle *Aspitates gilvaria*	9–6			SE	RDB

Laburnum *Laburnum anagyroides*

Sycamore *Acronicta aceris*	7–9			S, (C)	L

Lady's-mantle *Alchemilla vulgaris*

Dark Marbled Carpet *Chloroclysta citrata*	4–6		F		
Red Carpet *Xanthorhoe decoloraria*	9~5			C, N	

Lady's-smock *Cardamine pratensis* see under Cuckoo-flower

Larches *Larix* spp.

Autumnal Moth *Epirrita autumnata*	4–6				
Engrailed *Ectropis bistortata*	4–6 & 7–9	5–7			
Feathered Thorn *Colotois pennaria*	4–6				
Pine Beauty *Panolis flammea*	5–7				
Larch Pug *Eupithecia lariciata*	6–9				
Small Engrailed *Ectropis crepuscularia*	6–8			S, C, (N)	L
Tawny-barred Angle *Macaria liturata*	6–8 & 9–10	7–8			
Cloaked Pug *Eupithecia abietaria*	6–9		S	C, N, (S)	UC
Ochreous Pug *Eupithecia indigata*	6–9				
Scalloped Hazel *Odontopera bidentata*	6–9				
Bordered White *Bupalus piniaria*	6–10				
Pale Oak Beauty *Hypomecis punctinalis*	7–8			S, (C)	
Broom Moth *Melanchra pisi*	7–9				
Dot Moth *Melanchra persicariae*	8–10			S, C, (N)	
Satin Beauty *Deileptenia ribeata*	8–5				
Barred Red *Hylaea fasciaria*	9~5				

Larkspurs *Consolida* spp.

Golden Plusia *Polychrysia moneta*	9~6		B, L & S	S, C, (N)	

Laurustinus *Viburnum tinus*

Privet Hawk-moth *Sphinx ligustri*	7–9			S, (C)	

Lesser Celandine *Ranunculus ficaria*

Twin-spot Carpet *Perizoma didymata*	4–6				

Lettuces *Lactuca* spp.

Garden Dart *Euxoa nigricans*	2–6				
Grey Chi *Antitype chi*	4–6			C, N, (S)	
Shuttle-shaped Dart *Agrotis puta*	6–4	+		S, C, (N)	
Small Ranunculus *Hecatera dysodea*	7–8		F & S	SE	RDB
Shark *Cucullia umbratica*	7–9				
Pearly Underwing *Peridroma saucia*	7–10				Bm
Heart and Dart *Agrotis exclamationis*	7~3	+			
Broad-barred White *Hecatera bicolorata*	8–9		F & S		
Vine's Rustic *Hoplodrina ambigua*	9–4 & 7–8			S, (C)	L
Jersey Tiger *Euplagia quadripunctaria*	9–6			SW	Nb
Speckled Footman *Coscinia cribraria*	9~6			SW	RDB

Prickly Lettuce *L. serriola*

Small Ranunculus *Hecatera dysodea*	7–8		F & S	SE	RDB

Lichens

Orange Footman *Eilema sororcula*	6–9		S	L
Scalloped Hazel *Odontopera bidentata*	6–9			
Red-necked Footman *Atolmis rubricollis*	8–10		S, C	L
Beautiful Hook-tip *Laspeyria flexula*	8–5		S, C	L
Common Footman *Eilema lurideola*	8–5		S, C, (N)	
Four-dotted Footman *Cybosia mesomella*	8–5			L
Dew Moth *Setina irrorella*	8–6		S, C, NW	Na
Dingy Footman *Eilema griseola*	8–6		S, (C)	
Dotted Footman *Pelosia muscerda*	8–6		SE	RDB
Muslin Footman *Nudaria mundana*	8–6			L
Northern Footman *Eilema complana* f. *sericea*	8–6		WC	RDB
Pigmy Footman *Eilema pygmaeola*	8–6		SE	RDB
Scarce Footman *Eilema complana*	8–6		S, C	L
Small Dotted Footman *Pelosia obtusa*	8–6		SE	RDB
Brussels Lace *Cleorodes lichenaria*	9–5		SW, NW, (S, N)	L
Marbled Beauty *Cryphia domestica*	9–5		S, C, (N)	
Rosy Footman *Miltochrista miniata*	9–5		S, (C)	L
Round-winged Muslin *Thumatha senex*	9–5		S, C, (N)	L
Buff Footman *Eilema depressa*	9–6		S, (C)	L
Dotted Carpet *Alcis jubata*	9–6		W, N	L
Four-spotted Footman *Lithosia quadra*	9–6		SW	Na
Hoary Footman *Eilema caniola*	9–6		SW, (WC)	Nb
Marbled Green *Cryphia muralis*	9–6		S	L

Lilac *Syringa vulgaris*

Svensson's Copper Underwing *Amphipyra berbera*	4–5		S, C	
March Moth *Alsophila aescularia*	5–6			
August Thorn *Ennomos quercinaria*	5–7		S, C, (N)	L
Waved Umber *Menophra abruptaria*	6–9		S, C	
Privet Hawk-moth *Sphinx ligustri*	7–9		S, (C)	
Willow Beauty *Peribatodes rhomboidaria*	7–6	+		
Leopard Moth *Zeuzera pyrina*	8–5	*	ISt	S, C
Orange Moth *Angerona prunaria*	8–5		S, (C)	L
Lilac Beauty *Apeira syringaria*	9–5		S, C, (N)	L

Lily-of-the-valley *Convallaria majalis*

Grey Chi *Antitype chi*	4–6		C, N, (S)	

Limes *Tilia* spp.

Orange Sallow *Xanthia citrago*	3–6		B & L	
Svensson's Copper Underwing *Amphipyra berbera*	4–5		S, C	
Copper Underwing *Amphipyra pyramidea*	4–6		S, C, (N)	
December Moth *Poecilocampa populi*	4–6			
Hebrew Character *Orthosia gothica*	4–7			
Lunar-spotted Pinion *Cosmia pyralina*	4–6		S, (C)	L
Pale Brindled Beauty *Phigalia pilosaria*	4–6			
Satellite *Eupsilia transversa*	4–6			
Scarce Umber *Agriopis aurantiaria*	4–6			
Sprawler *Asteroscopus sphinx*	4–6		S, C	
Clouded Drab *Orthosia incerta*	4–6			
August Thorn *Ennomos quercinaria*	5–7		S, C, (N)	L
Brindled Beauty *Lycia hirtaria*	5–7		S, C, (N)	
Canary-shouldered Thorn *Ennomos alniaria*	5–7			
Pale Pinion *Lithophane hepatica*	5–7		S, WC	L

September Thorn *Ennomos erosaria*	5–7		S, C, (N)	
Sword-grass *Xylena exsoleta*	5–7		C, N	Nb
Vapourer *Orgyia antiqua*	5–8	+		
Coxcomb Prominent *Ptilodon capucina*	6–7 & 8–9	6–8		
Pauper (Fletcher's) Pug *Eupithecia egenaria*	6–7		S, (EC)	RDB
Autumn Green Carpet *Chloroclysta miata*	6–8			L
Least Black Arches *Nola confusalis*	6–8		S, C, (N)	L
Red-green Carpet *Chloroclysta siterata*	6–8			
Brindled White-spot *Parectropis similaria*	6–9		S, (C)	L
Lime Hawk-moth *Mimas tiliae*	6–9		S, C	
Scalloped Hazel *Odontopera bidentata*	6–9			
Pale Tussock *Calliteara pudibunda*	6–10		S, C	
Broken-barred Carpet *Electrophaes corylata*	7–9			
Grey Dagger *Acronicta psi*	7–9	+		
Lobster Moth *Stauropus fagi*	7–9		S, (WC)	
Peppered Moth *Biston betularia*	7–9			
Scarce Hook-tip *Sabra harpagula*	7–9		SW	RDB
Buff-tip *Phalera bucephala*	7–10			
Small Fan-foot *Herminia grisealis*	7–10	L & DL		
Common Emerald *Hemithea aestivaria*	8–5		S, C, (N)	

Liquorice, Wild *Astragalus glycyphyllos* see under Milk-vetch

Loosestrife, see Purple Loosestrife *Lythrum salicaria* & Yellow Loosestrife *Lysimachia vulgaris*

Louseworts *Pedicularis* spp.

Small Purple-barred *Phytometra viridaria*	7–9			L
Water Ermine *Spilosoma urticae*	7–9		SE, (SW)	Nb

Lucerne *Medicago sativa* ssp. *sativa*

Scarce Bordered Straw *Helicoverpa armigera*	?			Bm
Grass Eggar *Lasiocampa trifolii*	3–6		S, WC	Na
Clouded Yellow *Colias croceus*	6–7 & 8–11			Bm
Latticed Heath *Chiasmia clathrata*	6–7 & 8–9	7–8		
Shears *Hada plebeja*	7–8	+		
Mother Shipton *Callistege mi*	7–9			
Pale Clouded Yellow *Colias hyale*	7–4		S,C	Bm

Magnolia *Magnolia grandiflora*

Large Ranunculus *Polymixis flavicincta*	4–7		S, (C)	L

Male Fern *Dryopteris filix-mas*

Small Angle Shades *Euplexia lucipara*	7–9	+		

Mallows *Malva* spp.

Mallow *Larentia clavaria*	4–6		S, C, (SN)	
Painted Lady *Vanessa cardui*	5–10			Bm
Small Angle Shades *Euplexia lucipara*	7–9	+		
Least Yellow Underwing *Noctua interjecta*	9–5		S, C, (SN)	

Marigolds *Calendula* spp.

Dark-barred Twin-spot Carpet *Xanthorhoe ferrugata*	6–7 & 9	6–8	S, C, (N)	
Red Twin-spot Carpet *Xanthorhoe spadicearia*	7 & 9	6–8		
Bordered Straw *Heliothis peltigera*	7–10	F		Bm
Large Yellow Underwing *Noctua pronuba*	9–5			

Marjoram *Origanum vulgare*

Double-striped Pug *Gymnoscelis rufifasciata*	5–6 & 9–10		F		
Green Carpet *Colostygia pectinataria*	6–7 & 9–5	8–5			
Lace Border *Scopula ornata*	6–7 & 9–4			S	Na
Burnished Brass *Diachrysia chrysitis*	6–8 & 9–5	8–6			
Mullein Wave *Scopula marginepunctata*	7 & 9–5	9–5		S, C, (N)	L
Shaded Pug *Eupithecia subumbrata*	7–9		F	S, (C)	L
Black-veined Moth *Siona lineata*	7–5			SE	RDB
Wormwood Pug *Eupithecia absinthiata*	8–10		F		
Sub-angled Wave *Scopula nigropunctata*	8–5			SE	RDB

Marsh Cinquefoil *Potentilla palustris*

Purple-bordered Gold *Idaea muricata*	8–5			S, C	Nb

Marsh-mallow *Althaea officinalis*

Marsh Mallow Moth *Hydraecia osseola*	4–7		ISt & R	SE	RDB
Painted Lady *Vanessa cardui*	5–10				Bm

Mayweeds *Tripleurospermum* spp.

Chamomile Shark *Cucullia chamomillae*	5–7		F		L
Bordered Straw *Heliothis peltigera*	7–10		F		Bm
Lesser Broad-bordered Yellow Underwing *Noctua janthe*	9–4				

Meadow-rues *Thalictrum* spp.

Marsh Carpet *Perizoma sagittata*	7–9		S	SE, EC	Na

Meadowsweet *Filipendula ulmaria*

Brown-spot Pinion *Agrochola litura*	4–6				
Hebrew Character *Orthosia gothica*	4–7				
Powdered Quaker *Orthosia gracilis*	5–7				
Emperor Moth *Saturnia pavonia*	5–8				
Fox Moth *Macrothylacia rubi*	6–4				
Glaucous Shears *Papestra biren*	6–8			WC, N, (SW)	L
Satyr Pug *Eupithecia satyrata*	6–9		F		L
Sweet Gale Moth *Acronicta euphorbiae*	6–9			N	Na
Mullein Wave *Scopula marginepunctata*	7 & 9–5	9–5		S, C, (N)	L
Small Yellow Wave *Hydrelia flammeolaria*	7–9			S, C, (N)	
Buff Arches *Habrosyne pyritoides*	7–10			S, C	
Marsh Moth *Athetis pallustris*	7–4			EC	RDB
Scarlet Tiger *Callimorpha dominula*	8–5			S, (WC)	L
Scarce Vapourer *Orgyia recens*	8–6			EC	RDB
Least Yellow Underwing *Noctua interjecta*	9–5			S, C, (SN)	
Lesser Cream Wave *Scopula immutata*	9–5			S, C, (N)	L

Meadow Vetchling *Lathyrus pratensis* see under Peas

Melilots *Melilotus* spp.

Beaded Chestnut *Agrochola lychnidis*	3–6			S, C, (N)	
Grass Eggar *Lasiocampa trifolii*	3–6			S, WC	Na
Clouded Yellow *Colias croceus*	6–7 & 8–11				Bm
Mother Shipton *Callistege mi*	7–9				

Michaelmas-daisys *Aster* spp.

Large Ranunculus *Polymixis flavicincta*	4–7			S, (C)	L
Vapourer *Orgyia antiqua*	5–8	+			
Dot Moth *Melanchra persicariae*	8–10			S, C, (N)	

Mignonette *Reseda lutea*
Small White *Pieris rapae*	5–10				
Large White *Pieris brassicae*	5–12				

Milk Parsley *Peucedanum palustre*
Swallowtail *Papilio machaon*	6–8	+		SE	R

Milk-vetches *Astragalus* spp.
Blackneck *Lygephila pastinum*	8~5			S, C	L

Milkworts *Polygala* spp.
Small Purple-barred *Phytometra viridaria*	7–9				L
Marbled Clover *Heliothis viriplaca*	8–9	+	F & S	SE, (S)	RDB

Mints *Mentha* spp.
Large Ranunculus *Polymixis flavicincta*	4–7			S, (C)	L
Knot Grass *Acronicta rumicis*	7–9	+			
Water Ermine *Spilosoma urticae*	7–9			SE, (SW)	Nb
Orange Moth *Angerona prunaria*	8~5			S, (C)	L
Plain Golden Y *Autographa jota*	8~5				

Corn Mint *Mentha arvensis*
Deep-brown Dart *Aporophyla lutulenta*	10~6			S, EC	

Monk's-hood *Aconitum* spp. & Wolf's-bane *Aconitum* spp.
Golden Plusia *Polychrysia moneta*	9~6		B, L & S	S, C, (N)	

Morning-glories *Ipomoea* spp.
Convolvulus Hawk-Moth *Agrius convolvuli*	7–11			(S)	Bm

Mosses
Barred Carpet *Perizoma taeniata*	9~5			C, N, (SW)	Na
Rosy Footman *Miltochrista miniata*	9~5			S, C, (N)	L
Round-winged Muslin *Thumatha senex*	9~5			S, C, (N)	L

Mountain Avens *Dryas octopetala*
Emperor Moth *Saturnia pavonia*	5–8				

Mouse-ears *Cerastium* spp.
Coast Dart *Euxoa cursoria*	3–7			E, WC, N	Nb
White-line Dart *Euxoa tritici*	3–7				
Marsh Pug *Eupithecia pygmaeata*	6–7		F & S	C, N, (S)	Nb
Small Yellow Underwing *Panemeria tenebrata*	6–7		F & S	S, C, (N)	L
Cloaked Carpet *Euphyia biangulata*	8–9			S, W	Nb
Portland Moth *Actebia praecox*	9–6			SW, C, N, (S)	Nb

Snow-in-summer *C. tomentosum*
Marsh Pug *Eupithecia pygmaeata*	6–7		F & S	C, N, (S)	Nb

Mugworts *Artemisia* spp.
Mouse *Amphipyra tragopoginis*	4–6		L & F		
Northern Drab *Orthosia opima*	5–7				L
Lime-speck Pug *Eupithecia centaureata*	5–10	+	F		
V-Pug *Chloroclystis v-ata*	5–7 & 8–10	7–9	F	S, C, (N)	
Grey Pug *Eupithecia subfuscata*	6–10		F & L		
Mullein Wave *Scopula marginepunctata*	7 & 9–5	9–5		S, C, (N)	L
Peppered Moth *Biston betularia*	7–9				

Wormwood *Cucullia absinthii*	8–9		F & S	S, C	Nb
Bordered Pug *Eupithecia succenturiata*	8–10			S, C, (N)	
Wormwood Pug *Eupithecia absinthiata*	8–10		F		
Common Emerald *Hemithea aestivaria*	8–5			S, C, (N)	

Mulleins *Verbascum* spp.

Frosted Orange *Gortyna flavago*	4–8		lSt & R		
Mullein *Shargacucullia verbasci*	5–7			S, C	
Setaceous Hebrew Character *Xestia c-nigrum*	5–7 & 9–4	9–5			
Satyr Pug *Eupithecia satyrata*	6–9		F		L
Cinnabar *Tyria jacobaeae*	7–9			S, C, (N)	
Star-wort *Cucullia asteris*	7–9		F	S, C	Nb
Striped Lychnis *Shargacucullia lychnitis*	7–9		F & S	S	Na

Nasturtium *Tropaeolum majus*

Green-veined White *Pieris napi*	5–6 & 7–8	6–8			
Small White *Pieris rapae*	5–10				
Large White *Pieris brassicae*	5–12				
Garden Carpet *Xanthorhoe fluctuata*	6–10				

Navelwort *Umbilicus rupestris*

Weaver's Wave *Idaea contiguaria*	8–5			WC	Na

Nettles *Urtica* spp.

Angle Shades *Phlogophora meticulosa*	All				
Hebrew Character *Orthosia gothica*	4–7				
Frosted Orange *Gortyna flavago*	4–8		lSt & R		
Comma *Polygonia c-album*	5–6 & 7–8			S, C, (SN)	
Small Tortoiseshell *Aglais urticae*	5–6 & 7–8				
Bloxworth Snout *Hypena obsitalis*	5–7 & 8–4			SW	RDB
Peacock *Inachis io*	5–7			S, C, (N)	
Setaceous Hebrew Character *Xestia c-nigrum*	5–7 & 9–4	9–5			
Painted Lady *Vanessa cardui*	5–10				Bm
Silver Y *Autographa gamma*	5–10	+			Bm
Burnished Brass *Diachrysia chrysitis*	6–8 & 9–5	8–6			
Red Admiral *Vanessa atalanta*	6–5				Bm
Snout *Hypena proboscidalis*	7–8 & 9–5	8–5			
Bright-line Brown-eye *Lacanobia oleracea*	7–9	+			
Dark Spectacle *Abrostola triplasia*	7–9	+			
Flame *Axylia putris*	7–9			S, C, (N)	
Small Angle Shades *Euplexia lucipara*	7–9	+			
Spectacle *Abrostola tripartita*	7–9	+			
White Ermine *Spilosoma lubricipeda*	7–9				
Buff Ermine *Spilosoma luteum*	7–10				
Small Fan-foot *Herminia grisealis*	7–10		L & DL		
Dot Moth *Melanchra persicariae*	8–10			S, C, (N)	
Mottled Rustic *Caradrina morpheus*	8–11				
Beautiful Golden Y *Autographa pulchrina*	8–5				
Ghost Moth *Hepialus humuli*	8–5	*	R		
Plain Golden Y *Autographa jota*	8–5				
Scarlet Tiger *Callimorpha dominula*	8–5			S, (WC)	L
Garden Tiger *Arctia caja*	8–6				
Gold Spangle *Autographa bractea*	8–6			C, N	
Lesser Yellow Underwing *Noctua comes*	8–6				
Broad-bordered Yellow Underwing *Noctua fimbriata*	9–4				

Dotted Clay *Xestia baja*	9–5			
Plain Clay *Eugnorisma depuncta*	9–5		SW, WC, N	Nb
Square-spotted Clay *Xestia rhomboidea*	9–5		S, (WC, N)	Nb
Jersey Tiger *Euplagia quadripunctaria*	9–6		SW	Nb

Night-flowering Catchfly *Silene noctiflora* see under Campions

Nottingham Catchfly *Silene nutans* see under Campions

Oaks *Quercus* spp.

Deciduous Oaks *Quercus* spp.

Angle Shades *Phlogophora meticulosa*	All			
Brindled Green *Dryobotodes eremita*	3–6	B & L		
Dotted Chestnut *Conistra rubiginea*	3–6		S, (C)	Nb
Scalloped Oak *Crocallis elinguaria*	3–7			
Svensson's Copper Underwing *Amphipyra berbera*	4–5		S, C	
Autumnal Moth *Epirrita autumnata*	4–6			
Barred Sallow *Xanthia aurago*	4–6		S, C, (N)	
Black Arches *Lymantria monacha*	4–6		S, C	L
Brown-spot Pinion *Agrochola litura*	4–6			
Common Quaker *Orthosia cerasi*	4–6			
Copper Underwing *Amphipyra pyramidea*	4–6		S, C, (N)	
Dark Chestnut *Conistra ligula*	4–6		S, C, (N)	
Dark Crimson Underwing *Catocala sponsa*	4–6		S	RDB
December Moth *Poecilocampa populi*	4–6			
Dotted Border *Agriopis marginaria*	4–6			
Dun-bar *Cosmia trapezina*	4–6			
Engrailed *Ectropis bistortata*	4–6 & 7–9	5–7		
Feathered Thorn *Colotois pennaria*	4–6			
Flounced Chestnut *Agrochola helvola*	4–6			
Heart Moth *Dicycla oo*	4–6		S	RDB
Hebrew Character *Orthosia gothica*	4–7			
Lackey *Malacosoma neustria*	4–6		S, C, (N)	
Light Crimson Underwing *Catocala promissa*	4–6		S	RDB
Lunar-spotted Pinion *Cosmia pyralina*	4–6		S, (C)	L
Merveille du Jour *Dichonia aprilina*	4–6	B, L&F		
Mottled Umber *Erannis defoliaria*	4–6			
November Moth *Epirrita dilutata*	4–6			
Pale Brindled Beauty *Phigalia pilosaria*	4–6			
Pale Eggar *Trichiura crataegi*	4–6			
Pale November Moth *Epirrita christyi*	4–6		S, C, (N)	
Purple Hairstreak *Neozephyrus quercus*	4–6		S, C, (N)	
Satellite *Eupsilia transversa*	4–6			
Scarce Umber *Agriopis aurantiaria*	4–6			
Small Brindled Beauty *Apocheima hispidaria*	4–6		S, (C, N)	L
Small Quaker *Orthosia cruda*	4–6			
Sprawler *Asteroscopus sphinx*	4–6		S, C	
Spring Usher *Agriopis leucophaearia*	4–6		S, C, (N)	
Twin-spotted Quaker *Orthosia munda*	4–6		S, C, (N)	
White-marked *Cerastis leucographa*	4–6		S, C	L
Winter Moth *Operophtera brumata*	4–6			
Yellow-line Quaker *Agrochola macilenta*	4–6			
Grey Shoulder-knot *Lithophane ornitopus*	4–7		S, WC	
Orange Upperwing *Jodia croceago*	4–7		S	RDB
Blossom Underwing *Orthosia miniosa*	5–6		S, C	L

Species				
Chestnut Conistra vaccinii	5–6			
Clouded Drab Orthosia incerta	4–6			
March Moth Alsophila aescularia	5–6			
August Thorn Ennomos quercinaria	5–7		S, C, (N)	L
Brindled Beauty Lycia hirtaria	5–7		S, C, (N)	
Brindled Pug Eupithecia abbreviata	5–7	F		
Frosted Green Polyploca ridens	5–7		S, C	L
Lunar Marbled Brown Drymonia ruficornis	5–7		S, C, (N)	L
Marbled Pug Eupithecia irriguata	5–7		S, (C)	Nb
Nut-tree Tussock Colocasia coryli	5–7 & 9–10	7–9		
Oak Beauty Biston strataria	5–7		S, C, (N)	
Oak Lutestring Cymatophorima diluta	5–7		S, C	L
Oak Nycteoline Nycteola revayana	5–7	+	S, (C, N)	L
Pale Pinion Lithophane hepatica	5–7		S, WC	L
Purple Thorn Selenia tetralunaria	5–7 & 8–9	6–7	S, C, (N)	
September Thorn Ennomos erosaria	5–7		S, C, (N)	
Sword-grass Xylena exsoleta	5–7		C, N	Nb
Large Thorn Ennomos autumnaria	5–8		SE	Nb
Vapourer Orgyia antiqua	5–8	+		
Cabbage Moth Mamestra brassicae	5–10	+		
Coxcomb Prominent Ptilodon capucina	6–7 & 8–9	6–8		
False Mocha Cyclophora porata	6–7 & 9–10		S, C	Nb
Golden-rod Pug Eupithecia virgaureata	6–7 & 9–10	F		L
Iron Prominent Notodonta dromedarius	6–7 & 9–10	8		
Maiden's Blush Cyclophora punctaria	6–7 & 8–9		S, C, (N)	L
Oak Hook-tip Watsonalla binaria	6–7 & 8–9		S, C	
Autumn Green Carpet Chloroclysta miata	6–8			L
Barred Umber Plagodis pulveraria	6–8			L
Great Prominent Peridea anceps	6–8		S, WC, (EC, N)	L
Least Black Arches Nola confusalis	6–8		S, C, (N)	L
Lunar Thorn Selenia lunularia	6–8			L
Oak-tree Pug Eupithecia dodoneata	6–8		S, C	
Red-green Carpet Chloroclysta siterata	6–8			
Square Spot Paradarisa consonaria	6–8		S, C, SN	L
Brindled White-spot Parectropis similaria	6–9		S, (C)	L
Common White Wave Cabera pusaria	6–10			
Lime Hawk-moth Mimas tiliae	6–9		S, C	
Scalloped Hazel Odontopera bidentata	6–9			
Mottled Pug Eupithecia exiguata	6–10		S, C, (N)	
Pale Tussock Calliteara pudibunda	6–10		S, C	
Alder Moth Acronicta alni	7–8		S, C, (N)	L
Bordered Sallow Pyrrhia umbra	7–8		S, C, NE	L
Pale Oak Beauty Hypomecis punctinalis	7–8		S, (C)	
Broken-barred Carpet Electrophaes corylata	7–9			
Dark Dagger Acronicta tridens	7–9	+	S, C, (N)	
Green Silver-lines Pseudoips prasinana	7–9	+		
Lobster Moth Stauropus fagi	7–9		S, (WC)	
Marbled Brown Drymonia dodonaea	7–9		S, C, (NW)	L
Pale-shouldered Brocade Lacanobia thalassina	7–9	+		
Peppered Moth Biston betularia	7–9			
Scarce Merveille du Jour Moma alpium	7–9		S	RDB
Scorched Wing Plagodis dolabraria	7–9		S, (WC)	L
Small Angle Shades Euplexia lucipara	7–9	+		
Sycamore Acronicta aceris	7–9		S, (C)	L
Buff-tip Phalera bucephala	7–10			

Common Lutestring *Ochropacha duplaris*	7–10				
Fan-foot *Zanclognatha tarsipennalis*	7–10		DL	S, C, (N)	
Little Emerald *Jodis lactearia*	7–10			S, C, NW	
Miller *Acronicta leporina*	7–10				
Small Fan-foot *Herminia grisealis*	7–10		L & DL		
Triangle *Heterogenea asella*	7–10			S, (EC)	RDB
Common Fan-foot *Pechipogo strigilata*	7~4		DL	S, C	Na
Blotched Emerald *Comibaena bajularia*	7~5			S, C	L
Festoon *Apoda limacodes*	7–5			S, (C)	Nb
Beautiful Brocade *Lacanobia contigua*	8–9				L
Olive Crescent *Trisateles emortualis*	8–10		DL	SE	RDB
Common Emerald *Hemithea aestivaria*	8~5			S, C, (N)	
Double Dart *Graphiphora augur*	8~5				
Goat Moth *Cossus cossus*	8~5	★	ISt		Nb
Great Oak Beauty *Hypomecis roboraria*	8~5			S, (C)	Nb
Grey Arches *Polia nebulosa*	8~5				
Leopard Moth *Zeuzera pyrina*	8~5	★	ISt	S, C	
Light Emerald *Campaea margaritata*	8~5	+			
Mottled Beauty *Alcis repandata*	8~5				
Satin Beauty *Deileptenia ribeata*	8~5				
Scarce Silver-lines *Bena bicolorana*	8~5			S, C	L
Scarlet Tiger *Callimorpha dominula*	8~5			S, (WC)	L
Yellow-legged Clearwing *Synanthedon vespiformis*	8~5		ISt	S, C	Nb
Clay Fan-foot *Paracolax tristalis*	8~6		DL	SE	Na
Scarce Vapourer *Orgyia recens*	8~6			EC	RDB
Small Black Arches *Meganola strigula*	8~6			S	Na
Yellow-tail *Euproctis similis*	8~6			S, C, (N)	

Evergreen Oak *Q. ilex*

Purple Hairstreak *Neozephyrus quercus*	4–6			S, C, (N)	
Brindled Beauty *Lycia hirtaria*	5–7			S, C, (N)	
Least Black Arches *Nola confusalis*	6–8			S, C, (N)	L
Oak-tree Pug *Eupithecia dodoneata*	6–8			S, C	
Privet Hawk-moth *Sphinx ligustri*	7–9			S, (C)	
Yellow-legged Clearwing *Synanthedon vespiformis*	8–5		ISt	S, C	Nb

Oats *Avena* spp. see under Cereals

Olive *Olea europaea*

Privet Hawk-moth *Sphinx ligustri*	7–9			S, (C)	

Onions *Allium* spp.

Garden Dart *Euxoa nigricans*	2–6				
Nutmeg *Discestra trifolii*	6–7 & 9–10	8–9		S, C, (N)	

Oraches *Atriplex* spp.

Ground Lackey *Malacosoma castrensis*	4–7			SE, (SW)	Na
Nutmeg *Discestra trifolii*	6–7 & 9–10	8–9		S, C, (N)	
White Colon *Sideridis albicolon*	6–7 & 9		F		Nb
Blood-vein *Timandra comae*	7 & 9–4			S, C, (N)	
Bright-line Brown-eye *Lacanobia oleracea*	7–9	+			
Plain Pug *Eupithecia simpliciata*	8–9		F & S	S, C	L
Sand Dart *Agrotis ripae*	8–4			S, C, NE	Nb
Dark Spinach *Pelurga comitata*	9–10			S, C, (N)	
Lesser Broad-bordered Yellow Underwing *Noctua janthe*	9–4				

Oxeye Daisy *Leucanthemum vulgare*
Cinnabar *Tyria jacobaeae*	7–9		S, C, (N)	

Oxlip *Primula elatior*
Square-spotted Clay *Xestia rhomboidea*	9–5		S, (WC, N)	Nb

Oxtongues *Picris* spp.
Broad-barred White *Hecatera bicolorata*	8–9		F & S	

Pampas Grass see Grasses

Parsley *Petroselinum crispum*
Mouse *Amphipyra tragopoginis*	4–6		L & F	

Parsnip *Pastinaca sativa*
White-spotted Pug *Eupithecia tripunctaria*	6–7 & 9–10		F & S	S, C, (N)	L
Triple-spotted Pug *Eupithecia trisignaria*	8–9		F & S	S, C, (N)	L
Plain Golden Y *Autographa jota*	8~5				
Straw Belle *Aspitates gilvaria*	9–6			SE	RDB

Pears *Pyrus* spp.
Green Pug *Pasiphila rectangulata*	4–5		F		
Brindled Beauty *Lycia hirtaria*	5–7			S, C, (N)	
Figure of Eight *Diloba caeruleocephala*	5–7			S, C, (N)	
V-Pug *Chloroclystis v-ata*	5–7 & 8–10	7–9	F	S, C, (N)	
Chinese Character *Cilix glaucata*	6–7 & 8–9			S, C, (N)	
Dark Dagger *Acronicta tridens*	7 9	+		S, C, (N)	
Grey Dagger *Acronicta psi*	7–9	+			
Red-belted Clearwing *Synanthedon myopaeformis*	7–5	*	ISt	S, (C)	Nb
Gothic *Naenia typica*	8–3				L
Lappet *Gastropacha quercifolia*	8~5			S, EC	
Leopard Moth *Zeuzera pyrina*	8~5	*	ISt	S, C	
Short-cloaked Moth *Nola cucullatella*	8~5			S, C	
Yellow-tail *Euproctis similis*	8~6			S, C, (N)	
Brown-tail *Euproctis chrysorrhoea*	9~6			S, (EC)	L

Peas *Lathyrus* & *Pisum* spp.

Bitter-vetch *L. linifolius*
Wood White *Leptidea sinapis*	6–7 & 8–9	7–8	S	R
Narrow-bordered Five-spot Burnet *Zygaena lonicerae*	7–6		S, C, (N)	

Everlasting Peas *L. latifolius* & *L. sylvestris*
Long-tailed Blue *Lampides boeticus*	9–11		F&S	S	Bm

Field Pea *P. sativum var. arvense*
Pale Mottled Willow *Paradrina clavipalpis*	6–8 & 9–4		S	

Garden Pea *P. sativum*
Silver Y *Autographa gamma*	5–10	+		Bm
Pale Mottled Willow *Paradrina clavipalpis*	6–8 & 9–4		S	

Marsh Pea *L. palustris*
Scarce Blackneck *Lygephila craccae*	5–7		SW	RDB
Blackneck *Lygephila pastinum*	8–5		S, C	Na

Meadow Vetchling *L. pratensis*
Wood White *Leptidea sinapis*	6–7 & 8–9	7–8	S	R

Narrow-bordered Five-spot Burnet *Zygaena lonicerae*	7–6		S, C, (N)	
New Forest Burnet *Zygaena viciae*	7–6	*	NW	RDB

Tuberous Pea *L. tuberosus*

Scarce Blackneck *Lygephila craccae*	5–7		SW	RDB
Wood White *Leptidea sinapis*	6–7 & 8–9	7–8	S	R

Pellitory-of-the-wall *Parietaria judaica*

Bloxworth Snout *Hypena obsitalis*	5–7 & 8–4		SW	RDB
Red Admiral *Vanessa atalanta*	6–5			Bm

Pennyworts *Hydrocotyle* spp.

Weaver's Wave *Idaea contiguaria*	8–5		WC	Na
Magpie *Abraxas grossulariata*	9–6			

Periwinkles *Vinca* spp.

Six-striped Rustic *Xestia sexstrigata*	9–4			

Petty Whin *Genista anglica*

Silver-studded Blue *Plebejus argus*	4–6	F & L	S, WC	R
Green Hairstreak *Callophrys rubi*	5–8	F & L		L
Small Grass Emerald *Chlorissa viridata*	7–8		S, (WC)	Na
Lead Belle *Scotopteryx mucronata*	8–3		W, N	L
Grass Wave *Perconia strigillaria*	8–5		S, C, (N)	L
July Belle *Scotopteryx luridata*	9–4			
Grass Emerald *Pseudoterpna pruinata*	9–5			
Scotch Annulet *Gnophos obfuscatus*	9–6		N	Nb

Pignut *Conopodium majus*

Chimney Sweeper *Odezia atrata*	4–6	F	C, N, (S)	

Pines *Pinus* spp.

Unspecified

Square Spot *Paradarisa consonaria*	6–8		S, C, SN	L
Scalloped Hazel *Odontopera bidentata*	6–9			
Bordered White *Bupalus piniaria*	6–10			

Austrian Pine *P. nigra*

Pine Beauty *Panolis flammea*	5–7			
Bordered White *Bupalus piniaria*	6–10			
Dwarf Pug *Eupithecia tantillaria*	7–8			

Lodgepole Pine *P. contorta*

Twin-spot Carpet *Perizoma didymata*	4–6			
Winter Moth *Operophtera brumata*	4–6			
July Highflyer *Hydriomena furcata*	5–6			
Pine Beauty *Panolis flammea*	5–7			
Ochreous Pug *Eupithecia indigata*	6–9			
Satyr Pug *Eupithecia satyrata*	6–9	F		L
Bordered White *Bupalus piniaria*	6–10			

Maritime Pine *P. pinaster*

Pine Beauty *Panolis flammea*	5–7			

Scots Pine *P. sylvestris*

Autumnal Moth *Epirrita autumnata*	4–6			
Black Arches *Lymantria monacha*	4–6		S, C	L

Pine Beauty *Panolis flammea*	5–7				
Spruce Carpet *Thera britannica*	6–7 & 9–5			S, C, (N)	
Tawny-barred Angle *Macaria liturata*	6–8 & 9–10	7–8			
Ochreous Pug *Eupithecia indigata*	6–9				
Pine Hawk-moth *Hyloicus pinastri*	6–9			S, EC	L
Bordered White *Bupalus piniaria*	6–10				
Grey Pine Carpet *Thera obeliscata*	7–8 & 9–6				
Satin Beauty *Deileptenia ribeata*	8–5				
Barred Red *Hylaea fasciaria*	9–5				
Pine Carpet *Thera firmata*	11–7				

Pinks & Sweet William *Dianthus* spp.

Lychnis *Hadena bicruris*	6–8 & 9	7–8	S		
Mullein Wave *Scopula marginepunctata*	7 & 9–5	9–5		S, C, (N)	L
Tawny Shears *Hadena perplexa*	7–8	+	S		
White Spot *Hadena albimacula*	7–8		S	S	RDB
Bordered Gothic *Heliophobus reticulata*	7–9			S, C	RDB
Sharp-angled Carpet *Euphyia unangulata*	7–9			S, (C)	L
Varied Coronet *Hadena compta*	7–9		S	S, C	

Planes *Platanus* spp.

Lime Hawk-moth *Mimas tiliae*	6–9			S, C	
Sycamore *Acronicta aceris*	7–9			S, (C)	L

Plantains *Plantago* spp.

Unspecified

White-line Dart *Euxoa tritici*	3–7				
White-marked *Cerastis leucographa*	4–6			S, C	L
Large Ranunculus *Polymixis flavicincta*	4–7			S, (C)	L
Belted Beauty *Lycia zonaria*	5–7	*		NW	Na
Ruby Tiger *Phragmatobia fuliginosa*	5–7 & 7–4	7–5			
Flame Shoulder *Ochropleura plecta*	6–7 & 9–10	8–9			
Small Square-spot *Diarsia rubi*	6–7 & 9–4	8–5			
White Colon *Sideridis albicolon*	6–7 & 9		F		Nb
Yellow Belle *Semiaspilates ochrearia*	6–8 & 9–5			S, C	L
Muslin Moth *Diaphora mendica*	6–9			S, C, (N)	
Shuttle-shaped Dart *Agrotis puta*	6–4	+		S, C, (N)	
Green Carpet *Colostygia pectinataria*	6–7 & 9–5	8–5			
Mullein Wave *Scopula marginepunctata*	7 & 9–5	9–5		S, C, (N)	L
Bright-line Brown-eye *Lacanobia oleracea*	7–9	+			
Broom Moth *Melanchra pisi*	7–9				
Flame *Axylia putris*	7–9			S, C, (N)	
Uncertain *Hoplodrina alsines*	7–4			S, C, (N)	
Clouded Buff *Diacrisia sannio*	7–5				L
Rustic *Hoplodrina blanda*	7–5				
Dot Moth *Melanchra persicariae*	8–10			S, C, (N)	
Mottled Rustic *Caradrina morpheus*	8–11				
Gothic *Naenia typica*	8–3				L
Brown Rustic *Rusina ferruginea*	8–5				
Common Emerald *Hemithea aestivaria*	8–5			S, C, (N)	
Double Square-spot *Xestia triangulum*	8–5				
Plain Golden Y *Autographa jota*	8–5				
Satin Wave *Idaea subsericeata*	8–5	+		S, (C, NW)	
Silvery Arches *Polia trimaculosa*	8–5				Nb
Wood Tiger *Parasemia plantaginis*	8–5				L

Garden Tiger *Arctia caja*	8~6			
Lesser Yellow Underwing *Noctua comes*	8~6			
Ingrailed Clay *Diarsia mendica*	9~4			
Marsh Moth *Athetis pallustris*	9~4		S, C	RDB
Pale Mottled Willow *Paradrina clavipalpis*	9–4 & 6–8	S		
Square-spot Rustic *Xestia xanthographa*	9~4			
Vine's Rustic *Hoplodrina ambigua*	9–4 & 7–8		S, (C)	L
Clay *Mythimna ferrago*	9~5			
Gold Spot *Plusia festucae*	9~5 & 7–8	9~5		
Great Brocade *Eurois occulta*	9~6		N	Nb
Jersey Tiger *Euplagia quadripunctaria*	9~6		SW	Nb
Portland Moth *Actebia praecox*	9~6		SW, C, N, (S)	Nb
Black Rustic *Aporophyla nigra*	10–5			
Feathered Ranunculus *Polymixis lichenea*	10–5		S, C, (N)	L
Deep-brown Dart *Aporophyla lutulenta*	10~6		S, EC	

Buck's-horn Plantain *P. coronopus*

Yellow Belle *Semiaspilates ochrearia*	6–8 & 9–5		S, C	L
Glanville Fritillary *Melitaea cinxia*	7~4		S	R

Greater Plantain *P. major*

Garden Dart *Euxoa nigricans*	2–6			
Setaceous Hebrew Character *Xestia c-nigrum*	5–7 & 9~4	9~5		
Silver Cloud *Egira conspicillaris*	5–7		SW, WC	Na
Lime-speck Pug *Eupithecia centaureata*	5–10	+	F	
Treble Lines *Charanyca trigrammica*	6–4		S, C	
Dog's Tooth *Lacanobia suasa*	6–7 & 8–9	7–8	S, C, (N)	L
Knot Grass *Acronicta rumicis*	7–9	+		
Pearly Underwing *Peridroma saucia*	7–10			Bm
Heart and Dart *Agrotis exclamationis*	7~3	+		
Silver-ground Carpet *Xanthorhoe montanata*	7~5			
Heath Fritillary *Melitaea athalia*	7~6		SW, SE	R
Wood Tiger *Parasemia plantaginis*	8~5			L

Ribwort Plantain *P. lanceolata*

Garden Dart *Euxoa nigricans*	2–6			
Setaceous Hebrew Character *Xestia c-nigrum*	5–7 & 9~4			
Rosy Rustic *Hydraecia micacea*	5–8		ISt & R	
Painted Lady *Vanessa cardui*	5–10			Bm
Flame Shoulder *Ochropleura plecta*	6–7 & 9–10	8–9		
White Colon *Sideridis albicolon*	6–7 & 9	F		Nb
Sweet Gale Moth *Acronicta euphorbiae*	6–9		N	Na
Glanville Fritillary *Melitaea cinxia*	6–5		S	R
Knot Grass *Acronicta rumicis*	7–9	+		
Pearly Underwing *Peridroma saucia*	7–10			Bm
Heart and Dart *Agrotis exclamationis*	7~3	+		
Marsh Moth *Athetis pallustris*	7~4		EC	RDB
Heath Fritillary *Melitaea athalia*	7~6		SW, SE	R
Wood Tiger *Parasemia plantaginis*	8~5			L
Six-striped Rustic *Xestia sexstrigata*	9~4			
Square-spotted Clay *Xestia rhomboidea*	9–5		S, (WC, N)	Nb

Sea Plantain *P. maritima*

Black-banded *Polymixis xanthomista*	3–7	F & S	SW, WC	Na
Ground Lackey *Malacosoma castrensis*	4–7		SE, (SW)	Na
Rosy Rustic *Hydraecia micacea*	5–8		ISt & R	

Sweet Gale Moth *Acronicta euphorbiae*	6–9			N	Na
Glanville Fritillary *Melitaea cinxia*	6–5			S	R
Feathered Ranunculus *Polymixis lichenea*	10–5			S, C, (N)	L

Ploughman's-spikenard *Inula conyzae*

Small Marbled *Eublemma parva*	7–9		F	S, C, (N)	Bm

Plums, Wild Plum *Prunus domestica* & Cherry Plum *P. cerasifera* see also Bullace

Brimstone Moth *Opisthograptis luteolata*	All	7–9			
Grass Eggar *Lasiocampa trifolii*	3–6			S, WC	Na
Black Hairstreak *Satyrium pruni*	4–5		F & L	SE, EC	R
Early Moth *Theria primaria*	4–5			S, C, (N)	
Blue-bordered Carpet *Plemyria rubiginata*	4–6				
Copper Underwing *Amphipyra pyramidea*	4–6			S, C, (N)	
Dotted Border *Agriopis marginaria*	4–6				
Green-brindled Crescent *Allophyes oxyacanthae*	4–6				
Lackey *Malacosoma neustria*	4–6			S, C, (N)	
Lunar-spotted Pinion *Cosmia pyralina*	4–6			S, C	L
Northern Winter Moth *Operophtera fagata*	4–6				
November Moth *Epirrita dilutata*	4–6				
Pale Brindled Beauty *Phigalia pilosaria*	4–6				
Twin-spotted Quaker *Orthosia munda*	4–6			S, C, (N)	
Large Ranunculus *Polymixis flavicincta*	4–7			S, (C)	L
March Moth *Alsophila aescularia*	5–6				
Brindled Beauty *Lycia hirtaria*	5–7			S, C, N	
Figure of Eight *Diloba caeruleocephala*	5–7			S, C, (N)	
Tawny Pinion *Lithophane semibrunnea*	5–7			S, C	L
Large Thorn *Ennomos autumnaria*	5–8			SE	Nb
Lunar Thorn *Selenia lunularia*	6–8				L
White-pinion Spotted *Lomographa bimaculata*	6–8			S, C	
Scalloped Hazel *Odontopera bidentata*	6–9				
Clouded Silver *Lomographa temerata*	7–8			S, C, (N)	
Dark Dagger *Acronicta tridens*	7–9	+		S, C, (N)	
Grey Dagger *Acronicta psi*	7–9	+			
Peppered Moth *Biston betularia*	7–9				
Sycamore *Acronicta aceris*	7–9			S, (C)	L
Buff Ermine *Spilosoma luteum*	7–10				
Willow Beauty *Peribatodes rhomboidaria*	7–6	+			
Cream-spot Tiger *Arctia villica*	8–5			S	L
Lappet *Gastropacha quercifolia*	8–5			S, EC	
Leopard Moth *Zeuzera pyrina*	8–5	*	ISt	S, C	
Short-cloaked Moth *Nola cucullatella*	8–5			S, C	
Brown-tail *Euproctis chrysorrhoea*	9–6			S, (EC)	L

Poplars & Aspen *Populus* spp.

Unspecified

Pink-barred Sallow *Xanthia togata*	3–6		F		
Feathered Thorn *Colotois pennaria*	4–6				
Northern Winter Moth *Operophtera fagata*	4–6				
Pale Brindled Beauty *Phigalia pilosaria*	4–6				
Sprawler *Asteroscopus sphinx*	4–6			S, C	
Yellow-line Quaker *Agrochola macilenta*	4–6		F		
July Highflyer *Hydriomena furcata*	5–6				
Oak Beauty *Biston strataria*	5–7			S, C, (N)	
Scarce Chocolate-tip *Clostera anachoreta*	5–7 & 8–9			SE	RDB

Species					
Sword-grass *Xylena exsoleta*	5–7			C, N	Nb
Large Thorn *Ennomos autumnaria*	5–8			SE	Nb
Pebble Prominent *Notodonta ziczac*	6–7 & 8–9	7–8			
Sallow Kitten *Furcula furcula*	6–7 & 8–9	7–8			
Common White Wave *Cabera pusaria*	6–10				
Eyed Hawk-moth *Smerinthus ocellata*	6–9			S, C	
Puss Moth *Cerura vinula*	6–9				
Clouded Silver *Lomographa temerata*	7–8			S, C, (N)	
Clouded Border *Lomaspilis marginata*	7–9				
Green Silver-lines *Pseudoips prasinana*	7–9	+			
Peppered Moth *Biston betularia*	7–9				
Triangle *Heterogenea asella*	7–10			S, (EC)	RDB
Goat Moth *Cossus cossus*	8–5	*	ISt		Nb
Lunar Hornet Moth *Sesia bembeciformis*	8–5	*	ISt		
Hornet Moth *Sesia apiformis*	9–5	*	ISt	S, (C, N)	Nb

Aspen *P. tremula*

Species					
Olive *Ipimorpha subtusa*	4–5			S, C, (N)	L
Angle-striped Sallow *Enargia paleacea*	4–6			C, N	Nb
Autumnal Moth *Epirrita autumnata*	4–6				
Black Arches *Lymantria monacha*	4–6			S, C	L
Brick *Agrochola circellaris*	4–6		F, S & L		
December Moth *Poecilocampa populi*	4–6				
Dun-bar *Cosmia trapezina*	4–6				
Engrailed *Ectropis bistortata*	4–6 & 7–9	5–7			
Lead-coloured Drab *Orthosia populeti*	4–6		F & L		L
Minor Shoulder-knot *Brachylomia viminalis*	4–6				
November Moth *Epirrita dilutata*	4–6				
Twin-spotted Quaker *Orthosia munda*	4–6			S, C, (N)	
Chevron *Eulithis testata*	5–6				
Light Orange Underwing *Archiearis notha*	5–6			S, (EC)	Nb
Chocolate-tip *Closter curtula*	5–7 & 8–10	7–8		S, C, (N)	L
Dark Bordered Beauty *Epione vespertaria*	5–7			EC, NE	RDB
Oak Beauty *Biston strataria*	5–7			S, C, (N)	
Red Underwing *Catocala nupta*	5–7			S, C	
Scarce Chocolate-tip *Clostera anachoreta*	5–7 & 8–9			SE	RDB
Small Chocolate-tip *Clostera pigra*	5–7 & 8–9	7–9			Nb
Herald *Scoliopteryx libatrix*	5–9	+			
Common Wave *Cabera exanthemata*	6–7 & 8–9	7–8			
Coxcomb Prominent *Ptilodon capucina*	6–7 & 8–9	6–8			
Pale Prominent *Pterostoma palpina*	6–7 & 8–9	6–8			
Pebble Prominent *Notodonta ziczac*	6–7 & 8–9	7–8			
Sallow Kitten *Furcula furcula*	6–7 & 8–9	7–8			
Seraphim *Lobophora halterata*	6–7				L
Swallow Prominent *Pheosia tremula*	6–7 & 9	7–9			
Eyed Hawk-moth *Smerinthus ocellata*	6–9			S, C	
Poplar Hawk-moth *Laothoe populi*	6–9	+			
Puss Moth *Cerura vinula*	6–9				
Grey Pug *Eupithecia subfuscata*	6–10		F & L		
Clouded Silver *Lomographa temerata*	7–8			S, C, (N)	
Figure of Eighty *Tethea ocularis*	7–8			S, C, (N)	
Clouded Border *Lomaspilis marginata*	7–9				
Green Silver-lines *Pseudoips prasinana*	7–9	+			
Pale-shouldered Brocade *Lacanobia thalassina*	7–9	+			
Poplar Grey *Acronicta megacephala*	7–9			S, C, (N)	

Poplar Lutestring *Tethea or*	7–9				L
Miller *Acronicta leporina*	7–10				
Scallop Shell *Rheumaptera undulata*	7–10			S, C, (N)	L
Purple Emperor *Apatura iris*	8–6			S	R
White Satin Moth *Leucoma salicis*	8–6			S, C	L
Hornet Moth *Sesia apiformis*	9–5	*	ISt	S, (C, N)	Nb

Black-poplar *P. nigra*

Sallow *Xanthia icteritia*	3–6		F		
Double Kidney *Ipimorpha retusa*	4–5			S, WC, (EC)	L
Olive *Ipimorpha subtusa*	4–5			S, C, (N)	L
Brick *Agrochola circellaris*	4–6		F, S & L		
Copper Underwing *Amphipyra pyramidea*	4–6			S, C, (N)	
December Moth *Poecilocampa populi*	4–6				
Dingy Shears *Parastichtis ypsillon*	4–6			S, C, (N)	L
Feathered Thorn *Colotois pennaria*	4–6				
Lead-coloured Drab *Orthosia populeti*	4–6		F & L		L
Minor Shoulder-knot *Brachylomia viminalis*	4–6				
Pale-lemon Sallow *Xanthia ocellaris*	4–6		F & L	SE	Na
Yellow-line Quaker *Agrochola macilenta*	4–6		F		
Clouded Drab *Orthosia incerta*	4–6				
Bordered Beauty *Epione repandaria*	5–7				
Chocolate-tip *Clostera curtula*	5–7 & 8–10	7–8		S, C, (N)	L
Powdered Quaker *Orthosia gracilis*	5–7				
Red Underwing *Catocala nupta*	5–7			S, C	
Scarce Chocolate-tip *Clostera anachoreta*	5–7 & 8–9			SE	RDB
Herald *Scoliopteryx libatrix*	5–9	+			
Pale Prominent *Pterostoma palpina*	6–7 & 8–9	6–8			
Seraphim *Lobophora halterata*	6–7				L
Swallow Prominent *Pheosia tremula*	6–7 & 9	7–9			
Poplar Hawk-moth *Laothoe populi*	6–9	+			
Poplar Kitten *Furcula bifida*	6–9			S, C	L
Puss Moth *Cerura vinula*	6–9				
Figure of Eighty *Tethea ocularis*	7–8			S, C, (N)	
Clouded Border *Lomaspilis marginata*	7–9				
Poplar Grey *Acronicta megacephala*	7–9			S, C, (N)	
Poplar Lutestring *Tethea or*	7–9				L
Miller *Acronicta leporina*	7–10				
Lunar Hornet Moth *Sesia bembeciformis*	8–5	*	ISt		
White Satin Moth *Leucoma salicis*	8–6			S, C	L
Hornet Moth *Sesia apiformis*	9–5	*	ISt	S, (C, N)	Nb
Brown-tail *Euproctis chrysorrhoea*	9–6			S, (EC)	L

Eastern Balsam-poplar *P. balsamifera*

Miller *Acronicta leporina*	7–10				

Lombardy-poplar *P. nigra var. 'italica'*

Pale-lemon Sallow *Xanthia ocellaris*	4–6		F & L	SE	Na
Pale Prominent *Pterostoma palpina*	6–7 & 8–9	6–8			
Poplar Hawk-moth *Laothoe populi*	6–9	+			
Poplar Kitten *Furcula bifida*	6–9			S, C	L
Puss Moth *Cerura vinula*	6–9				
Poplar Grey *Acronicta megacephala*	7–9			S, C, (N)	
Hornet Moth *Sesia apiformis*	9–5	*	ISt	S, (C, N)	Nb

White Poplar *P. alba*

Chocolate-tip *Clostera curtula*	5–7 & 8–10	7–8		S, C, (N)	L
Red Underwing *Catocala nupta*	5–7			S, C	
Seraphim *Lobophora halterata*	6–7				L
Swallow Prominent *Pheosia tremula*	6–7 & 9	7–9			
Figure of Eighty *Tethea ocularis*	7–8			S, C, (N)	
Poplar Grey *Acronicta megacephala*	7–9			S, C, (N)	

Poppy see under Californian Poppy

Potato *Solanum tuberosum*

Rosy Rustic *Hydraecia micacea*	5–8		ISt & R		
Death's-head Hawk-moth *Acherontia atropos*	7–10				Bm

Potentilla (Garden Shrubs) *Potentilla* spp.

Lackey *Malacosoma neustria*	4–6			S, C, (N)	

Primrose *Primula vulgaris*

Twin-spot Carpet *Perizoma didymata*	4–6		F		
Duke of Burgundy *Hamearis lucina*	6–8			S, (C, N)	S
Uncertain *Hoplodrina alsines*	7–4			S, C, (N)	
Riband Wave *Idaea aversata*	7~5	+			
Silver-ground Carpet *Xanthorhoe montanata*	7~5				
Gothic *Naenia typica*	8–3				L
Clouded-bordered Brindle *Apamea crenata*	8–4				
Double Square-spot *Xestia triangulum*	8–5				
Green Arches *Anaplectoides prasina*	8–5				
Large Twin-spot Carpet *Xanthorhoe quadrifasiata*	8–5			S, C	L
Triple-spotted Clay *Xestia ditrapezium*	8–5		B		L
Broad-bordered Yellow Underwing *Noctua fimbriata*	9~4				
Ingrailed Clay *Diarsia mendica*	9~4				
Lesser Broad-bordered Yellow Underwing *Noctua janthe*	9~4				
Square-spot Rustic *Xestia xanthographa*	9~4				
Vine's Rustic *Hoplodrina ambigua*	9~4 & 7–8			S, (C)	L
Dotted Clay *Xestia baja*	9~5				
Least Yellow Underwing *Noctua interjecta*	9~5			S, C, (SN)	
Plain Clay *Eugnorisma depuncta*	9~5			SW, WC, N	Nb
Square-spotted Clay *Xestia rhomboidea*	9~5			S, (WC, N)	Nb
Great Brocade *Eurois occulta*	9~6			N	Nb
Feathered Ranunculus *Polymixis lichenea*	10–5			S, C, (N)	L

Privets *Ligustrum* spp.

Barred Tooth-striped *Trichopteryx polycommata*	4–6			S, N, (C)	Na
Copper Underwing *Amphipyra pyramidea*	4–6			S, C, (N)	
Engrailed *Ectropis bistortata*	4–6 & 7–9	5–7			
March Moth *Alsophila aescularia*	5–6				
Dusky Thorn *Ennomos fuscantaria*	5–7			S, C	
Pale Pinion *Lithophane hepatica*	5–7			S, WC	L
Tawny Pinion *Lithophane semibrunnea*	5–7			S, C	L
Yellow-barred Brindle *Acasis viretata*	6–7	+	F, S & L	S, C, (NW)	L
Eyed Hawk-moth *Smerinthus ocellata*	6–9			S, C	
Scalloped Hazel *Odontopera bidentata*	6–9				
Waved Umber *Menophra abruptaria*	6–9			S, C	
Common Marbled Carpet *Chloroclysta truncata*	7–8 & 9~5	8~6			
Privet Hawk-moth *Sphinx ligustri*	7–9			S, (C)	

Death's-head Hawk-moth *Acherontia atropos*	7–10				Bm
Willow Beauty *Peribatodes rhomboidaria*	7–6	+			
Coronet *Craniophora ligustri*	8–9				L
Grey Arches *Polia nebulosa*	8–5				
Leopard Moth *Zeuzera pyrina*	8–5	*	lSt	S, C	
Orange Moth *Angerona prunaria*	8–5			S, (C)	L
Swallow-tailed Moth *Ourapteryx sambucaria*	8–6				
Broad-bordered Yellow Underwing *Noctua fimbriata*	9–4				
Lilac Beauty *Apeira syringaria*	9–5			S, C, (N)	L
Small Blood-vein *Scopula imitaria*	9–5			S, C	
Magpie *Abraxas grossulariata*	9–6				

Purple Loosestrife *Lythrum salicaria*

Powdered Quaker *Orthosia gracilis*	5–7				
Emperor Moth *Saturnia pavonia*	5–8				
V-Pug *Chloroclystis v-ata*	5–7 & 8–10	7–9	F	S, C, (N)	
Common Heath *Ematurga atomaria*	6–9	+			
Small Elephant Hawk-moth *Deilephila porcellus*	7–9			S, C, (N)	L

Pyracanthas *Pyracantha* spp. see under Firethorns

Radish, Wild *Raphanus raphanistrum* ssp. *raphanistrum*

Green-veined White *Pieris napi*	5–6 & 7–8	6–8			

Ragged-Robin *Lychnis flos-cuculi*

Marbled Coronet *Hadena confusa*	5–8	+	S		L
Campion *Hadena rivularis*	6–7 & 8–9	7–9	S		
Lychnis *Hadena bicruris*	6–8 & 9	7–8	S		
Rivulet *Perizoma affinitata*	7–9		F & S		

Ragworts *Senecio* spp.

Large Ranunculus *Polymixis flavicincta*	4–7			S, (C)	L
Frosted Orange *Gortyna flavago*	4–8		lSt & R		
Double-striped Pug *Gymnoscelis rufifasciata*	5–6 & 9–10		F		
Northern Drab *Orthosia opima*	5–7				L
Ruby Tiger *Phragmatobia fuliginosa*	5–7 & 7–4	7–5			
Lime-speck Pug *Eupithecia centaureata*	5–10	+	F		
Common Pug *Eupithecia vulgata*	6–7 & 8–10	7–8			
Golden-rod Pug *Eupithecia virgaureata*	6–7 & 9–10		F		L
White-spotted Pug *Eupithecia tripunctaria*	6–7 & 9–10		F & S	S, C, (N)	L
Satyr Pug *Eupithecia satyrata*	6–9		F		L
Sweet Gale Moth *Acronicta euphorbiae*	6–9			N	Na
Grey Pug *Eupithecia subfuscata*	6–10		F & L		
Cinnabar *Tyria jacobaeae*	7–9			S, C, (N)	
Shaded Pug *Eupithecia subumbrata*	7–9		F	S, (C)	L
Water Ermine *Spilosoma urticae*	7–9			SE, (SW)	Nb
Tawny Speckled Pug *Eupithecia icterata*	8–10		F & L		
Wormwood Pug *Eupithecia absinthiata*	8–10		F		
Beautiful Golden Y *Autographa pulchrina*	8–5				
Cream-spot Tiger *Arctia villica*	8–5			S	L
Sussex Emerald *Thalera fimbrialis*	8–6			SE	RDB
Archer's Dart *Agrotis vestigialis*	9–6				L
Feathered Ranunculus *Polymixis lichenea*	10–5			S, C, (N)	L

Rape *Brassica napus*

Green-veined White *Pieris napi*	5–6 & 7–8	6–8			

Large White *Pieris brassicae*	5–12				
Garden Carpet *Xanthorhoe fluctuata*	6–10				
Pearly Underwing *Peridroma saucia*	7–10				Bm

Raspberry *Rubus idaeus*

Early Thorn *Selenia dentaria*	5–6 & 8–9	6–8			
Common Pug *Eupithecia vulgata*	6–7 & 8–10	7–8			
Beautiful Carpet *Mesoleuca albicillata*	7–9				
Grizzled Skipper *Pyrgus malvae*	7–9	+		S, C	S
Sharp-angled Carpet *Euphyia unangulata*	7–9			S, (C)	L
Buff Arches *Habrosyne pyritoides*	7–10			S, C	
Fan-foot *Zanclognatha tarsipennalis*	7–10		DL	S, C, (N)	
Saxon *Hyppa rectilinea*	7–10			N	Nb
Small Fan-foot *Herminia grisealis*	7–10		L & DL		
Double Square-spot *Xestia triangulum*	8–5				
Kent Black Arches *Meganola albula*	8–6			SE	Nb
Silver-washed Fritillary *Argynnis paphia*	8–6			S, (WC)	L

Red Bartsia *Odontites vernus*

Barred Rivulet *Perizoma bifaciata*	8–10		S	S, C, (N)	L

Redshank *Persicaria maculosa*

Blood-vein *Timandra comae*	7 & 9–4			S, C, (N)	
Light Brocade *Lacanobia w-latinum*	7–8			S, C, (N)	L
Heart and Club *Agrotis clavis*	8–5		L & R		

Reeds *Phragmites* & *Calamagrostis* spp.

Unspecified

Lempke's Gold Spot *Plusia putnami*	8–5			C, (S, N)	L
Striped Wainscot *Mythimna pudorina*	8–5			S, (C)	L
Drinker *Euthrix potatoria*	8–6			S, C, NW	
Southern Wainscot *Mythimna straminea*	8–6			S, C	L

Common Reed *P. australis*

Fenn's Wainscot *Chortodes brevilinea*	4–6		lSt & L	SE	RDB
Fen Wainscot *Arenostola phragmitidis*	4–6		lSt	S, C	L
Brown-veined Wainscot *Archanara dissoluta*	4–7		lSt	S, C	L
Large Wainscot *Rhizedra lutosa*	4–7		lSt & R		
White-mantled Wainscot *Archanara neurica*	5–6		lSt	SE	RDB
Twin-spotted Wainscot *Archanara geminipuncta*	5–7		lSt	S, (EC)	L
Reed Dagger *Simyra albovenosa*	6–7 & 8–9			SE	Nb
Mother Shipton *Callistege mi*	7–9				
Flame Wainscot *Mythimna flammea*	7–10			S	Na
Obscure Wainscot *Mythimna obsoleta*	7–4		lSt	S, EC, (WC)	L
Smoky Wainscot *Mythimna impura*	7–5				
Reed Leopard *Phragmataecia castaneae*	8–5	*	lSt & R	E, (SW)	RDB
Striped Wainscot *Mythimna pudorina*	8–5			S, (C)	L
Drinker *Euthrix potatoria*	8–6			S, C, NW	
Southern Wainscot *Mythimna straminea*	8–6			S, C	L
Silky Wainscot *Chilodes maritimus*	9–4		lSt	S, C, (N)	L

Purple Small-reed *C. canescens*

Concolorous *Chortodes extrema*	7–5		lSt	SE, EC	RDB
Lempke's Gold Spot *Plusia putnami*	8–5			C, (S, N)	L
Mere Wainscot *Chortodes fluxa*	9–6		lSt	S, EC	Nb

Wood Small-reed *C. epigejos*

Concolorous *Chortodes extrema*	8–5		lSt	SE, EC	RDB
Lempke's Gold Spot *Plusia putnami*	8–5			C, (S, N)	L
Drinker *Euthrix potatoria*	8–6			S, C, NW	
Mere Wainscot *Chortodes fluxa*	9–6		lSt	S, EC	Nb

Restharrows *Ononis* spp.

Grass Eggar *Lasiocampa trifolii*	3–6			S, WC	Na
Silver-studded Blue *Plebejus argus*	4–6		F & L	S, WC	R
Sword-grass *Xylena exsoleta*	5–7			C, N	Nb
Common Blue *Polyommatus icarus*	6–7 & 8~4	8~5			
White Colon *Sideridis albicolon*	6–7 & 9		F		Nb
Yellow Belle *Semiaspilates ochrearia*	6–8 & 9–5			S, C	L
Bordered Sallow *Pyrrhia umbra*	7–8		F & S	S, C, NE	L
Bordered Straw *Heliothis peltigera*	7–10		F		Bm
Pale Shining Brown *Polia bombycina*	7–5			S	RDB
Rest Harrow *Aplasta ononaria*	7~5	+		SE	RDB
Yellow Shell *Camptogramma bilineata*	7–5				
Marbled Clover *Heliothis viriplaca*	8–9	+	F & S	SE, (S)	RDB
Plain Wave *Idaea straminata*	8–5				L
Portland Moth *Actebia praecox*	9–6			SW, C, N, (S)	Nb
Six-spot Burnet *Zygaena filipendulae*	9–6	*			

Rhododendrons & Azaleas *Rhododendron* spp.

Svensson's Copper Underwing *Amphipyra berbera*	4–5			S, C	

Rhubarbs *Rheum* spp.

Rosy Rustic *Hydraecia micacea*	5–8		lSt & R		
Knot Grass *Acronicta rumicis*	7–9	+			

Rock-cresses *Arabis* spp. see under White Arabis

Rock-roses *Helianthemum* spp.

Square-spot Dart *Euxoa obelisca*	3–7				Nb
Silver-studded Blue *Plebejus argus*	4–6		F & L	S, WC	R
Green Hairstreak *Callophrys rubi*	5–8		F & L		L
Brown Argus *Aricia agestis*	6–7 & 8~4			S, C	L
Satyr Pug *Eupithecia satyrata*	6–9		F		L
Cistus Forester *Adscita geryon*	7–5			S, C	Nb
Northern Brown Argus *Aricia artaxerxes*	7~5			C, N	S
Silky Wave *Idaea dilutaria*	8~5			W	RDB
Wood Tiger *Parasemia plantaginis*	8~5				L
Ashworth's Rustic *Xestia ashworthii*	8~6			WC	Na
Annulet *Charissa obscurata*	9~5				L

Rock Sea-spurrey *Spergularia rupicola* see under Spurrey

Root Vegetables

Heart and Dart *Agrotis exclamationis*	7~3	+			
Turnip Moth *Agrotis segetum*	7–4	+	St & R		

Roses *Rosa* spp.

Brown-spot Pinion *Agrochola litura*	4–6				
Common Quaker *Orthosia cerasi*	4–6				
Copper Underwing *Amphipyra pyramidea*	4–6			S, C, (N)	
Feathered Thorn *Colotois pennaria*	4–6				

Green-brindled Crescent *Allophyes oxyacanthae*	4–6			
Mottled Umber *Erannis defoliaria*	4–6			
November Moth *Epirrita dilutata*	4–6			
Scarce Umber *Agriopis aurantiaria*	4–6			
Small Quaker *Orthosia cruda*	4–6			
Shoulder Stripe *Anticlea badiata*	4–7		S, C, (N)	
Small Eggar *Eriogaster lanestris*	4–7	*	S, C	Nb
Barred Yellow *Cidaria fulvata*	5–6			
Chevron *Eulithis testata*	5–6			
Double-striped Pug *Gymnoscelis rufifasciata*	5–6 & 9–10	F		
March Moth *Alsophila aescularia*	5–6			
Figure of Eight *Diloba caeruleocephala*	5–7		S, C, (N)	
Northern Drab *Orthosia opima*	5–7			L
Streamer *Anticlea derivata*	5–7			
Coxcomb Prominent *Ptilodon capucina*	6–7 & 8–9	6–8		
V-Pug *Chloroclystis v-ata*	5–7 & 8–10	7–9	F S, C, (N)	
Autumn Green Carpet *Chloroclysta miata*	6–8			L
Lunar Thorn *Selenia lunularia*	6–8			L
Red-green Carpet *Chloroclysta siterata*	6–8			
Common Marbled Carpet *Chloroclysta truncata*	7–8 & 9–5	8–6		
Little Thorn *Cepphis advenaria*	7–8		S, (C)	Nb
Small White Wave *Asthena albulata*	7–8	+	S, C, (N)	
Broom Moth *Melanchra pisi*	7–9			
Dark Dagger *Acronicta tridens*	7–9	+	S, C, (N)	
Elephant Hawk-moth *Deilephila elpenor*	7–9	+	S, C, (N)	
Grey Dagger *Acronicta psi*	7–9	+		
Grizzled Skipper *Pyrgus malvae*	7–9	+	S, C	S
Lobster Moth *Stauropus fagi*	7–9		S, (WC)	
Peppered Moth *Biston betularia*	7–9			
Sycamore *Acronicta aceris*	7–9		S, (C)	L
Willow Beauty *Peribatodes rhomboidaria*	7–6	+		
Common Emerald *Hemithea aestivaria*	8–5		S, C, (N)	
Cream-spot Tiger *Arctia villica*	8–5		S	L
Yellow-tail *Euproctis similis*	8–6		S, C, (N)	
Dotted Clay *Xestia baja*	9–5			
Brown-tail *Euproctis chrysorrhoea*	9–6		S, (EC)	L
Jersey Tiger *Euplagia quadripunctaria*	9–6		SW	Nb

Burnet Rose *R. pimpinellifolia*

Shoulder Stripe *Anticlea badiata*	4–7		S, C, (N)	
Barred Yellow *Cidaria fulvata*	5–6			
Belted Beauty *Lycia zonaria*	5–7		NW	Na
Fox Moth *Macrothylacia rubi*	6–4			
Knot Grass *Acronicta rumicis*	7–9	+		

Rosebay Willowherb *Chamerion angustifolium* see under Willowherb

Roseroot *Sedum rosea*

Yellow-ringed Carpet *Entephria flavicinctata*	6–7 & 9–5	9–6	C, N	Nb

Rowan *Sorbus aucuparia*

Brimstone Moth *Opisthograptis luteolata*	All	7–9		
Green-brindled Crescent *Allophyes oxyacanthae*	4–6			
Orange Underwing *Archiearis parthenias*	4–6	F		L
Chevron *Eulithis testata*	5–6			

Double-striped Pug *Gymnoscelis rufifasciata*	5–6 & 9–10		F		
Emperor Moth *Saturnia pavonia*	5–8				
Herald *Scoliopteryx libatrix*	5–9	+			
Chinese Character *Cilix glaucata*	6–7 & 8–9			S, C, (N)	
Coxcomb Prominent *Ptilodon capucina*	6–7 & 8–9	6–8			
Yellow-barred Brindle *Acasis viretata*	6–7	+	F, S & L	S, C, (NW)	L
Autumn Green Carpet *Chloroclysta miata*	6–8				L
Red-green Carpet *Chloroclysta siterata*	6–8				
Mottled Pug *Eupithecia exiguata*	6–10			S, C, (N)	
Grey Dagger *Acronicta psi*	7–9	+			
Privet Hawk-moth *Sphinx ligustri*	7–9			S, (C)	
Small Yellow Wave *Hydrelia flammeolaria*	7–9			S, C, (N)	
Welsh Wave *Venusia cambrica*	7–9			W, N	L
Buff-tip *Phalera bucephala*	7–10				
Red-belted Clearwing *Synanthedon myopaeformis*	7–5	*	ISt	S, (C)	Nb
Oak Eggar *Lasiocampa quercus*	All	*			

Rushes *Juncus, Typha, Bolboschoenus* & *Scirpus* spp.

Unspecified

Haworth's Minor *Celaena haworthii*	4–7		ISt	C, N, (S)	L
Small Wainscot *Chortodes pygmina*	9–7		ISt		

Bulrushes & Reed-maces *Typha* spp.

Bulrush Wainscot *Nonagria typhae*	4–7		ISt		
Rush Wainscot *Archanara algae*	6–8		ISt	SE, EC	RDB
Webb's Wainscot *Archanara sparganii*	6–8		ISt	S, (EC)	Nb

Club-rushes *Scirpus* & *Schoenoplectus* spp.

Haworth's Minor *Celaena haworthii*	4–7		ISt	C, N, (S)	L
Rush Wainscot *Archanara algae*	6–8		ISt	SE, EC	RDB
Webb's Wainscot *Archanara sparganii*	6–8		ISt	S, (EC)	Nb

Compact Rush *J. conglomeratus*

Red Sword-grass *Xylena vetusta*	5–7		F		L

Heath Rush *J. squarrosus*

Antler Moth *Cerapteryx graminis*	3–6				

Jointed Rush *J. articulatus*

Antler Moth *Cerapteryx graminis*	3–6				
Large Heath *Coenonympha tullia*	7~5			WC, N, (EC)	S
Small Rufous *Coenobia rufa*	9~6		ISt	S, C, (N)	L

Sea Club-rush *B. maritimus*

Saltern Ear *Amphipoea fucosa*	5–7		St & R		L

Sharp-flowered Rush *J. acutiflorus*

Small Rufous *Coenobia rufa*	9~6		ISt	S, C, (N)	L

Soft Rush *J. effusus*

Red Sword-grass *Xylena vetusta*	5–7		F		L
Small Rufous *Coenobia rufa*	9~6		ISt	S, C, (N)	L

Sage *Salvia officinalis*

Bordered Straw *Heliothis peltigera*	7–10		F		Bm

Sainfoin *Onobrychis viciifolia*

Latticed Heath *Chiasmia clathrata*	6–7 & 8–9	7–8			
Narrow-bordered Five-spot Burnet *Zygaena lonicerae*	7–6			S, C, (N)	

St. John's-worts *Hypericum* spp.

Powdered Quaker *Orthosia gracilis*	5–7				
V-Pug *Chloroclystis v-ata*	5–7 & 8–10	7–9	F	S, C, (N)	
Lesser Treble-bar *Aplocera efformata*	6–8 & 9–5			S, C	
Treble-bar *Aplocera plagiata*	6–8 & 9–5				
Satyr Pug *Eupithecia satyrata*	6–9		F		L
Bright-line Brown-eye *Lacanobia oleracea*	7–9	+			
Shaded Pug *Eupithecia subumbrata*	7–9		F	S, (C)	L
Mottled Beauty *Alcis repandata*	8–5				

Salad Burnet *Sanguisorba minor* ssp. *minor*

Mouse *Amphipyra tragopoginis*	4–6		L & F		
Fox Moth *Macrothylacia rubi*	6–4				
Reddish Buff *Acosmetia caliginosa*	7–8			S	RDB
Grizzled Skipper *Pyrgus malvae*	7–9	+		S, C	S
Wood Tiger *Parasemia plantaginis*	8–5				L
Ashworth's Rustic *Xestia ashworthii*	8–6			WC	Na
Annulet *Charissa obscurata*	9–5				L
Feathered Ranunculus *Polymixis lichenea*	10–5			S, C, (N)	L

Sallow see under Willows

Saltworts *Salsola* spp.

Sand Dart *Agrotis ripae*	8–10			S, C, NE	Nb

Saw-wort *Serratula tinctoria*

Mouse *Amphipyra tragopoginis*	4–6		L & F		
Reddish Buff *Acosmetia caliginosa*	7–8			S	RDB
Sharp-angled Carpet *Euphyia unangulata*	7–9			S, (C)	L

Saxifrages *Saxifraga* spp.

Small Autumnal Moth *Epirrita filigrammaria*	4–5			C, N	
Twin-spot Carpet *Perizoma didymata*	4–6		F		
Lime-speck Pug *Eupithecia centaureata*	5–10	+	F		
Yellow-ringed Carpet *Entephria flavicinctata*	6–7 & 9–5	9–6		C, N	Nb
Grey Mountain Carpet *Entephria caesiata*	8–6			C, N	
Red Carpet *Xanthorhoe decoloraria*	9–5			C, N	
Scotch Annulet *Gnophos obfuscatus*	9–6			N	Nb
Feathered Ranunculus *Polymixis lichenea*	10–5			S, C, (N)	L
Northern Rustic *Standfussiana lucernea*	10–5			SW, WC, N	L

Scabious *Knautia, Scabiosa* & *Succisa* spp.

Unspecified

Lime-speck Pug *Eupithecia centaureata*	5–10	+	F		
Striped Hawk-moth *Hyles livornica*	6–7 & 9–10				Bm
Narrow-bordered Bee Hawk-moth *Hemaris tityus*	6–8				Nb
Satyr Pug *Eupithecia satyrata*	6–9		F		L
Red Admiral *Vanessa atalanta*	6–5				Bm
Shaded Pug *Eupithecia subumbrata*	7–9		F	S, (C)	L
Clouded Buff *Diacrisia sannio*	7–5				L
Marsh Fritillary *Euphydryas aurinia*	7–5			W, NW	S

Marbled Clover *Heliothis viriplaca*	8–9	+	F & S	SE, (S)	RDB
Feathered Ranunculus *Polymixis lichenea*	10–5			S, C, (N)	L
Deep-brown Dart *Aporophyla lutulenta*	10~6			S, EC	

Devil's–bit Scabious *Succisa pratensis*

Narrow-bordered Bee Hawk-moth *Hemaris tityus*	6–8				Nb

Field Scabious *Knautia arvensis*

Lime-speck Pug *Eupithecia centaureata*	5–10	+	F		
Narrow-bordered Bee Hawk-moth *Hemaris tityus*	6–8				Nb
Shaded Pug *Eupithecia subumbrata*	7–9		F	S, (C)	L

Small Scabious *Scabiosa columbaria*

Narrow-bordered Bee Hawk-moth *Hemaris tityus*	6–8				Nb

Sea Aster *Aster tripolium*

Double-striped Pug *Gymnoscelis rufifasciata*	5–6 & 9–10		F		
Broom Moth *Melanchra pisi*	7–9				
Star-wort *Cucullia asteris*	7–9		F & L	S, C	Nb
Wormwood Pug *Eupithecia absinthiata*	8–10		F		

Sea Beet *Beta vulgaris* ssp. *maritima*

Nutmeg *Discestra trifolii*	6–7 & 9–10	8–9		S, C, (N)	
Rosy Wave *Scopula emutaria*	8~5			S, C	Nb

Sea-blite *Suaeda maritima*

Sand Dart *Agrotis ripae*	8–10			S, C, NE	Nb

Sea-buckthorn *Hippophae rhamnoides*

Ash Pug *Eupithecia fraxinata*	6–7 & 8–9				
Sharp-angled Peacock *Macaria alternata*	7 & 9			S, (C)	L
Broom Moth *Melanchra pisi*	7–9				
Sand Dart *Agrotis ripae*	8–10			S, C, NE	Nb
Brown-tail *Euproctis chrysorrhoea*	9–6			S, (EC)	L
Oak Eggar *Lasiocampa quercus*	All	*			

Sea Club-rush *Bolboschoenus maritimus* see under Rushes

Sea-holly *Eryngium maritimum*

Sand Dart *Agrotis ripae*	8–10			S, C, NE	Nb

Sea-lavenders *Limonium* spp.

Ground Lackey *Malacosoma castrensis*	4–7			SE, (SW)	Na
Northern Drab *Orthosia opima*	5–7				L
Rosy Rustic *Hydraecia micacea*	5–8		lSt & R		
Dog's Tooth *Lacanobia suasa*	6–7 & 8–9	7–8		S, C, (N)	L

Sea-milkwort *Glaux maritima*

Sand Dart *Agrotis ripae*	8–10			S, C, NE	Nb

Sea-purslane *Atriplex portulacoides*

Ground Lackey *Malacosoma castrensis*	4–7			SE, (SW)	Na
Sand Dart *Agrotis ripae*	8–10			S, C, NE	Nb

Sea Rocket *Cakile maritima*

White Colon *Sideridis albicolon*	6–7 & 9				Nb
Sand Dart *Agrotis ripae*	8–10			S, C, NE	Nb

Sea Sandwort *Honckenya peploides*

Coast Dart *Euxoa cursoria*	3–7			E, WC, N	Nb
White Colon *Sideritis albicolon*	6–7 & 9		F		Nb
Bordered Sallow *Pyrrhia umbra*	7–8		F & S	S, C, NE	L
Bright Wave *Idaea ochrata*	8–5			SE	RDB
Archer's Dart *Agrotis vestigialis*	9–6				L

Sea Wormwood *Seriphidium maritimum*

Ground Lackey *Malacosoma castrensis*	4–7			SE, (SW)	Na
Lime-speck Pug *Eupithecia centaureata*	5–10	+	F		
Yellow Belle *Semiaspilates ochrearia*	6–8 & 9–5			S, C	L
Star-wort *Cucullia asteris*	7–9		F	S, C	Nb
Yellow Shell *Camptogramma bilineata*	7–5				
Scarce Pug *Eupithecia extensaria*	8–9		F & L	SE, EC	RDB
Bordered Pug *Eupithecia succenturiata*	8–10			S, C, (N)	
Wormwood Pug *Eupithecia absinthiata*	8–10		F		

Sedges *Carex, Cladium & Rhynchospora* spp.

Unspecified

Antler Moth *Cerapteryx graminis*	3–6				
Red Sword-grass *Xylena vetusta*	5–7				L
Lesser Treble-bar *Aplocera efformata*	6–8 & 9–5			S, C	
Mother Shipton *Callistege mi*	7–9				
Silver Hook *Deltote uncula*	7–9			S, C, NW	L
Flame Wainscot *Mythimna flammea*	7–10			S	Na
Large Heath *Coenonympha tullia*	7–5			WC, N, (EC)	S
Ringlet *Aphantopus hyperantus*	7–6				
Small Wainscot *Chortodes pygmina*	9–7		ISt		

Bladder-sedge *Carex vesicaria*

Gold Spot *Plusia festucae*	9~5 & 7–8	9~5	

Carnation Sedge *C. panicea*

Gold Spot *Plusia festucae*	9~5 & 7–8	9~5	

Common Sedge *C. nigra*

Crescent *Celaena leucostigma*	3–7		ISt	L

Glaucous Sedge *C. flacca*

Least Minor *Photedes captiuncula*	8~5		ISt	SN	RDB
Gold Spot *Plusia festucae*	9~5 & 7–8	9~5			
Rosy Minor *Mesoligia literosa*	9–6		ISt & R		
Small Wainscot *Chortodes pygmina*	9–7		ISt		

Great Fen-sedge *Cladium mariscus*

Crescent *Celaena leucostigma*	3–7		ISt	L
Reed Dagger *Simyra albovenosa*	6–7 & 8–9			SE	Nb

Lesser Pond-sedge *Carex acutiformis*

Crescent *Celaena leucostigma*	3–7		ISt		L
Blair's Wainscot *Sedina buettneri*	4–8		ISt	S	RDB
Small Wainscot *Chortodes pygmina*	9–7		ISt		

Tufted-sedge *Carex elata*

Reed Dagger *Simyra albovenosa*	6–7 & 8–9			SE	Nb
Smoky Wainscot *Mythimna impura*	7–5				

Gold Spot *Plusia festucae*	9–5 & 7–8	9–5			
Small Wainscot *Chortodes pygmina*	9–7		ISt		

Wood-sedge *Carex sylvatica*

Silver Hook *Deltote uncula*	7–9			S, C, NW	L
Ringlet *Aphantopus hyperantus*	7–6				
Dotted Fan-foot *Macrochilo cribrumalis*	8–5		DL	SE, (EC)	Nb
Gold Spot *Plusia festucae*	9–5 & 7–8	9–5			

White Beak-sedge *Rhynchospora alba*

Large Heath *Coenonympha tullia*	7–5			WC, N, (EC)	S

Selfheal *Prunella vulgaris*

Shaded Pug *Eupithecia subumbrata*	7–9		F	S, (C)	L

Service-tree *Sorbus domestica*

Brimstone Moth *Opisthograptis luteolata*	All	7–9			
Dun-bar *Cosmia trapezina*	4–6				
Feathered Thorn *Colotois pennaria*	4–6				
Winter Moth *Operophtera brumata*	4–6				

Sheep's-bit *Jasione montana*

Jasione Pug *Eupithecia denotata* ssp. *jasioneata*	8–10		F	S, E	Na

Shepherd's-purse *Capsella bursa-pastoris*

Garden Carpet *Xanthorhoe fluctuata*	6–10				

Silverweed *Potentilla anserina*

Rosy Marbled *Elaphria venustula*	6–8		F	SE	Nb
Grizzled Skipper *Pyrgus malvae*	7–9	+		S, C	S
Scarce Black Arches *Nola aerugula*	8–6				Bm

Smooth Tare *Vicia tetrasperma* see under Vetches

Snapdragon *Antirrhinum majus*

Striped Hawk-moth *Hyles livornica*	6–7 & 9–10				Bm
Toadflax Pug *Eupithecia linariata*	6–10		F & S	S, C, (N)	
Feathered Ranunculus *Polymixis lichenea*	10–5			S, C, (N)	L

Sneezewort *Achillea ptarmica*

Tawny Speckled Pug *Eupithecia icterata*	8–10		F & L		

Snowberries *Symphoricarpos* spp.

Holly Blue *Celastrina argiolus*	5–7 & 8–9		B, F & S	S, C, (SN)	
Mottled Pug *Eupithecia exiguata*	6–10			S, C, (N)	
Broad-bordered Bee Hawk-moth *Hemaris fuciformis*	7–8			S, C	Nb
Privet Hawk-moth *Sphinx ligustri*	7–9			S, (C)	
Death's-head Hawk-moth *Acherontia atropos*	7–10				Bm
Marsh Fritillary *Euphydryas aurinia*	7–5			W, NW	S
Lilac Beauty *Apeira syringaria*	9–5			S, C, (N)	L

Snow-in-Summer *Cerastium tomentosum* see under Mouse-ears

Soapwort *Saponaria officinalis*

The Grey *Hadena caesia*	6–9		S, R & L	NW	RDB
Bordered Gothic *Heliophobus reticulata*	7–9			S, C	RDB

Sorrels *Rumex* spp.

Unspecified

Grey Chi *Antitype chi*	4–6			C, N, (S)	
Striped Hawk-moth *Hyles livornica*	6–7 & 9–10				Bm
Blood-vein *Timandra comae*	7 & 9–4			S, C, (N)	
Yellow Shell *Camptogramma bilineata*	7–5				
Fiery Clearwing *Pyropteron chrysidiformis*	8–5	*	R	SE	RDB
Bordered Grey *Selidosema brunnearia*	9–6		F		Na
Autumnal Rustic *Eugnorisma glareosa*	10–5				
Feathered Brindle *Aporophyla australis*	10–5			S	Nb
Feathered Ranunculus *Polymixis lichenea*	10–5			S, C, (N)	L
Deep-brown Dart *Aporophyla lutulenta*	10–6			S, EC	

Common Sorrel *R. acetosa*

Brown-spot Pinion *Agrochola litura*	4–6				
Small Copper *Lycaena phlaeas*	5–4	+			
Sweet Gale Moth *Acronicta euphorbiae*	6–9			N	Na
Green Carpet *Colostygia pectinataria*	6–7 & 9–5	8–5			
Blood-vein *Timandra comae*	7 & 9–4			S, C, (N)	
Bird's Wing *Dypterygia scabriuscula*	7–8	+		S, C	L
Knot Grass *Acronicta rumicis*	7–9	+			
Shoulder-striped Wainscot *Mythimna comma*	7–4			S, C, (N)	
Uncertain *Hoplodrina alsines*	7–4			S, C, (N)	
Forester *Adscita statices*	7–5			S, C, (NW)	L
Yellow Shell *Camptogramma bilineata*	7–5				
Fiery Clearwing *Pyropteron chrysidiformis*	8–5	*	R	SE	RDB
Plain Clay *Eugnorisma depuncta*	9–5			SW, WC, N	Nb
Feathered Brindle *Aporophyla australis*	10–5			S	Nb

Sheep's Sorrel *R. acetosella*

Small Copper *Lycaena phlaeas*	5–4	+			
Green Carpet *Colostygia pectinataria*	6–7 & 9–5	8–5			
Shoulder-striped Wainscot *Mythimna comma*	7–4			S, C, (N)	
Clouded Buff *Diacrisia sannio*	7–5				L
Forester *Adscita statices*	7–5			S, C, (NW)	L
Ashworth's Rustic *Xestia ashworthii*	8–6			WC	Na
Plain Clay *Eugnorisma depuncta*	9–5			SW, WC, N	Nb
Autumnal Rustic *Eugnorisma glareosa*	10–5				
Black Rustic *Aporophyla nigra*	10–5				

Southernwood *Artemisia abrotanum*

Bordered Pug *Eupithecia succenturiata*	8–10			S, C, (N)	
Tawny Speckled Pug *Eupithecia icterata*	8–10		F & L		

Sow-thistles *Sonchus* spp.

Striped Hawk-moth *Hyles livornica*	6–7 & 9–10				Bm
Shark *Cucullia umbratica*	7–9				
Broad-barred White *Hecatera bicolorata*	8–9		F & S		
Dot Moth *Melanchra persicariae*	8–10			S, C, (N)	

Spanish Catchfly see under Campions

Speedwells *Veronica* spp.

Heath Fritillary *Melitaea athalia*	7–6			SW, SE	R
Sub-angled Wave *Scopula nigropunctata*	8–5			SE	RDB

Straw Belle *Aspitates gilvaria*	9–6			SE	RDB

Spindles *Euonymus* spp.

Evergreen Spindle *E. japonicus*
Magpie *Abraxas grossulariata*	9–6				

Spindle *E. europaeus*
Engrailed *Ectropis bistortata*	4–6 & 7–9	5–7			
Small Eggar *Eriogaster lanestris*	4–7	*		S, C	Nb
Holly Blue *Celastrina argiolus*	5–7 & 8–9		B, F & S	S, C, (SN)	
Ruby Tiger *Phragmatobia fuliginosa*	5–7 & 7–4	7–5			
Scorched Carpet *Ligdia adusta*	6–7 & 8–9	7–8		S, (C)	L
Old Lady *Mormo maura*	9–5			S, C, (N)	L
Magpie *Abraxas grossulariata*	9–6				

Spruces *Picea* & *Tsuga* spp.

Norway Spruce *P. abies*
Black Arches *Lymantria monacha*	4–6			S, C	L
Spruce Carpet *Thera britannica*	6–7 & 9–5			S, C, (N)	
Tawny-barred Angle *Macaria liturata*	6–8 & 9–10	7–8			
Cloaked Pug *Eupithecia abietaria*	6–9		S	C, N, (S)	UC
Ochreous Pug *Eupithecia indigata*	6–9				
Pine Hawk-moth *Hyloicus pinastri*	6–9			S, EC	L
Scalloped Hazel *Odontopera bidentata*	6–9				
Bordered White *Bupalus piniaria*	6–10				
Dwarf Pug *Eupithecia tantillaria*	7 8				
Grey Pine Carpet *Thera obeliscata*	7–8 & 9–6				
Willow Beauty *Peribatodes rhomboidaria*	7–6	+			
Mottled Beauty *Alcis repandata*	8–5				
Satin Beauty *Deileptenia ribeata*	8–5				
Barred Red *Hylaea fasciaria*	9–5				
Feathered Beauty *Peribatodes secundaria*	9–6			SE	UC

Sitka Spruce *P. sitchensis*
Engrailed *Ectropis bistortata*	4–6 & 7–9	5–7			
Mottled Umber *Erannis defoliaria*	4–6				
Twin-spot Carpet *Perizoma didymata*	4–6				
Winter Moth *Operophtera brumata*	4–6				
July Highflyer *Hydriomena furcata*	5–6				
Spruce Carpet *Thera britannica*	6–7 & 9–5			S, C, (N)	
Tawny-barred Angle *Macaria liturata*	6–8 & 9–10	7–8			
Cloaked Pug *Eupithecia abietaria*	6–9		S	C, N, (S)	UC
Satyr Pug *Eupithecia satyrata*	6–9		F		L
Scalloped Hazel *Odontopera bidentata*	6–9				
Dwarf Pug *Eupithecia tantillaria*	7–8				

Western Hemlock-spruce *T. heterophylla*
Spruce Carpet *Thera britannica*	6 7 & 9–5			S, C, (N)	
Tawny-barred Angle *Macaria liturata*	6–8 & 9–10	7–8			
Dwarf Pug *Eupithecia tantillaria*	7–8				
Grey Pine Carpet *Thera obeliscata*	7–8 & 9–6				
Mottled Beauty *Alcis repandata*	8–5				
Barred Red *Hylaea fasciaria*	9–5				

Spurges *Euphorbia* spp.

Sea Spurge *E. paralias*
Coast Dart *Euxoa cursoria*	3–7		E, WC, N	Nb

Wood Spurge *E. amygdaloides*
Drab Looper *Minoa murinata*	6–9	F &L	S, (WC)	Nb
Double Square-spot *Xestia triangulum*	8~5			

Spurreys *Spergula* & *Spergularia* spp.

Corn Spurrey *Spergula arvensis*
White-line Dart *Euxoa tritici*	3–7

Rock Sea-spurrey *Spergularia rupicola*
Marbled Coronet *Hadena confusa*	5–8	+	S		L
Tawny Shears *Hadena perplexa*	7–8	+	S		
Barrett's Marbled Coronet *Hadena luteago*	7–9		lSt & R	SW	Nb

Sand Spurrey *S. rubra*
White Colon *Sideridis albicolon*	6–7 & 9	F		Nb
Barrett's Marbled Coronet *Hadena luteago*	7–9	lSt & R	SW	Nb
Bordered Straw *Heliothis peltigera*	7–10	F		Bm

Stitchworts *Stellaria* spp. see also under Chickweed
Twin-spot Carpet *Perizoma didymata*	4–6			
Marsh Pug *Eupithecia pygmaeata*	6–7	F & S	C, N, (S)	Nb
Cloaked Carpet *Euphyia biangulata*	8–9		S, W	Nb
Bright Wave *Idaea ochrata*	8–5		SE	RDB
Plain Clay *Eugnorisma depuncta*	9~5		SW, WC, N	Nb
Archer's Dart *Agrotis vestigialis*	9–6			L

Stonecrops *Sedum* spp.
Sword-grass *Xylena exsoleta*	5–7		C, N	Nb
Common Pug *Eupithecia vulgata*	6–7 & 8–10	7–8		
Yellow-ringed Carpet *Entephria flavicinctata*	6–7 & 9–5	9–6	C, N	Nb
Mullein Wave *Scopula marginepunctata*	7 & 9–5	9–5	S, C, (N)	L
Magpie *Abraxas grossulariata*	9–6			
Scotch Annulet *Gnophos obfuscatus*	9~6		N	Nb
Feathered Ranunculus *Polymixis lichenea*	10–5		S, C, (N)	L
Northern Rustic *Standfussiana lucernea*	10–5		SW, WC, N	L

Stork's-bill *Erodium cicutarium*
Brown Argus *Aricia agestis*	6–7 & 8~4		S, C	L
Bordered Straw *Heliothis peltigera*	7–10	F		Bm

Strawberry, Wild *Fragaria vesca*
Dark Marbled Carpet *Chloroclysta citrata*	4–6			
Mouse *Amphipyra tragopoginis*	4–6	L & F		
Rosy Rustic *Hydraecia micacea*	5–8	lSt & R		
Fox Moth *Macrothylacia rubi*	6~4			
Common Marbled Carpet *Chloroclysta truncata*	7–8 & 9~5	8~6		
Beautiful Carpet *Mesoleuca albicillata*	7–9			
Grizzled Skipper *Pyrgus malvae*	7–9	+	S, C	S
Knot Grass *Acronicta rumicis*	7–9	+		
Yellow Shell *Camptogramma bilineata*	7–5			
Ghost Moth *Hepialus humuli*	8–5	*	R	

Kent Black Arches *Meganola albula*	8~6			SE	Nb
Six-striped Rustic *Xestia sexstrigata*	9~4				
Annulet *Charissa obscurata*	9~5				L

Sweet Chestnut *Castanea sativa*

Engrailed *Ectropis bistortata*	4–6 & 7–9	5–7			
Mottled Umber *Erannis defoliaria*	4–6				
Small Brindled Beauty *Apocheima hispidaria*	4–6			S, (C, N)	L
Green Silver-lines *Pseudoips prasinana*	7–9	+			
Peppered Moth *Biston betularia*	7–9				
Scarce Merveille du Jour *Moma alpium*	7–9			S	RDB
Scorched Wing *Plagodis dolabraria*	7–9			S, (WC)	L
Waved Carpet *Hydrelia sylvata*	7–9			S, W	Nb
Little Emerald *Jodis lactearia*	7–10			S, C, NW	
Olive Crescent *Trisateles emortualis*	8–10		DL	SE	RDB
Light Emerald *Campaea margaritata*	8~5	+			
Yellow-legged Clearwing *Synanthedon vespiformis*	8–5		ISt	S, C	Nb

Sweet William *Dianthus barbatus* see under Pinks

Sycamore *Acer pseudoplatanus*

Barred Sallow *Xanthia aurago*	4–6			S, C, (N)	
Copper Underwing *Amphipyra pyramidea*	4–6			S, C, (N)	
Mottled Umber *Erannis defoliaria*	4–6				
Plumed Prominent *Ptilophora plumigera*	4–6			S	Na
Winter Moth *Operophtera brumata*	4–6				
Large Thorn *Ennomos autumnaria*	5–8			SE	Nb
Yellow-barred Brindle *Acasis viretata*	6–7	+	F, S & L	S, C, (NW)	L
Maple Prominent *Ptilodon cucullina*	6–9			SE, (SW)	L
Mottled Pug *Eupithecia exiguata*	6–10			S, C, (N)	
Mocha *Cyclophora annularia*	7 & 8–9			S, (C)	Nb
Alder Moth *Acronicta alni*	7–8			S, C, (N)	
Pale Oak Beauty *Hypomecis punctinalis*	7–8			S, (C)	
Small Yellow Wave *Hydrelia flammeolaria*	7–9			S, C, (N)	
Sycamore *Acronicta aceris*	7–9			S, (C)	L
Buff-tip *Phalera bucephala*	7–10				
Leopard Moth *Zeuzera pyrina*	8–5	*	ISt	S, C	

Tamarisk *Tamarix gallica*

Vapourer *Orgyia antiqua*	5–8	+			
Ash Pug *Eupithecia fraxinata*	6–7 & 8–9				
Channel Islands Pug *Eupithecia ultimaria*	8–9		F & L	S	UC
Bright-line Brown-eye *Lacanobia oleracea*	7–9	+			

Tansy *Tanacetum vulgare*

Bordered Pug *Eupithecia succenturiata*	8–10			S, C, (N)	
Tawny Speckled Pug *Eupithecia icterata*	8–10		F & L		
Wormwood Pug *Eupithecia absinthiata*	8–10		F		

Teasels *Dipsacus fullonum* & *D. pilosus*

Mouse *Amphipyra tragopoginis*	4–6		L & F		
Marsh Fritillary *Euphydryas aurinia*	7–5			W, NW	S
Mottled Rustic *Caradrina morpheus*	8–11				

Thistles *Carduus, Carlina* & *Cirsium* spp.

Frosted Orange *Gortyna flavago*	4–8		ISt & R		

Belted Beauty *Lycia zonaria*	5–7			NW	Na
Sword-grass *Xylena exsoleta*	5–7			C, N	Nb
Painted Lady *Vanessa cardui*	5–10				Bm
Burnished Brass *Diachrysia chrysitis*	6–8 & 9–5	8–6			
Treble Lines *Charanyca trigrammica*	6–4			S, C	
Knot Grass *Acronicta rumicis*	7–9	+			
Purple Marbled *Eublemma ostrina*	8			S	Bm

Thorn-apple *Datura stramonium*

Bordered Straw *Heliothis peltigera*	7–10		F		Bm

Thrift *Armeria maritima*

Grass Eggar *Lasiocampa trifolii*	3–6			S, WC	Na
Black-banded *Polymixis xanthomista*	3–7		F & S	SW, WC	Na
Ground Lackey *Malacosoma castrensis*	4–7			SE, (SW)	Na
Sweet Gale Moth *Acronicta euphorbiae*	6–9			N	Na
Cinnabar *Tyria jacobaeae*	7–9			S, C, (N)	
Crescent Dart *Agrotis trux*	8–3			SW, WC, NW	L
Thrift Clearwing *Synansphecia muscaeformis*	8–5		ISt & R	W, NE	Nb
Annulet *Charissa obscurata*	9–5		F		L
Feathered Ranunculus *Polymixis lichenea*	10–5			S, C, (N)	L

Thymes *Thymus* spp.

Silver-studded Blue *Plebejus argus*	4–6		F & L	S, WC	R
V-Pug *Chloroclystis v-ata*	5–7 & 8–10	7–9	F	S, C, (N)	
Lace Border *Scopula ornata*	6–7 & 9–4			S	Na
Satyr Pug *Eupithecia satyrata*	6–9		F		
Light Feathered Rustic *Agrotis cinerea*	7–9			S, (C)	Nb
Thyme Pug *Eupithecia distinctaria*	7–9		F		Nb
Transparent Burnet *Zygaena purpuralis*	7–5	*		NW	Na
Large Blue *Maculinea arion*	8–5		F	SW	R
Ashworth's Rustic *Xestia ashworthii*	8–6			WC	Na
Annulet *Charissa obscurata*	9–5				L
Straw Belle *Aspitates gilvaria*	9–6			SE	RDB

Toadflaxes *Linaria* spp.

Silver Y *Autographa gamma*	5–10	+			Bm
Striped Hawk-moth *Hyles livornica*	6–7 & 9–10				Bm
Toadflax Brocade *Calophasia lunula*	6–7 & 8–9			SE	RDB
Yellow Belle *Semiaspilates ochrearia*	6–8 & 9–5			S, C	L
Broom Moth *Melanchra pisi*	7–9				
Marbled Clover *Heliothis viriplaca*	8–9	+	F & S	SE, (S)	RDB
Toadflax Pug *Eupithecia linariata*	6–10		F & S	S, C, (N)	
Dot Moth *Melanchra persicariae*	8–10			S, C, (N)	
Feathered Ranunculus *Polymixis lichenea*	10–5			S, C, (N)	L

Tobacco Plants *Nicotiana* spp.

Scarce Bordered Straw *Helicoverpa armigera*	?				Bm
Pearly Underwing *Peridroma saucia*	7–10				Bm

Tomato *Lycopersicon esculentum*

Bright-line Brown-eye *Lacanobia oleracea*	6-9	+	S		
Golden Twin-spot *Chrysodeixis chalcites*					Bm
Ni Moth *Trichoplusia ni*					Bm
Scarce Bordered Straw *Helicoverpa armigera*	?				Bm

Tormentil *Potentilla erecta*

Rosy Marbled *Elaphria venustula*	6–8		F	SE	Nb
Small Grass Emerald *Chlorissa viridata*	7–8			S, (WC)	Na
Grizzled Skipper *Pyrgus malvae*	7–9	+		S, C	S

Tower Mustard *Arabis glabra*

Orange-tip *Anthocharis cardamines*	5–7				

Traveller's-joy *Clematis vitalba*

Double-striped Pug *Gymnoscelis rufifasciata*	5–6 & 9–10		F		
Lime-speck Pug *Eupithecia centaureata*	5–10	+	F		
Small Waved Umber *Horisme vitalbata*	6–7 & 9–10			S, C	
V-Pug *Chloroclystis v-ata*	5–7 & 8–10	7–9	F	S, C, (N)	
Haworth's Pug *Eupithecia haworthiata*	7–8		F	S, C	L
Fern *Horisme tersata*	7–9			S, (C)	
Small Fan-foot *Herminia grisealis*	7–10		L & DL		
Willow Beauty *Peribatodes rhomboidaria*	7~6	+			
Pretty Chalk Carpet *Melanthia procellata*	8–9			S, C, (N)	
Least Carpet *Idaea rusticata*	8~5			SE	L
Mottled Beauty *Alcis repandata*	8~5				
Orange Moth *Angerona prunaria*	8~5			S, (C)	L
Sub-angled Wave *Scopula nigropunctata*	8~5			SE	RDB
Small Emerald *Hemistola chrysoprasaria*	8~6			S, (C)	L

Treacle-mustard *Erysimum cheiranthoides*

Grey Carpet *Lithostege griseata*	6–8		S	SE	RDB

Tree Lupin *Lupinus arboreus*

Grass Eggar *Lasiocampa trifolii*	3–6			S, WC	Na
Streak *Chesias legatella*	4–6				
Portland Moth *Actebia praecox*	9–6			SW, C, N, (S)	Nb

Tree Mallow *Lavatera arborea*

Scarce Bordered Straw *Helicoverpa armigera*	?				Bm

Trefoils *Trifolium* spp.

Grass Eggar *Lasiocampa trifolii*	3–6			S, WC	Na
Silver-studded Blue *Plebejus argus*	4–6		F & L	S, WC	R
Belted Beauty *Lycia zonaria*	5–7			NW	Na
Scarce Blackneck *Lygephila craccae*	5–7			SW	RDB
Silver Cloud *Egira conspicillaris*	5–7			SW, WC	Na
Green Hairstreak *Callophrys rubi*	5–8		F & L		L
Common Blue *Polyommatus icarus*	6–7 & 8~4	8~5			
Latticed Heath *Chiasmia clathrata*	6–7 & 8–9	7–8			
Common Heath *Ematurga atomaria*	6–9	+			
Five-spot Burnet *Zygaena trifolii*	6–5			S, WC	L
Mother Shipton *Callistege mi*	7–9				
Bordered Straw *Heliothis peltigera*	7–10		F		Bm
Narrow-bordered Five-spot Burnet *Zygaena lonicerae*	7–6			S, C, (N)	
Six-belted Clearwing *Bembecia ichneumoniformis*	7–6		R	S, C	Nb
Blackneck *Lygephila pastinum*	8~5			S, C	Na
Least Carpet *Idaea rusticata*	8~5			SE	L
Scotch Burnet *Zygaena exulans*	8–5	*	L & S	N	RDB
Chalk Carpet *Scotopteryx bipunctaria*	8~6			S, C, (N)	Nb
Scarce Black Arches *Nola aerugula*	8~6				Bm
Annulet *Charissa obscurata*	9~5				L

Northern Deep-brown Dart *Aporophyla lueneburgensis*	9–5		WC, N	
Six-spot Burnet *Zygaena filipendulae*	9–6			
Feathered Ranunculus *Polymixis lichenea*	10–5		S, C, (N)	L

Twayblade *Listera ovata*

Red Chestnut *Cerastis rubricosa*	5–6			

Valerians *Valeriana* & *Centranthus* spp.

Unspecified

Angle Shades *Phlogophora meticulosa*	All			
Large Ranunculus *Polymixis flavicincta*	4–7		S, (C)	L
Humming-bird Hawk-moth *Macroglossum stellatarum*	6–9			Bm
Small Blue *Cupido minimus*	6~4	F	S, NE, (NW)	S
Mullein Wave *Scopula marginepunctata*	7 & 9–5	9–5	S, C, (N)	L
Valerian Pug *Eupithecia valerianata*	7–8	F & S		Nb
Lesser Cream Wave *Scopula immutata*	9–5		S, C, (N)	L
Feathered Ranunculus *Polymixis lichenea*	10–5		S, C, (N)	L

Common Valerian *V. officinalis*

Valerian Pug *Eupithecia valerianata*	7–8	F & S		Nb

Marsh Valerian *V. dioica*

Marsh Fritillary *Euphydryas aurinia*	7~5		W, NW	S
Valerian Pug *Eupithecia valerianata*	7–8	F & S		Nb

Vetches *Vicia, Hippocrepis* & *Anthyllis* spp.

Unspecified

Clouded Yellow *Colias croceus*	6–7 & 8–11			Bm
Common Heath *Ematurga atomaria*	6–9	+		
Shears *Hada plebeja*	7–8	+		
Narrow-bordered Five-spot Burnet *Zygaena lonicerae*	7–6		S, C, (N)	
Six-belted Clearwing *Bembecia ichneumoniformis*	7–6	R	S, C	Nb
Bright Wave *Idaea ochrata*	8–5		SE	RDB
Scarce Black Arches *Nola aerugula*	8~6			Bm
Shaded Broad-bar *Scotopteryx chenopodiata*	8~6			
Hoary Footman *Eilema caniola*	9–6		SW, (WC)	Nb
Six-spot Burnet *Zygaena filipendulae*	9–6			

Bush Vetch *V. sepium*

Scarce Blackneck *Lygephila craccae*	5–7		SW	RDB
Cream Wave *Scopula floslactata*	7~4			L

Horseshoe Vetch *H. comosa*

Chalkhill Blue *Lysandra coridon*	3–6		S	S
Silver-studded Blue *Plebejus argus*	4–6	F & L	S, WC	R
Adonis Blue *Lysandra bellargus*	6–7 & 9~5		S	R
Dingy Skipper *Erynnis tages*	6~4	+	S, C, N	L
Mullein Wave *Scopula marginepunctata*	7 & 9–5	9–5	S, C, (N)	L
Six-belted Clearwing *Bembecia ichneumoniformis*	7–6	R	S, C	Nb
Chalk Carpet *Scotopteryx bipunctaria*	8~6		S, C, (N)	Nb

Kidney Vetch *A. vulneraria*

Chalkhill Blue *Lysandra coridon*	3–6		S	S
Grass Eggar *Lasiocampa trifolii*	3–6		S, SW	Na
Black–banded *Polymixis xanthomista*	3–7	F & S	SW, WC	Na

Belted Beauty *Lycia zonaria*	5–7			NW	Na
Small Blue *Cupido minimus*	6–4	+	F	S, NE, (NW)	S
Six-belted Clearwing *Bembecia ichneumoniformis*	7–6		R	S, C	Nb
Annulet *Charissa obscurata*	9–5				L
Hoary Footman *Eilema caniola*	9–6			SW, (WC)	Nb

Smooth Tare *V. tetrasperma*

Yellow Belle *Semiaspilates ochrearia*	6–8 & 9–5			S, C	L
Bright Wave *Idaea ochrata*	8–5			SE	RDB

Tufted Vetch *V. cracca*

Scarce Blackneck *Lygephila craccae*	5–7			SW	RDB
Wood White *Leptidea sinapis*	6–7 & 8–9	7–8		S	R
Mother Shipton *Callistege mi*	7–9				
Blackneck *Lygephila pastinum*	8–5			S, C	Na
Sub-angled Wave *Scopula nigropunctata*	8–5			SE	RDB

Wood Vetch *V. sylvatica*

Scarce Blackneck *Lygephila craccae*	5–7			SW	RDB

Violets *Viola* spp.

Unspecified

Coast Dart *Euxoa cursoria*	3–7			E, WC, N	Nb
Large Twin-spot Carpet *Xanthorhoe quadrifasiata*	8–5			S, C	L
Plain Wave *Idaea straminata*	8–5				L
Sub-angled Wave *Scopula nigropunctata*	8–5			SE	RDB
Silver-washed Fritillary *Argynnis paphia*	8–6			S, (WC)	L
Broad-bordered Yellow Underwing *Noctua fimbriata*	9–4				
Ingrailed Clay *Diarsia mendica*	9–4				

Common Dog-violet *V. riviniana*

High Brown Fritillary *Argynnis adippe*	4–6			SW, WC	R
Pearl-bordered Fritillary *Boloria euphrosyne*	6–4			S, N, (WC)	S
Small Pearl-bordered Fritillary *Boloria selene*	6–5	+			S
Clouded Buff *Diacrisia sannio*	7–5				L
Dark Green Fritillary *Argynnis aglaja*	7–5				L
Silver-washed Fritillary *Argynnis paphia*	8–6			S, (WC)	L

Heath Dog-violet *V. canina*

High Brown Fritillary *Argynnis adippe*	4–6			SW, WC	R
Pearl-bordered Fritillary *Boloria euphrosyne*	6–4			S, N, (WC)	S
Small Pearl-bordered Fritillary *Boloria selene*	6–5	+			S
Clouded Buff *Diacrisia sannio*	7–5				L
Dark Green Fritillary *Argynnis aglaja*	7–5				L
Silver-washed Fritillary *Argynnis paphia*	8–6			S, (WC)	L

Hairy Violet *V. hirta*

Pearl-bordered Fritillary *Boloria euphrosyne*	6–4			S, N, (WC)	S
Small Pearl-bordered Fritillary *Boloria selene*	6–5	+			S
Dark Green Fritillary *Argynnis aglaja*	7–5				L

Heartsease (Wild Pansy) *V. tricolor*

Pearl-bordered Fritillary *Boloria euphrosyne*	6–4			S, N, (WC)	S
Small Pearl-bordered Fritillary *Boloria selene*	6–5	+			S
Dark Green Fritillary *Argynnis aglaja*	7–5				L

Marsh Violet *V. palustris*
Small Pearl-bordered Fritillary *Boloria selene*	6~5	+			S
Dark Green Fritillary *Argynnis aglaja*	7~5				L

Sweet Violet *V. odorata*
High Brown Fritillary *Argynnis adippe*	4–6			SW, WC	R
Pearl-bordered Fritillary *Boloria euphrosyne*	6~4			S, N, (WC)	S
Small Pearl-bordered Fritillary *Boloria selene*	6~5	+			S
Silver-washed Fritillary *Argynnis paphia*	8~6			S, (WC)	L

Viper's-buglosses *Echium* spp.
Painted Lady *Vanessa cardui*	5–10				Bm
Orange Swift *Hepialus sylvina*	9~5	*	IR		

Virginia-creepers *Parthenocissus* spp.
Elephant Hawk-moth *Deilephila elpenor*	7–9	+		S, C, (N)	
Buff Ermine *Spilosoma luteum*	7–10				
Silver-striped Hawk-moth *Hippotion celerio*	10				Bm

Virginia Stock *Malcolmia maritima*
Garden Carpet *Xanthorhoe fluctuata*	6–10

Wallflowers *Erysimum* spp.
Flame Carpet *Xanthorhoe designata*	6–7 & 8–9	7–8
Garden Carpet *Xanthorhoe fluctuata*	6–10	

Wall-rockets *Diplotaxis* spp.
Garden Carpet *Xanthorhoe fluctuata*	6–10

Water-cresses *Rorippa* spp.
Green-veined White *Pieris napi*	5–6 & 7–8	6–8
Orange-tip *Anthocharis cardamines*	5–7	
Small White *Pieris rapae*	5–10	

Water-plantain *Alisma plantago-aquatica*
Gold Spot *Plusia festucae*	9~5 & 7–8	9~5

Wayfaring-tree *Viburnum lantana*
Brimstone Moth *Opisthograptis luteolata*	All	7–9			
Sprawler *Asteroscopus sphinx*	4–6			S, C	
Privet Hawk-moth *Sphinx ligustri*	7–9			S, (C)	
Orange-tailed Clearwing *Synanthedon andrenaeformis*	7–5	*	ISt	S	Nb
Leopard Moth *Zeuzera pyrina*	8–5	*	ISt	S, C	

Western Hemlock-spruce *Tsuga heterophylla* see under Spruce

Wheats *Triticum* spp. see under Cereals

White Arabis *Arabis* spp.
Garden Carpet *Xanthorhoe fluctuata*	6–10

Whorl-grass *Catabrosa aquatica* see under grasses

Wild Madder *Rubia peregrina*
Humming-bird Hawk-moth *Macroglossum stellatarum*	6–9				Bm

Wild-oat *Avena fatua*
Grass Eggar *Lasiocampa trifolii*	3–6			S, SW	Na

Wild Pansy *Viola tricolor* see under Violets

Willows & Sallows *Salix* spp.

Unspecified Willows

Angle Shades *Phlogophora meticulosa*	All			
Scalloped Oak *Crocallis elinguaria*	3–7			
Double Kidney *Ipimorpha retusa*	4–5	S, WC, (EC)	L	
Svensson's Copper Underwing *Amphipyra berbera*	4–5		S, C	
Angle-striped Sallow *Enargia paleacea*	4–6		C, N	Nb
Brown-spot Pinion *Agrochola litura*	4–6			
Dark Chestnut *Conistra ligula*	4–6		S, C, (N)	
Dark Marbled Carpet *Chloroclysta citrata*	4–6			
Dingy Shears *Parastichtis ypsillon*	4–6		S, C, (N)	L
Dotted Border *Agriopis marginaria*	4–6			
Dun-bar *Cosmia trapezina*	4–6			
Feathered Thorn *Colotois pennaria*	4–6			
Flounced Chestnut *Agrochola helvola*	4–6			
Grey Chi *Antitype chi*	4–6		C, N, (S)	
Hebrew Character *Orthosia gothica*	4–7			
Lackey *Malacosoma neustria*	4–6		S, C, (N)	
Minor Shoulder-knot *Brachylomia viminalis*	4–6			
Mottled Umber *Erannis defoliaria*	4–6			
Pale Brindled Beauty *Phigalia pilosaria*	4–6			
Pale Eggar *Trichiura crataegi*	4–6			
Red-line Quaker *Agrochola lota*	4–6			
Sprawler *Asteroscopus sphinx*	4–6		S, C	
Twin-spot Carpet *Perizoma didymata*	4–6			
Twin-spotted Quaker *Orthosia munda*	4–6		S, C, (N)	
Yellow-line Quaker *Agrochola macilenta*	4–6			
Golden-rod Brindle *Lithomoia solidaginis*	4–7		WC, N	L
Comma *Polygonia c-album*	5–6 & 7–8		S, C, (SN)	
Early Thorn *Selenia dentaria*	5–6 & 8–9	6–8		
March Moth *Alsophila aescularia*	5–6			
Bordered Beauty *Epione repandaria*	5–7			
Chocolate-tip *Clostera curtula*	5–7 & 8–10	7–8	S, C, (N)	L
Early Tooth-striped *Trichopteryx carpinata*	5–7			
Pale Pinion *Lithophane hepatica*	5–7		S, WC	L
Purple Thorn *Selenia tetralunaria*	5–7 & 8–9	6–7	S, C, (N)	
Red Underwing *Catocala nupta*	5–7		S, C	
Scarce Chocolate-tip *Clostera anachoreta*	5–7 & 8–9		SE	RDB
Small Chocolate-tip *Clostera pigra*	5–7 & 8–9	7–9		Nb
Emperor Moth *Saturnia pavonia*	5–8			
Rannoch Brindled Beauty *Lycia lapponaria*	5–8		N	Na
Herald *Scoliopteryx libatrix*	5–9	+		
Common Pug *Eupithecia vulgata*	6–7 & 8–10	7–8		
Pale Prominent *Pterostoma palpina*	6–7 & 8–9	6–8		
Pebble Prominent *Notodonta ziczac*	6–7 & 8–9	7–8		
Reed Dagger *Simyra albovenosa*	6–7 & 8–9		SE	Nb
Sallow Kitten *Furcula furcula*	6–7 & 8–9	7–8	F	
Swallow Prominent *Pheosia tremula*	6–7 & 9	7–9		
Autumn Green Carpet *Chloroclysta miata*	6–8			L
Cream-bordered Green Pea *Earias clorana*	6–8 & 9–10		S, EC	Nb
Ringed Carpet *Cleora cinctaria*	6–8		S, WC, N	Na
Brindled White-spot *Parectropis similaria*	6–9		S, (C)	L

Eyed Hawk-moth *Smerinthus ocellata*	6–9			S, C	
Poplar Hawk-moth *Laothoe populi*	6–9	+			
Poplar Kitten *Furcula bifida*	6–9			S, C	L
Puss Moth *Cerura vinula*	6–9				
Satyr Pug *Eupithecia satyrata*	6–9		F		L
Grey Pug *Eupithecia subfuscata*	6–10		F & L		
Mottled Pug *Eupithecia exiguata*	6–10			S, C, (N)	
Sharp-angled Peacock *Macaria alternata*	7 & 9			S, (C)	L
Bordered Sallow *Pyrrhia umbra*	7–8			S, C, NE	L
Small Grass Emerald *Chlorissa viridata*	7–8			S, (WC)	Na
Broom Moth *Melanchra pisi*	7–9				
Clouded Border *Lomaspilis marginata*	7–9				
Grey Dagger *Acronicta psi*	7–9	+			
Knot Grass *Acronicta rumicis*	7–9	+			
Lobster Moth *Stauropus fagi*	7–9			S, (WC)	
Peppered Moth *Biston betularia*	7–9				
Poplar Grey *Acronicta megacephala*	7–9			S, C, (N)	
Privet Hawk-moth *Sphinx ligustri*	7–9			S, (C)	
Small Angle Shades *Euplexia lucipara*	7–9	+			
Buff-tip *Phalera bucephala*	7–10				
Dot Moth *Melanchra persicariae*	8–10			S, C, (N)	
Gothic *Naenia typica*	8–3				L
Common Emerald *Hemithea aestivaria*	8–5			S, C, (N)	
Dotted Fan-foot *Macrochilo cribrumalis*	8–5		DL, ISt	SE, (EC)	Nb
Goat Moth *Cossus cossus*	8–5	*	ISt		Nb
Leopard Moth *Zeuzera pyrina*	8–5	*	ISt	S, C	
Lunar Hornet Moth *Sesia bembeciformis*	8–5	*	ISt		
Red-tipped Clearwing *Synanthedon formicaeformis*	8–5		ISt	S, C, (N)	Nb
Satin Beauty *Deileptenia ribeata*	8–5				
Scarlet Tiger *Callimorpha dominula*	8–5			S, (WC)	L
Silvery Arches *Polia trimaculosa*	8–5				Nb
Triple-spotted Clay *Xestia ditrapezium*	8–5		B		L
Lesser Yellow Underwing *Noctua comes*	8–6				
Sallow Clearwing *Synanthedon flaviventris*	8–6	*	ISt	S	Nb
White Satin Moth *Leucoma salicis*	8–6			S, C	L
Yellow-tail *Euproctis similis*	8–6			S, C, (N)	
Barred Chestnut *Diarsia dahlii*	9–4			C, N, (S)	L
Lesser Broad-bordered Yellow Underwing *Noctua janthe*	9–4				
Dotted Clay *Xestia baja*	9–5				
Old Lady *Mormo maura*	9–5			S, C, (N)	L
Brown-tail *Euproctis chrysorrhoea*	9–6			S, (EC)	L
Great Brocade *Eurois occulta*	9–6			N	Nb
Magpie *Abraxas grossulariata*	9–6				
Oak Eggar *Lasiocampa quercus*	All	*			

Trees (>10m High)

Crack Willow *S. fragilis*

Dingy Shears *Parastichtis ypsillon*	4–6			S, C, (N)	L
Red-line Quaker *Agrochola lota*	4–6				
Red Underwing *Catocala nupta*	5–7			S, C	
Lunar Hornet Moth *Sesia bembeciformis*	8–5	*	ISt		
Purple Emperor *Apatura iris*	8–6			S	R

White Willow *S. alba*

Double Kidney *Ipimorpha retusa*	4–5			S, WC, (EC)	L

Black Arches *Lymantria monacha*	4–6		S, C	L
Copper Underwing *Amphipyra pyramidea*	4–6		S, C, (N)	
Dingy Shears *Parastichtis ypsillon*	4–6		S, C, (N)	L
Minor Shoulder-knot *Brachylomia viminalis*	4–6			
Red-line Quaker *Agrochola lota*	4–6			
Clouded Drab *Orthosia incerta*	4–6			
July Highflyer *Hydriomena furcata*	5–6			
Satellite *Eupsilia transversa*	5–6			
Bordered Beauty *Epione repandaria*	5–7			
Powdered Quaker *Orthosia gracilis*	5–7			
Red Underwing *Catocala nupta*	5–7		S, C	
Small Chocolate-tip *Clostera pigra*	5–7 & 8–9	7–9		Nb
Herald *Scoliopteryx libatrix*	5–9	+		
Pale Prominent *Pterostoma palpina*	6–7 & 8–9	6–8		
Sallow Kitten *Furcula furcula*	6–7 & 8–9	7–8		
Small Seraphim *Pterapherapteryx sexalata*	6–7 & 8–9	7–8	S, (C, N)	L
Swallow Prominent *Pheosia tremula*	6–7 & 9	7–9		
Eyed Hawk-moth *Smerinthus ocellata*	6–9		S, C	
Poplar Hawk-moth *Laothoe populi*	6–9	+		
Puss Moth *Cerura vinula*	6–9			
Ruddy Highflyer *Hydriomena ruberata*	6–9		W, N, (S, E)	L
Clouded Border *Lomaspilis marginata*	7–9			
Pale Shining Brown *Polia bombycina*	7–5		S	RDB
Lappet *Gastropacha quercifolia*	8–5		S, EC	
Scarce Vapourer *Orgyia recens*	8–6		EC	RDB
White Satin Moth *Leucoma salicis*	8–6		S, C	L
Old Lady *Mormo maura*	9–5		S, C, (N)	L
Rosy Marsh Moth *Coenophila subrosea*	9–6		WC	RDB

Shrubs & Small Trees (<10m High)

Unspecified 'Sallows'

Angle Shades *Phlogophora meticulosa*	All			
Slender Pug *Eupithecia tenuiata*	2–4	F		
Grass Eggar *Lasiocampa trifolii*	3–6		S, WC	Na
Pink-barred Sallow *Xanthia togata*	3–6	F		
Sallow *Xanthia icteritia*	3–6			
Scalloped Oak *Crocallis elinguaria*	3–7			
Double Kidney *Ipimorpha retusa*	4–5		S, WC, (EC)	L
Svensson's Copper Underwing *Amphipyra berbera*	4–5		S, C	
Autumnal Moth *Epirrita autumnata*	4–6		C, W, N	
Brick *Agrochola circellaris*	4–6	F, S & L		
Brown-spot Pinion *Agrochola litura*	4–6			
Common Quaker *Orthosia cerasi*	4–6			
Copper Underwing *Amphipyra pyramidea*	4–6		S, C, (N)	
Dark Chestnut *Conistra ligula*	4–6		S, C, (N)	
Dark Marbled Carpet *Chloroclysta citrata*	4–6			
December Moth *Poecilocampa populi*	4–6			
Dingy Shears *Parastichtis ypsillon*	4–6		S, C, (N)	L
Dotted Border *Agriopis marginaria*	4–6			
Dun-bar *Cosmia trapezina*	4–6			
Engrailed *Ectropis bistortata*	4–6 & 7–9	5–7		
Feathered Thorn *Colotois pennaria*	4–6			
Flounced Chestnut *Agrochola helvola*	4–6			
Hebrew Character *Orthosia gothica*	4–7			

Species				
Lackey *Malacosoma neustria*	4–6		S, C, (N)	
Minor Shoulder-knot *Brachylomia viminalis*	4–6			
Mottled Umber *Erannis defoliaria*	4–6			
Mouse *Amphipyra tragopoginis*	4–6	L & F		
November Moth *Epirrita dilutata*	4–6			
Pale Brindled Beauty *Phigalia pilosaria*	4–6			
Pale Eggar *Trichiura crataegi*	4–6			
Pale November Moth *Epirrita christyi*	4–6		S, C, (N)	
Red-line Quaker *Agrochola lota*	4–6			
Scarce Umber *Agriopis aurantiaria*	4–6			
Silver-studded Blue *Plebejus argus*	4–6	F & L	S, WC	R
Small Quaker *Orthosia cruda*	4–6			
Sprawler *Asteroscopus sphinx*	4–6		S, C	
Suspected *Parastichtis suspecta*	4–6			L
Twin–spot Carpet *Perizoma didymata*	4–6			
Twin-spotted Quaker *Orthosia munda*	4–6		S, C, (N)	
White-marked *Cerastis leucographa*	4–6		S, C	L
Winter Moth *Operophtera brumata*	4–6			
Yellow-line Quaker *Agrochola macilenta*	4–6			
Golden-rod Brindle *Lithomoia solidaginis*	4–7		WC, N	L
Chevron *Eulithis testata*	5–6			
Clouded Drab *Orthosia incerta*	4–6			
Early Thorn *Selenia dentaria*	5–6 & 8–9	6–8		
July Highflyer *Hydriomena furcata*	5–6			
Red Chestnut *Cerastis rubricosa*	5–6			
Satellite *Eupsilia transversa*	5–6			
Belted Beauty *Lycia zonaria*	5–7	*	NW	Na
Bordered Beauty *Epione repandaria*	5–7			
Brindled Beauty *Lycia hirtaria*	5–7		S, C, (N)	
Canary-shouldered Thorn *Ennomos alniaria*	5–7			
Chocolate-tip *Clostera curtula*	5–7 & 8–10	7–8	S, C, (N)	L
Early Tooth-striped *Trichopteryx carpinata*	5–7			
Northern Drab *Orthosia opima*	5–7			L
Oak Beauty *Biston strataria*	5–7		S, C, (N)	
Pale Pinion *Lithophane hepatica*	5–7		S, WC	L
Powdered Quaker *Orthosia gracilis*	5–7			
Red Underwing *Catocala nupta*	5–7		S, C	
Scarce Chocolate-tip *Clostera anachoreta*	5–7 & 8–9		SE	RDB
Emperor Moth *Saturnia pavonia*	5–8			
Large Thorn *Ennomos autumnaria*	5–8		SE	Nb
Vapourer *Orgyia antiqua*	5–8	+		
Herald *Scoliopteryx libatrix*	5–9	+		
Cabbage Moth *Mamestra brassicae*	5–10	+		
Common Pug *Eupithecia vulgata*	6–7 & 8–10	7–8		
Common Wave *Cabera exanthemata*	6–7 & 8–9	7–8		
Coxcomb Prominent *Ptilodon capucina*	6–7 & 8–9	6–8		
Dingy Mocha *Cyclophora pendularia*	6–7 & 8–9		S	RDB
Pale Prominent *Pterostoma palpina*	6–7 & 8–9	6–8		
Pebble Prominent *Notodonta ziczac*	6–7 & 8–9	7–8		
Reed Dagger *Simyra albovenosa*	6–7 & 8–9		SE	Nb
Sallow Kitten *Furcula furcula*	6–7 & 8–9	7–8	F	
Small Seraphim *Pterapherapteryx sexalata*	6–7 & 8–9	7–8	S, (C, N)	L
Swallow Prominent *Pheosia tremula*	6–7 & 9	7–9		
Autumn Green Carpet *Chloroclysta miata*	6–8			L
Barred Umber *Plagodis pulveraria*	6–8			L

Cream-bordered Green Pea *Earias clorana*	6–8 & 9–10			S, EC	Nb
Glaucous Shears *Papestra biren*	6–8			WC, N, (SW)	L
Peacock Moth *Macaria notata*	6–8	+		S, WC, NW	L
Small Engrailed *Ectropis crepuscularia*	6–8			S, C, (N)	L
Common White Wave *Cabera pusaria*	6–10				
Eyed Hawk-moth *Smerinthus ocellata*	6–9			S, C	
Light Knot Grass *Acronicta menyanthidis*	6–9			C, N, (SE)	L
Poplar Hawk-moth *Laothoe populi*	6–9	+			
Puss Moth *Cerura vinula*	6–9				
Ruddy Highflyer *Hydriomena ruberata*	6–9			W, N, (S, E)	L
Scalloped Hazel *Odontopera bidentata*	6–9				
Sweet Gale Moth *Acronicta euphorbiae*	6–9			N	Na
Grey Pug *Eupithecia subfuscata*	6–10		F & L		
Mottled Pug *Eupithecia exiguata*	6–10			S, C, (N)	
Fox Moth *Macrothylacia rubi*	6~4				
Sharp-angled Peacock *Macaria alternata*	7 & 9			S, (C)	L
Common Marbled Carpet *Chloroclysta truncata*	7–8 & 9~5	8~6			
Little Thorn *Cepphis advenaria*	7–8			S, (C)	Nb
Pale Oak Beauty *Hypomecis punctinalis*	7–8			S, (C)	
Broom Moth *Melanchra pisi*	7–9				
Clouded Border *Lomaspilis marginata*	7–9				
Dark Dagger *Acronicta tridens*	7–9	+		S, C, (N)	
Grey Dagger *Acronicta psi*	7–9	+			
Knot Grass *Acronicta rumicis*	7–9	+			
Pale-shouldered Brocade *Lacanobia thalassina*	7–9	+			
Peppered Moth *Biston betularia*	7–9				
Scorched Wing *Plagodis dolabraria*	7–9			S, (WC)	L
Small Angle Shades *Euplexia lucipara*	7–9	+			
Sycamore *Acronicta aceris*	7–9			S, (C)	L
Waved Carpet *Hydrelia sylvata*	7–9			S, W	Nb
Buff-tip *Phalera bucephala*	7–10				
Little Emerald *Jodis lactearia*	7–10			S, C, NW	
Miller *Acronicta leporina*	7–10				
Saxon *Hyppa rectilinea*	7–10			N	Nb
Scallop Shell *Rheumaptera undulata*	7–10			S, C, (N)	L
Beautiful Brocade *Lacanobia contigua*	8–9				L
Gothic *Naenia typica*	8–3				L
Common Emerald *Hemithea aestivaria*	8–5			S, C, (N)	
Double Dart *Graphiphora augur*	8–5				
Double Square-spot *Xestia triangulum*	8–5				
Goat Moth *Cossus cossus*	8–5	*	ISt		Nb
Great Oak Beauty *Hypomecis roboraria*	8–5			S, (C)	Nb
Green Arches *Anaplectoides prasina*	8–5				
Grey Arches *Polia nebulosa*	8–5				
Lappet *Gastropacha quercifolia*	8–5			S, EC	
Light Emerald *Campaea margaritata*	8–5	+			
Lunar Hornet Moth *Sesia bembeciformis*	8–5	*	ISt		
Purple Clay *Diarsia brunnea*	8–5				
Scarlet Tiger *Callimorpha dominula*	8–5			S, (WC)	L
Silvery Arches *Polia trimaculosa*	8–5				Nb
Triple-spotted Clay *Xestia ditrapezium*	8–5		B		L
Dark Tussock *Dicallomera fascelina*	8–6			S, WC, N	L
Lesser Yellow Underwing *Noctua comes*	8–6				
Sallow Clearwing *Synanthedon flaviventris*	8–6	*	ISt	S	Nb
Scarce Vapourer *Orgyia recens*	8–6			EC	RDB

Species	Months			
White Satin Moth *Leucoma salicis*	8~6		S, C	L
Yellow-tail *Euproctis similis*	8~6		S, C, (N)	
Barred Chestnut *Diarsia dahlii*	9~4		C, N, (S)	L
Broad-bordered Yellow Underwing *Noctua fimbriata*	9~4			
Ingrailed Clay *Diarsia mendica*	9~4			
Lesser Broad-bordered Yellow Underwing *Noctua janthe*	9~4			
Least Yellow Underwing *Noctua interjecta*	9~5		S, C, (SN)	
Old Lady *Mormo maura*	9~5		S, C, (N)	L
Brown-tail *Euproctis chrysorrhoea*	9~6		S, (EC)	L
Great Brocade *Eurois occulta*	9~6		N	Nb
Magpie *Abraxas grossulariata*	9~6			
Oak Eggar *Lasiocampa quercus*	All	*		
Autumnal Rustic *Eugnorisma glareosa*	10~5			

Almond (French) Willow *S. triandra*

Species	Months			
Cream-bordered Green Pea *Earias clorana*	6–8 & 9–10		S, EC	Nb

Eared Willow *S. aurita*

Species	Months			
Slender Pug *Eupithecia tenuiata*	2–4		F	
Minor Shoulder-knot *Brachylomia viminalis*	4–6			
Red-line Quaker *Agrochola lota*	4–6			
July Highflyer *Hydriomena furcata*	5–6			
Northern Drab *Orthosia opima*	5–7			L
Ruby Tiger *Phragmatobia fuliginosa*	5–7 & 7–4	7–5		
Small Chocolate-tip *Clostera pigra*	5–7 & 8–9	7–9		Nb
Rannoch Brindled Beauty *Lycia lapponaria*	5–8		N	Na
Dingy Mocha *Cyclophora pendularia*	6–7 & 8–9		S	RDB
Sallow Kitten *Furcula furcula*	6–7 & 8–9	7–8	F	
Common Heath *Ematurga atomaria*	6–9	+		
Light Knot Grass *Acronicta menyanthidis*	6–9		C, N, (SE)	L
Poplar Hawk-moth *Laothoe populi*	6–9	+		
Puss Moth *Cerura vinula*	6–9			
Ruddy Highflyer *Hydriomena ruberata*	6–9		W, N, (S, E)	L
Sweet Gale Moth *Acronicta euphorbiae*	6–9		N	Na
Cousin German *Protolampra sobrina*	9~6		N	Na

Goat Willow *S. caprea*

Species	Months			
Slender Pug *Eupithecia tenuiata*	2–4		F	
Pink-barred Sallow *Xanthia togata*	3–6		F	
Sallow *Xanthia icteritia*	3–6		F	
Double Kidney *Ipimorpha retusa*	4–5		S, WC, (EC)	L
Brick *Agrochola circellaris*	4–6		F, S & L	
Copper Underwing *Amphipyra pyramidea*	4–6		S, C, (N)	
Dotted Border *Agriopis marginaria*	4–6			
Feathered Thorn *Colotois pennaria*	4–6			
Minor Shoulder-knot *Brachylomia viminalis*	4–6			
Mouse *Amphipyra tragopoginis*	4–6		L & F	
Northern Spinach *Eulithis populata*	4–6		SW, C, N	
Pale Brindled Beauty *Phigalia pilosaria*	4–6			
Pale November Moth *Epirrita christyi*	4–6		S, C, (N)	
Red-line Quaker *Agrochola lota*	4–6			
Scarce Umber *Agriopis aurantiaria*	4–6			
Sprawler *Asteroscopus sphinx*	4–6		S, C	
Chestnut *Conistra vaccinii*	5–6			
Chevron *Eulithis testata*	5–6			
Clouded Drab *Orthosia incerta*	4–6			

July Highflyer *Hydriomena furcata*	5–6				
Canary-shouldered Thorn *Ennomos alniaria*	5–7				
Chocolate-tip *Clostera curtula*	5–7 & 8–10	7–8		S, C, (N)	L
Early Tooth-striped *Trichopteryx carpinata*	5–7				
Northern Drab *Orthosia opima*	5–7				L
Powdered Quaker *Orthosia gracilis*	5–7				
Scarce Chocolate-tip *Clostera anachoreta*	5–7 & 8–9			SE	RDB
Herald *Scoliopteryx libatrix*	5–9	+			
Common Pug *Eupithecia vulgata*	6–7 & 8–10	7–8			
Common Wave *Cabera exanthemata*	6–7 & 8–9	7–8			
Coxcomb Prominent *Ptilodon capucina*	6–7 & 8–9	6–8			
Dingy Mocha *Cyclophora pendularia*	6–7 & 8–9			S	RDB
Pale Prominent *Pterostoma palpina*	6–7 & 8–9	6–8			
Sallow Kitten *Furcula furcula*	6–7 & 8–9	7–8			
Seraphim *Lobophora halterata*	6–7				
Small Seraphim *Pterapherapteryx sexalata*	6–7 & 8–9	7–8		S, (C, N)	L
Barred Umber *Plagodis pulveraria*	6–8				L
Glaucous Shears *Papestra biren*	6–8			WC, N, (SW)	L
Peacock Moth *Macaria notata*	6–8	+		S, WC, NW	L
Dark Brocade *Blepharita adusta*	6–9				
Eyed Hawk-moth *Smerinthus ocellata*	6–9			S, C	
Poplar Hawk-moth *Laothoe populi*	6–9	+			
Puss Moth *Cerura vinula*	6–9				
Ruddy Highflyer *Hydriomena ruberata*	6–9			W, N, (S, E)	L
Mottled Pug *Eupithecia exiguata*	6–10			S, C, (N)	
Sharp-angled Peacock *Macaria alternata*	7 & 9			S, (C)	L
Alder Moth *Acronicta alni*	7–8			S, C, (N)	L
Common Marbled Carpet *Chloroclysta truncata*	7–8 & 9–5	8–6			
Clouded Border *Lomaspilis marginata*	7–9				
Dark Dagger *Acronicta tridens*	7–9	+		S, C, (N)	
Poplar Grey *Acronicta megacephala*	7–9			S, C, (N)	
Fan-foot *Zanclognatha tarsipennalis*	7–10		DL	S, C, (N)	
Saxon *Hyppa rectilinea*	7–10			N	Nb
Scallop Shell *Rheumaptera undulata*	7–10			S, C, (N)	
Mottled Rustic *Caradrina morpheus*	8–11				
Double Dart *Graphiphora augur*	8–5				
Grey Arches *Polia nebulosa*	8–5				
Lunar Hornet Moth *Sesia bembeciformis*	8–5	*	lSt		
Purple Clay *Diarsia brunnea*	8–5				
Red-tipped Clearwing *Synanthedon formicaeformis*	8–5		lSt	S, C, (N)	Nb
Purple Emperor *Apatura iris*	8–6			S	R
Sallow Clearwing *Synanthedon flaviventris*	8–6	*	lSt	S	Nb
Scarce Vapourer *Orgyia recens*	8–6			EC	RDB
Swallow-tailed Moth *Ourapteryx sambucaria*	8–6				
White Satin Moth *Leucoma salicis*	8–6			S, C	L
Ingrailed Clay *Diarsia mendica*	9–4				
Dotted Clay *Xestia baja*	9–5				
Square-spotted Clay *Xestia rhomboidea*	9–5			S, (WC, N)	Nb
Neglected Rustic *Xestia castanea*	10–5				L

Grey Willow *S. cinerea*

Slender Pug *Eupithecia tenuiata*	2–4		F		
Pink-barred Sallow *Xanthia togata*	3–6		F		
Sallow *Xanthia icteritia*	3–6		F		
Double Kidney *Ipimorpha retusa*	4–5			S, WC, (EC)	L

Common name / Scientific name					
Copper Underwing *Amphipyra pyramidea*	4–6			S, C, (N)	
Dotted Border *Agriopis marginaria*	4–6				
Minor Shoulder-knot *Brachylomia viminalis*	4–6				
Northern Spinach *Eulithis populata*	4–6			SW, C, N	
Red-line Quaker *Agrochola lota*	4–6				
Small Eggar *Eriogaster lanestris*	4–7	*		S, C	Nb
Chevron *Eulithis testata*	5–6				
July Highflyer *Hydriomena furcata*	5–6				
Bordered Beauty *Epione repandaria*	5–7				
Chocolate-tip *Clostera curtula*	5–7 & 8–10	7–8		S, C, (N)	L
Netted Mountain Moth *Macaria carbonaria*	5–7			N	RDB
Northern Drab *Orthosia opima*	5–7				L
Scarce Chocolate-tip *Clostera anachoreta*	5–7 & 8–9			SE	RDB
Small Chocolate-tip *Clostera pigra*	5–7 & 8–9	7–9			Nb
Herald *Scoliopteryx libatrix*	5–9	+			
Common Wave *Cabera exanthemata*	6–7 & 8–9	7–8			
Coxcomb Prominent *Ptilodon capucina*	6–7 & 8–9	6–8			
Dingy Mocha *Cyclophora pendularia*	6–7 & 8–9			S	RDB
Golden-rod Pug *Eupithecia virgaureata*	6–7 & 9–10		F		L
Iron Prominent *Notodonta dromedarius*	6–7 & 9–10	8			
Pale Prominent *Pterostoma palpina*	6–7 & 8–9	6–8			
Reed Dagger *Simyra albovenosa*	6–7 & 8–9			SE	Nb
Sallow Kitten *Furcula furcula*	6–7 & 8–9	7–8			
Seraphim *Lobophora halterata*	6–7				
Small Seraphim *Pterapherapteryx sexalata*	6–7 & 8–9	7–8		S, (C, N)	L
Barred Umber *Plagodis pulveraria*	6–8				L
Glaucous Shears *Papestra biren*	6–8			WC, N, (SW)	L
Peacock Moth *Macaria notata*	6–8	+		S, WC, NW	L
Eyed Hawk-moth *Smerinthus ocellata*	6–9			S, C	
Poplar Hawk-moth *Laothoe populi*	6–9	+			
Puss Moth *Cerura vinula*	6–9				
Ruddy Highflyer *Hydriomena ruberata*	6–9			W, N, (S, E)	L
Sweet Gale Moth *Acronicta euphorbiae*	6–9			N	Na
Bright-line Brown-eye *Lacanobia oleracea*	7–9	+			
Clouded Border *Lomaspilis marginata*	7–9				
Dark Dagger *Acronicta tridens*	7–9	+		S, C, (N)	
Pale-shouldered Brocade *Lacanobia thalassina*	7–9	+			
Miller *Acronicta leporina*	7–10				
Scallop Shell *Rheumaptera undulata*	7–10			S, C, (N)	
Pale Shining Brown *Polia bombycina*	7~5			S	RDB
Double Dart *Graphiphora augur*	8~5				
Double Square-spot *Xestia triangulum*	8~5				
Lappet *Gastropacha quercifolia*	8~5			S, EC	
Lunar Hornet Moth *Sesia bembeciformis*	8~5	*	lSt		
Purple Clay *Diarsia brunnea*	8~5				
Red-tipped Clearwing *Synanthedon formicaeformis*	8~5		lSt	S, C, (N)	Nb
Dark Tussock *Dicallomera fascelina*	8~6			S, WC, N	L
Purple Emperor *Apatura iris*	8~6			S	R
Sallow Clearwing *Synanthedon flaviventris*	8~6	*	lSt	S	Nb
Scarce Vapourer *Orgyia recens*	8~6			EC	RDB
White Satin Moth *Leucoma salicis*	8~6			S, C	L
Ingrailed Clay *Diarsia mendica*	9~4				
Square-spot Rustic *Xestia xanthographa*	9~4				
Dotted Clay *Xestia baja*	9~5				
Neglected Rustic *Xestia castanea*	10~5				L

Osier *S. viminalis*

Double Kidney *Ipimorpha retusa*	4–5		S, WC, (EC)	L
Minor Shoulder-knot *Brachylomia viminalis*	4–6			
Northern Drab *Orthosia opima*	5–7			L
Herald *Scoliopteryx libatrix*	5–9	+		
Cream-bordered Green Pea *Earias clorana*	6–8 & 9–10		S, EC	Nb
Eyed Hawk-moth *Smerinthus ocellata*	6–9		S, C	
Clouded Border *Lomaspilis marginata*	7–9			
Knot Grass *Acronicta rumicis*	7–9	+		
Double Dart *Graphiphora augur*	8–5			

Purple Willow *S. purpurea*

Swallow Prominent *Pheosia tremula*	6–7 & 9	7–9		

Tea-leafed Willow *S. phylicifolia*

Dark Bordered Beauty *Epione vespertaria*	5–7		EC, NE	RDB

Dwarf Shrubs (<1.5m High)

Creeping Willow *S. repens*

Grass Eggar *Lasiocampa trifolii*	3–6		S, WC	Na
Chevron *Eulithis testata*	5–6			
July Highflyer *Hydriomena furcata*	5–6			
Belted Beauty *Lycia zonaria*	5–7		NW	Na
Bordered Beauty *Epione repandaria*	5–7			
Dark Bordered Beauty *Epione vespertaria*	5–7		EC, NE	RDB
Northern Drab *Orthosia opima*	5–7			L
Powdered Quaker *Orthosia gracilis*	5–7			
Small Chocolate-tip *Clostera pigra*	5–7 & 8–9	7–9		Nb
Cream-bordered Green Pea *Earias clorana*	6–8 & 9–10		S, EC	Nb
Glaucous Shears *Papestra biren*	6–8		WC, N, (SW)	L
Light Knot Grass *Acronicta menyanthidis*	6–9		C, N, (SE)	L
Sweet Gale Moth *Acronicta euphorbiae*	6–9		N	Na
Fox Moth *Macrothylacia rubi*	6–4			
Small Grass Emerald *Chlorissa viridata*	7–8		S, (WC)	Na
Red-tipped Clearwing *Synanthedon formicaeformis*	8–5	lSt	S, C, (N)	Nb
Smoky Wave *Scopula ternata*	8–5		W, N	L
Ashworth's Rustic *Xestia ashworthii*	8–6		WC	Na
Dark Tussock *Dicallomera fascelina*	8–6		S, WC, N	L
Grey Mountain Carpet *Entephria caesiata*	8–6		C, N	
Portland Moth *Actebia praecox*	9–6		SW, C, N, (S)	Nb
Autumnal Rustic *Eugnorisma glareosa*	10–5			

Dwarf Willow *S. herbacea*

Grass Eggar *Lasiocampa trifolii*	3–6		S, WC	Na

Willowherbs *Epilobium & Chamerion* spp.

Twin-spot Carpet *Perizoma didymata*	4–6			
Large Ranunculus *Polymixis flavicincta*	4–7		S, (C)	L
Setaceous Hebrew Character *Xestia c-nigrum*	5–7 & 9–4	9–5		
Small Phoenix *Ecliptopera silaceata*	6–7	+		
White-banded Carpet *Spargania luctuata*	6–7 & 9		SE	Na
Bedstraw Hawk-moth *Hyles gallii*	7–9			Bm
Bright-line Brown-eye *Lacanobia oleracea*	7–9	+		
Elephant Hawk-moth *Deilephila elpenor*	7–9	+	S, C, (N)	
Small Angle Shades *Euplexia lucipara*	7–9	+		

Small Elephant Hawk-moth *Deilephila porcellus*	7–9		S, C, (N)	L
Gothic *Naenia typica*	8–3			L
Scarce Vapourer *Orgyia recens*	8–6		EC	RDB
Silver-striped Hawk-moth *Hippotion celerio*	10			Bm
Black Rustic *Aporophyla nigra*	10–5			

Winter-cress *Barbarea vulgaris*

Green-veined White *Pieris napi*	5–6 & 7–8	6–8		
Orange-tip *Anthocharis cardamines*	5–7			

Wolf's-bane see Monk's-hood and Wolf's-bane

Wood Anemone *Anemone nemorosa*

Twin-spot Carpet *Perizoma didymata*	4–6			
Fern *Horisme tersata*	7–9		S, (C)	

Wood Avens *Geum urbanum*

Grizzled Skipper *Pyrgus malvae*	7–9	+	S, C	S
Riband Wave *Idaea aversata*	7~5	+		
Beautiful Golden Y *Autographa pulchrina*	8–5			

Woodruff *Galium odoratum*

Barred Straw *Eulithis pyraliata*	4–6			
Dark-barred Twin-spot Carpet *Xanthorhoe ferrugata*	6–7 & 9	6–8	S, C, (N)	
Flame Shoulder *Ochropleura plecta*	6–7 & 9–10	8–9		
Green Carpet *Colostygia pectinataria*	6–7 & 9–5	8~5		
Red Twin-spot Carpet *Xanthorhoe spadicearia*	7 & 9	6–8		
Cream Wave *Scopula floslactata*	7~4			L

Wood-rushes *Luzula* spp.

Unspecified

Twin-spot Carpet *Perizoma didymata*	4–6			
Double Line *Mythimna turca*	8~5		S, (WC)	Nb
Purple Clay *Diarsia brunnea*	8~5			
Broad-bordered Yellow Underwing *Noctua fimbriata*	9~4			
Slender Brindle *Apamea scolopacina*	9–5		lSt & L	S, C

Field Wood-rush *L. campestris*

Smoky Wainscot *Mythimna impura*	7–5	+		
Dotted Fan-foot *Macrochilo cribrumalis*	8–5		SE, (EC)	Nb
Double Line *Mythimna turca*	8–5		S, (WC)	Nb

Hairy Wood-rush *L. pilosa*

Smoky Wainscot *Mythimna impura*	7–5	+		
Dotted Fan-foot *Macrochilo cribrumalis*	8–5		SE, (EC)	Nb
Double Line *Mythimna turca*	8~5		S, (WC)	Nb
Common Rustic *Mesapamea secalis*	9–5		lSt	
Lesser Common Rustic *Mesapamea didyma*	10–5		lSt	

Wood Sage *Teucrium scorodonia*

Twin-spot Carpet *Perizoma didymata*	4–6			
Speckled Yellow *Pseudopanthera macularia*	6–8		S, WC, N, (EC)	
Mullein Wave *Scopula marginepunctata*	7 & 9–5	9–5	S, C, (N)	L
Heath Fritillary *Melitaea athalia*	7–6		SW, SE	R
Feathered Brindle *Aporophyla australis*	10–5		S	Nb

Wormwood Artemisia absinthium

Coast Dart Euxoa cursoria	3–7			E, WC, N	Nb
Wormwood Cucullia absinthii	8–9		F & S	S, C	Nb
Bordered Pug Eupithecia succenturiata	8–10			S, C, (N)	L
Wormwood Pug Eupithecia absinthiata	8–10		F & L		
Archer's Dart Agrotis vestigialis	9–6				L
Portland Moth Actebia praecox	9–6			SW, C, N, (S)	Nb

Woundworts Stachys spp.

Rosy Rustic Hydraecia micacea	5–8		lSt & R		
Speckled Yellow Pseudopanthera macularia	6–8			S, WC, N, (EC)	
Small Rivulet Perizoma alchemillata	7–9		S		
Beautiful Golden Y Autographa pulchrina	8–5				
Plain Golden Y Autographa jota	8–5				
Sub-angled Wave Scopula nigropunctata	8–5			SE	RDB

Yarrow Achillea millefolium

Belted Beauty Lycia zonaria	5–7	*		NW	Na
Lime-speck Pug Eupithecia centaureata	5–10	+	F		
Common Pug Eupithecia vulgata	6–7 & 8–10	7–8	F & L		
Ruby Tiger Phragmatobia fuliginosa	5–7 & 7–4	7–5			
V-Pug Chloroclystis v-ata	5–7 & 8–10	7–9	F	S, C, (N)	
Grey Pug Eupithecia subfuscata	6–10		F & L		
Mullein Wave Scopula marginepunctata	7 & 9–5	9–5		S, C, (N)	L
Cinnabar Tyria jacobaeae	7–9			S, C, (N)	
Heath Fritillary Melitaea athalia	7-6			SW, SE	R
Bordered Pug Eupithecia succenturiata	8–10			S, C, (N)	
Tawny Speckled Pug Eupithecia icterata	8–10		F & L		
Wormwood Pug Eupithecia absinthiata	8–10		F & L		
Mottled Beauty Alcis repandata	8–5				
Sussex Emerald Thalera fimbrialis	8–6			SE	RDB
Yarrow Pug Eupithecia millefoliata	8–11		F & S	S	Nb
Straw Belle Aspitates gilvaria	9–6			SE	RDB
Deep-brown Dart Aporophyla lutulenta	10–6			S, EC	

Yellow Archangel Lamiastrum galeobdolon

Speckled Yellow Pseudopanthera macularia	6–8			S, WC, N, (EC)	

Yellow Iris Iris pseudacorus

Crescent Celaena leucostigma	3–7		lSt		L
Belted Beauty Lycia zonaria	5–7			NW	Na
Crinan Ear Amphipoea crinanensis	5–7		lSt & R	WC, N	L
Red Sword-grass Xylena vetusta	5–7				L
Sword-grass Xylena exsoleta	5–7			C, N	Nb
Rush Wainscot Archanara algae	6–8		lSt	SE, EC	RDB
Webb's Wainscot Archanara sparganii	6–8		lSt & L	S, (EC)	Nb
Water Ermine Spilosoma urticae	7–9			SE, (SW)	Nb
Gold Spot Plusia festucae	9–5 & 7–8	9–5			

Yellow Loosestrife Lysimachia vulgaris

Powdered Quaker Orthosia gracilis	5–7				
Reed Dagger Simyra albovenosa	6–7 & 8–9			SE	Nb
V-Pug Chloroclystis v-ata	5–7 & 8–10	7–9	F	S, C, (N)	
Dentated Pug Anticollix sparsata	7–9		F & L	S, C	Na

Water Ermine *Spilosoma urticae*	7–9		SE, (SW)	Nb
Plain Wave *Idaea straminata*	8–5			L

Yellow-rattles *Rhinanthus* spp.

Scarce Bordered Straw *Helicoverpa armigera*	?			Bm
Grass Rivulet *Perizoma albulata*	6–8	S		L
Satyr Pug *Eupithecia satyrata*	6–9	F		L
Lead-coloured Pug *Eupithecia plumbeolata*	7–8	F	S, C, (N)	Nb

Yew *Taxus baccata*

Engrailed *Ectropis bistortata*	4–6 & 7–9	5–7		
Square Spot *Paradarisa consonaria*	6–8		S, C, SN	L
Willow Beauty *Peribatodes rhomboidaria*	7–6	+		
Satin Beauty *Deileptenia ribeata*	8–5			

No Plant Confirmed In Wild

Autumnal Snout *Schrankia intermedialis*	?		SE	RDB
Dotted Border Wave *Idaea sylvestraria*	8–5		S, C	Nb
Marsh Oblique-barred *Hypenodes humidalis*	8–5		S, C, NW	Nb
Pinion-streaked Snout *Schrankia costaestrigalis*	?		S, C, NW	L
Portland Ribbon Wave *Idaea degeneraria*	?		S	RDB

PLANT INDEX • LATIN – ENGLISH

In this book, the plants are entered alphabetically by English name. To assist those who use Latin nomenclature, the index below provides the English equivalent of the Latin to allow easy reference to the various plants in the main list. As described in the introduction to the book, many plants are listed by genus only as the authorities only mention the genus, e.g. Heather, the various species often being unspecified. A small number of genii have more than one entry, e.g. *Senecio* which is a large genus with Ragworts, Groundsels and Garden Senecios which are separately listed in the body of the work.

Abies **Firs** 47
   alba **Silver Fir** 48
   procera **Noble Fir** 48
Acer campestre **Field Maple** 47
   pseudoplatanus **Sycamore** 98
Achillea millefolium **Yarrow** 114
   ptarmica **Sneezewort** 94
Aconitum **Monk's-hood & Wolf's-bane** ...73
Actaea spicata **Baneberry** 17
Aesculus hippocastanum **Horse-chestnut** ...67
Agrimonia eupatoria **Agrimony** 14
Agrostis **Bents** 51
   curtisii **Bristle Bent** 52
Aira praecox **Early Hair-grass** 53
Alchemilla vulgaris **Lady's-mantle** 69
Alisma plantagoaquatica **Water-plantain** ...103
Alliaria petiolata **Garlic Mustard** 48
Allium **Onions** 77
Alnus glutinosa **Alder** 14
Alopecurus pratensis **Meadow Foxtail** ...55
Althaea officinalis **Marsh-mallow** 72
   rosea **Hollyhock** 65
Alyssum **Alyssum (Garden)** 15
Ammophila arenaria **Marram** 50
Andromeda polifolia **Bog-rosemary** ...29
Anemone nemorosa **Wood Anemone** ...113
Angelica sylvestris **Angelica** 15
Anisantha **Bromes** 52
Anthemis **Chamomiles** 34
Anthriscus sylvestris **Cow Parsley** 38
Anthyllis **Vetches** 101
   vulneraria **Kidney Vetch** 101
Antirrhinum majus **Snapdragon** 94
Aquilegia vulgaris **Columbine** 38
Arabis **White Arabis** 103
   glabra **Tower Mustard** 100
   hirsuta **Hairy Rock-cress** 59
Arctium **Burdocks** 32
Arctostaphylos uva-ursi **Bearberry** 17
Armeria maritima **Thrift** 99
Armoracia rusticana **Horse-radish** 67
Arrhenatherum elatius **False Oat-grass** ...53
Artemisia **Mugworts** 73

abrotanum **Southernwood** 95
absinthium **Wormwood** 114
Arum maculatum **Cuckoo-pint** 39
Aster **Michaelmas-daisies** 72
   tripolium **Sea Aster** 92
Astragalus **Milk-vetches** 73
Atriplex **Oraches** 77
   portulacoides **Sea-purslane** 92
Avena **Oats** 34
   fatua **Wild-oat** 103
Ballota nigra **Black Horehound** 26
Barbarea vulgaris **Winter-cress** 113
Bellis perennis **Daisy** 41
Berberis **Barberry or Berberis** 17
Beta vulgaris ssp. maritima **Sea Beet** ...92
Betula **Birches** 22
Bolboschoenus **Rushes** 90
   maritimus **Sea Club-rush** 90
Borago officinalis **Borage** 29
Brachypodium pinnatum **Tor-grass** 57
   sylvaticum **False-brome** 53
Brassica **Cabbage family** 32
   napus **Rape** 86
Briza **Quaking-grasses** 56
Bromopsis **Bromes** 52
Bromus **Bromes** 52
Buddleia **Buddleias** 31
Buxus sempervirens **Box** 29
Cakile maritima **Sea Rocket** 92
Calamagrostis **Reeds** 87
   canescens **Purple Small-reed** 87
   epigejos **Wood Small-reed** 87
Calendula **Marigolds** 71
Callistephus chinensis **China Aster** 36
Calluna vulgaris **Heathers** 63
Calystegia soldanella **Sea Bindweed** ...22
Campanula **Bellflowers** 21
   rotundifolia **Harebell** 59
Capsella bursa-pastoris **Shepherd's-purse** ...94
Cardamine **Bitter-cresses** 26
   amara **Large Bitter-cress** 26
   hirsuta **Hairy Bitter-cress** 26
   pratensis **Cuckooflower** 39

Carduus **Thistles**	98
Carex **Sedges**	93
acutiformis **Lesser Pond-sedge**	93
elata **Tufted-sedge**	93
flacca **Glaucous Sedge**	93
nigra **Common Sedge**	93
panicea **Carnation Sedge**	93
sylvatica **Wood-sedge**	94
vesicaria **Bladder-sedge**	93
Carlina **Thistles**	98
Carpinus betulus **Hornbeam**	66
Castanea sativa **Sweet Chestnut**	98
Catabrosa aquatica **Whorl-grass**	57
Cedrus **Cedars**	34
Centaurea **Knapweeds**	68
Centranthus **Valerians**	101
Cerastium **Mouse-ears**	73
tomentosum **Snow-in-summer**	73
Chaerophyllum **Chervils**	35
Chamaecyparis **Cypress**	40
lawsoniana **Lawson's Cypress**	40
Chamaemelum **Chamomiles**	34
Chamerion **Willowherbs**	112
Chenopodium **Goosefoots**	49
bonus-henricus **Good-King-Henry**	49
Cichorium intybus **Chicory**	36
Cicuta virosa **Cowbane**	38
Circaea lutetiana **Enchanter's-nightshade**	46
Cirsium **Thistles**	98
Cladium mariscus **Great Fen-sedge**	93
Clarkia amoena **Godetia**	49
Clematis **Clematis (Garden)**	37
vitalba **Traveller's-joy**	100
Colutea arborescens **Bladder-senna**	28
Conopodium majus **Pignut**	79
Consolida **Larkspurs**	69
Consolida **Delphiniums**	42
Convallaria majalis **Lily-of-the-valley**	70
Convolvulus **Bindweeds**	22
Cornus **Dogwoods**	45
Cortaderia selloana **Pampas-grass**	56
Corylus avellana **Hazel**	61
Cotoneaster **Cotoneasters**	38
Crataegus **Hawthorns**	59
Crepis **Hawk's-beards**	54
Cupressocyparis leylandii **Cypress**	40
Cupressus **Cypress**	40
macrocarpa **Monterey Cypress**	40
Cynara cardunculus **Globe Artichoke**	16
Cynoglossum officinale **Hound's-tongue**	67
Cynosurus cristatus **Crested Dog's-tail**	53
Cyperus longus **Galingale**	48
Cytisus scoparius **Broom**	30
Dactylis glomerata **Cock's-foot**	52
Datura stramonium **Thorn-apple**	99
Daucus **Carrots**	34
Deschampsia cespitosa **Tufted Hair-grass**	57
flexuosa **Wavy Hair-grass**	57
Descurainia sophia **Flixweed**	48
Dianthus **Pinks & Sweet William**	80
Digitalis **Foxgloves**	48
Diplotaxis **Wall-rockets**	103
Dipsacus **Teasels**	98
Dryas octopetala **Mountain Avens**	73
Dryopteris filix-mas **Male Fern**	71
Echium **Viper's-buglosses**	103
Elytrigia **Couches**	52
juncea **Sand Couch**	51
Empetrum nigrum **Crowberry**	39
Epilobium **Willowherbs**	112
Equisetum **Horsetails**	67
Erica **Heathers**	63
Eriophorum **Cottongrasses**	38
Erodium cicutarium **Stork's-bill**	97
Eryngium maritimum **Sea-holly**	92
Erysimum **Wallflowers**	103
cheiranthoides **Treacle-mustard**	100
Eschscholzia californica **Californian Poppy**	32
Euonymus **Spindles**	96
europaeus **Spindle**	96
japonicus **Evergreen Spindle**	96
Eupatorium cannabinum **Hemp-agrimony**	64
Euphorbia amygdaloides **Wood Spurge**	97
paralias **Sea Spurge**	97
Euphrasia **Eyebrights**	46
Fagopyrum **Buckwheats**	31
Fagus sylvatica **Beeches**	20
Festuca **Fescues**	54
arenaria **Rush-leaved Fescue**	51
arundinacea **Tall Fescue**	54
ovina **Sheep's-fescue**	54
pratensis **Meadow Fescue**	54
rubra **Red Fescue**	54
Filago vulgaris **Cudweed**	39
Filipendula ulmaria **Meadowsweet**	72
Foeniculum vulgare **Fennel**	47
Fragaria vesca **Wild Strawberry**	97
Frangula **Buckthorns**	31
alnus **Alder Buckthorn**	31
Fraxinus excelsior **Ash**	16
Fuchsia **Fuchsias**	48
Galeopsis **Hemp-nettles**	64
Galium **Bedstraws**	18
aparine **Goosegrass (Cleavers)**	18
mollugo **Hedge Bedstraw**	18
palustre **Common Marsh-bedstraw**	18
saxatile **Heath Bedstraw**	18
uliginosum **Fen Bedstraw**	18
verum **Lady's Bedstraw**	18
odoratum **Woodruff**	113

Genista anglica **Petty Whin** 79
   tinctoria **Dyer's Greenweed** 45
Gentiana **Gentians** 49
Geranium **Crane's-bills** 39
Geum urbanum **Wood Avens** 113
Glaux maritima **Sea-milkwort** 92
Glechoma hederacea **Ground-ivy** 58
Glyceria maxima **Reed Sweet-grass** 56
Hedera **Ivys** 67
Helianthemum **Rock-roses** 88
Helictotrichon pubescens **Downy Oat-grass** 53
Heracleum sphondylium **Hogweed** 65
Hesperis matronalis **Dame's-violet** 41
Hieracium **Hawkweeds** 59
Hippocrepis **Vetches** 101
   comosa **Horseshoe Vetch** 101
Hippophae rhamnoides **Sea-buckthorn** 92
Holcus lanatus **Yorkshire-fog** 57
   mollis **Creeping Soft-grass** 53
Honckenya peploides **Sea Sandwort** 93
Hordeum **Barley** 34
Humulus lupulus **Hop** 66
Hyacinthoides non-scripta **Bluebell** 28
Hydrocotyle **Pennyworts** 79
Hyoscyamus niger **Henbane** 65
Hypericum **St. John's-worts** 91
Iberis **Candytufts** 34
Ilex aquifolium **Holly** 65
Impatiens **Balsams** 17
Inula conyzae **Ploughman's-spikenard** 82
   crithmoides **Golden Samphire** 49
Ipomoea **Morning-glories** 73
Iris pseudacorus **Yellow Iris** 114
Jasione montana **Sheep's-bit** 94
Jasminum **Jasmines** 67
Juncus **Rushes** 86
   acutiflorus **Sharp-flowered Rush** 90
   articulatus **Jointed Rush** 90
   conglomeratus **Compact Rush** 90
   effusus **Soft Rush** 90
   squarrosus **Heath Rush** 90
Juniperus communis **Common Juniper** 67
Knautia **Scabious** 91
   arvensis **Field Scabious** 92
Koeleria **Hair-grasses** 54
Laburnum anagyroides **Laburnum** 69
Lactuca **Lettuces** 69
   serriola **Prickly Lettuce** 69
Lamiastrum galeobdolon **Yellow Archangel** 114
Lamium **Dead-nettles** 42
Larix **Larches** 69
Lathyrus **Peas** 78
   latifolius **Everlasting Peas** 78
   linifolius **Bitter-vetch** 78
   palustris **Marsh Pea** 78

   pratensis **Meadow Vetchling** 78
   sylvestris **Everlasting Peas** 78
   tuberosus **Tuberous Pea** 78
Lavatera arborea **Tree Mallow** 100
Leontodon **Hawkbits** 59
Lepidium draba **Hoary Cress** 65
Leucanthemum vulgare **Oxeye Daisy** 78
Leymus arenarius **Lyme Grass** 50
Ligustrum **Privets** 85
Limonium **Sea-lavenders** 92
Linaria **Toadflaxes** 99
Linum catharticum **Fairy Flax** 46
Listera ovata **Twayblade** 101
Lithospermum arvense **Field Gromwell** 47
Lolium **Ryegrasses** 57
Lonicera **Honeysuckles** 65
Lotus corniculatus **Common Birds-foot-trefoil** 25
   pedunculatus **Greater Birds-foot-trefoil** 25
Lunaria annua **Honesty** 65
Lupinus arboreus **Tree Lupin** 100
Luzula **Wood-rushes** 113
   campestris **Field Wood-rush** 113
   pilosa **Hairy Wood-rush** 113
Lychnis flos-cuculi **Ragged-Robin** 86
Lycopersicon esculentum **Tomato** 99
Lysimachia vulgaris **Yellow Loosestrife** 114
Lythrum salicaria **Purple Loosestrife** 86
Magnolia grandiflora **Magnolia** 71
Malcolmia maritima **Virginia Stock** 103
Malus **Apples, Cultivated & Crab** 15
Malva **Mallows** 71
Medicago lupulina **Black Medick** 26
   sativa ssp. *sativa* **Lucerne** 71
Melampyrum **Cow-wheats** 39
Melica uniflora **Wood Melick** 57
Melilotus **Melilots** 72
Mentha **Mints** 73
   arvensis **Corn Mint** 73
Menyanthes trifoliata **Bogbean** 28
Mercurialis perennis **Dog's Mercury** 44
Milium effusum **Wood Millet** 57
Molinia caerulea **Purple Moor-grass** 56
Myrica gale **Bog-myrtle** 28
Nardus stricta **Mat Grass** 55
Narthecium ossifragum **Bog Asphodel** 28
Nicotiana **Tobacco Plants** 99
Nothofagus **Beeches** 20
Odontites vernus **Red Bartsia** 87
Oenothera **Evening-primroses** 46
Olea europaea **Olive** 77
Onobrychis viciifolia **Sainfoin** 91
Ononis **Restharrows** 88
Origanum vulgare **Marjoram** 72
Ornithopus perpusillus **Bird's-foot** 25
Parapholis **Hard-grasses** 50

Parietaria judaica **Pellitory-of-the-wall**	79
Parthenocissus **Virginia-creepers**	103
Pastinaca sativa **Parsnip**	78
Pedicularis **Louseworts**	71
Pelargonium **Geraniums (Garden)**	49
Persicaria **Bistorts**	26
maculosa **Redshank**	87
Petasites hybridus **Butterbur**	32
Petroselinum crispum **Parsley**	78
Peucedanum officinale **Hog's Fennel**	65
palustre **Milk Parsley**	73
Phalaris arundinacea **Reed Canary-grass**	56
Phleum **Cat's-tails**	52
pratense **Timothy**	57
Phragmites **Reeds**	87
australis **Common Reed**	87
Picea **Spruces**	96
abies **Norway Spruce**	96
sitchensis **Sitka Spruce**	96
Picris **Oxtongues**	78
Pimpinella **Burnet-saxifrages**	32
Pinus **Pines**	79
contorta **Lodgepole Pine**	79
nigra **Austrian Pine**	79
pinaster **Maritime Pine**	79
sylvestris **Scots Pine**	79
Pisum **Peas**	78
sativum var. *arvense* **Field Pea**	78
sativum **Garden Pea**	78
Plantago **Plantains**	80
coronopus **Buck's-horn Plantain**	81
lanceolata **Ribwort Plantain**	81
major **Greater Plantain**	81
maritima **Sea Plantain**	81
Platanus **Planes**	80
Poa **Meadowgrasses**	55
alpina **Alpine Meadow-grass**	55
annua **Annual Meadow-grass**	55
bulbosa **Bulbous Meadow-grass**	56
nemoralis **Wood Meadow-grass**	56
pratensis **Smooth Meadow-grass**	56
trivialis **Rough Meadow-grass**	56
Polygala **Milkworts**	73
Polygonum aviculare **Knotgrass**	68
Populus **Poplars & Aspen**	82
alba **White Poplar**	84
balsamifera **Eastern Balsam-poplar**	84
nigra **Black-poplar**	84
nigra italica **Lombardy-poplar**	84
tremula **Aspen**	84
Potentilla **Potentilla (Garden Shrubs)**	85
Potentilla **Cinquefoils**	36
anserina **Silverweed**	94
erecta **Tormentil**	100
palustris **Marsh Cinquefoil**	72
Primula elatior **Oxlip**	78
veris **Cowslip**	39
vulgaris **Primrose**	85
Prunella vulgaris **Selfheal**	94
Prunus **Cherrys**	35
Prunus **Plums**	82
Prunus domestica ssp. *insititia* **Bullace**	32
dulcis **Almond**	15
spinosa **Blackthorn**	26
Pseudotsuga **Firs**	47
menziesii **Douglas Fir**	47
Pteridium aquilinum **Bracken**	29
Puccinellia **Saltmarsh-grasses**	51
Pulicaria dysenterica **Fleabane**	48
Pyracantha **Firethorns**	47
Pyrus **Pears**	78
Quercus **Oaks**	75
ilex **Evergreen Oak**	77
Ranunculus **Buttercups**	32
ficaria **Lesser Celandine**	69
Raphanus raphanistrum ssp. *raphanistrum* **Wild Radish**	86
Reseda lutea **Mignonette**	73
Rhamnus **Buckthorns**	31
Rheum **Rhubarbs**	88
Rhinanthus **Yellow-rattles**	115
Rhododendron **Rhododendrons & Azaleas**	88
Rhynchospora alba **White Beak-sedge**	94
Ribes **Currants**	39
alpinum **Mountain Currant**	40
nigrum **Black Currant**	40
rubrum **Red Currant**	40
sanguineum **Flowering Currant**	40
uvacrispa **Gooseberry**	49
Rorippa **Water-cresses**	103
Rosa **Roses**	88
pimpinellifolia **Burnet Rose**	89
Rubia peregrina **Wild Madder**	103
Rubus caesius **Dewberry**	43
fruticosus **Bramble**	29
idaeus **Raspberry**	87
Rumex **Docks**	43
Rumex **Sorrels**	95
acetosa **Common Sorrel**	95
acetosella **Sheep's Sorrel**	95
hydrolapathum **Water Dock**	44
Salix **Willows & Sallows**	104
alba **White Willow**	105
aurita **Eared Willow**	109
caprea **Goat Willow**	109
cinerea **Grey Willow**	110
fragilis **Crack Willow**	105
herbacea **Dwarf Willow**	112
phylicifolia **Tea-leafed Willow**	112
purpurea **Purple Willow**	112

repens **Creeping Willow**	112	*Tamarix gallica* **Tamarisk**	98
triandra **Almond (French) Willow**	112	*Tanacetum parthenium* **Feverfew**	47
viminalis **Osier**	112	*vulgare* **Tansy**	98
Salsola **Saltworts**	91	*Taraxacum* **Dandelions**	41
Salvia **Clarys**	37	*Taxus baccata* **Yew**	115
officinalis **Sage**	90	*Teucrium scorodonia* **Wood Sage**	113
Sambucus **Elders**	45	*Thalictrum* **Meadow-rues**	72
Sanguisorba minor ssp. *minor* **Salad Burnet**	91	*Thymus* **Thymes**	99
Saponaria officinalis **Soapwort**	94	*Tilia* **Limes**	70
Saxifraga **Saxifrages**	91	*Trichophorum cespitosum* **Deergrass**	42
Scabiosa **Scabious**	91	*Trifolium* **Trefoils**	100
columbaria **Small Scabious**	92	*Trifolium* **Clovers**	37
Schoenoplectus **Club-rushes**	90	*arvense* **Hare's-foot Clover**	37
Scirpus **Club-rushes**	90	*pratense* **Red Clover**	37
Scirpus **Rushes**	90	*repens* **White Clover**	37
Scrophularia **Figworts**	47	*Tripleurospermum* **Mayweeds**	72
Sedum **Stonecrops**	97	*Triticum* **Wheats**	34
rosea **Roseroot**	89	*Trollius europaeus* **Globeflower**	49
Senecio **Groundsel & Ragworts**	58	*Tropaeolum majus* **Nasturtium**	74
Seriphidium maritimum **Sea Wormwood**	93	*Tsuga* **Spruces**	96
Serratula tinctoria **Saw-wort**	91	*heterophylla* **Western Hemlock-spruce**	96
Sesleria caerulea **Blue Moor-grass**	52	*Tussilago farfara* **Colt's-foot**	38
Silene **Campions**	33	*Typha* **Bulrushes & Reedmaces**	90
acaulis **Moss Campion**	33	*Ulex europaeus* **Gorse**	50
dioica **Red Campion**	33	*Ulmus* **Elms**	45
latifolia **White Campion**	33	*Umbilicus rupestris* **Navelwort**	74
noctiflora **Night-flowering Catchfly**	33	*Urtica* **Nettles**	74
nutans **Nottingham Catchfly**	33	*Vaccinium myrtillus* **Bilberry**	21
otites **Spanish Catchfly**	33	*oxycoccos* **Cranberry**	39
uniflora **Sea Campion**	33	*vitis-idaea* **Cowberry**	38
vulgaris **Bladder Campion**	33	*Valeriana* **Valerians**	101
Sinapis arvensis **Charlock**	34	*dioica* **Marsh Valerian**	101
Sisymbrium officinale **Hedge Mustard**	64	*officinalis* **Common Valerian**	101
Solanum dulcamara **Bittersweet**	26	*Verbascum* **Mulleins**	74
tuberosum **Potato**	85	*Veronica* **Speedwells**	95
Solidago **Goldenrods**	49	*Viburnum opulus* **Guelder-rose**	58
Sonchus **Sow-thistles**	95	*lantana* **Wayfaring-tree**	103
Sorbus aucuparia **Rowan**	89	*tinus* **Laurustinus**	69
domestica **Service-tree**	94	*Vicia* **Vetches**	101
Sparganium **Bur-reeds**	32	*cracca* **Tufted Vetch**	102
Spergula arvensis **Corn Spurrey**	97	*sepium* **Bush Vetch**	101
Spergularia rubra **Sand Spurrey**	97	*sylvatica* **Wood Vetch**	102
rupicola **Rock Sea-spurrey**	97	*tetrasperma* **Smooth Tare**	102
Stachys **Woundworts**	114	*Vinca* **Periwinkles**	79
officinalis **Betony**	21	*Viola* **Violets**	102
Stellaria **Stitchworts**	97	*canina* **Heath Dog-violet**	102
Stellaria **Chickweeds**	35	*hirta* **Hairy Violet**	102
Suaeda maritima **Sea-blite**	92	*odorata* **Sweet Violet**	103
Succisa **Scabious**	91	*palustris* **Marsh Violet**	103
pratensis **Devil's-bit Scabious**	92	*riviniana* **Common Dog-violet**	102
Symphoricarpos **Snowberries**	94	*tricolor* **Heartsease (Wild Pansy)**	102
Symphytum officinale **Comfrey**	38	*Vitis* **Grape-vines**	50
Syringa vulgaris **Lilac**	70	*Zantedeschia aethiopica* **Arum Lily**	15

NOTES

NOTES

NOTES

NOTES